This book was a prize a[warded to] Mr. C. W. Perry by Radi[o ...] in September 1989, in re[sponse to a] correct answer to their "Guess my Secret" radio contest.

"Ann" of Sussex clues to her secret were :-
    a) "It's supposed to be unlucky indoors"
& b) "I was rather high at the time."

The correct answer was :-
    Ann was in a small aeroplane flying in a rainstorm and the roof started leaking. She opened an umbrella to keep dry.

[signature] C. W. Perry
Oct. '89

P.S. See "Aeroplane monthly" September 1989 p.557 for description of actual incident in a Consul (Airspeed) flying to UK from Belfast!

Window on to Annapurna

Window on to Annapurna

JOY STEPHENS

LONDON
VICTOR GOLLANCZ LTD
1988

First published in Great Britain in 1988
by Victor Gollancz Ltd
14 Henrietta Street London WC2E 8QJ

Copyright © 1988 by Joy Stephens

British Library Cataloguing in Publication Data
Stephens, Joy
    Window on to Annapurna.
    1. Nepal——Description and travel
    I. Title
    915.49'604   DS493.53

ISBN 0–575–04290–7

Typeset at The Spartan Press Ltd, Lymington, Hants
and printed in Great Britain by
St Edmundsbury Press Ltd, Bury St Edmunds, Suffolk
Illustrations originated and printed by
Acolortone Ltd, Ipswich

To Duane and Naina Singh's family

Acknowledgements

I would like to express my thanks to His Majesty's Government of Nepal and the United Mission to Nepal for the opportunity to work in the country, and to the Nepali people for making it an unforgettable experience. Also to Carol Philby who read through the manuscript and gave invaluable criticism and advice, and to Ruth Taunt for her comments. Finally a special thank you to my husband for all his support and to my father who started me writing in the first place and encouraged me to keep going.

J.S.
1987

Contents

1. Plans in the air   13

2. Village on the mountainside   28

3. First encounters with pigs and patukas   36

4. We're all one family   50

5. Lighting the lamp in Titeng   63

6. An invitation to a wedding   81

7. New developments   95

8. The eyes of the stomach   106

9. Off with their heads   119

10. Water from the twelve-month-flower   126

11. The sky is weeping   136

12. Rice-planting   143

13. Season of festivals and fertility   152

14. Too many people; too little land   156

15. When the flies stopped biting   164

16. Babies, witches and broomsticks   176

17. Death and Dasain   186

18. Farewell   199

Glossary of Nepali words   206

Colour illustrations

Facing page 32 A heavily-laden porter on the route to Baglung

Kali Gandaki river on the walk from Naudara to Baglung

Facing page 33 The children: Laute, Kali, Bhakhu, Devi and Gophle

Grandmother spinning in the courtyard

Facing page 64 The fields of Titeng

Our 'house' on the day we arrived

Facing page 65 Tiring work. Wife One and Wife Two working the rice *dhiki*

Children on the ladder leading to our upper room

Wife One, Wife Two and Maila preparing the evening meal inside their house

Facing page 128 Wife Two spreads a fresh layer of mud and dung over the courtyard

Threshing the grain in the courtyard

Facing page 129 Rice-planting Naina Singh's fields

Looking towards Annapurna

Facing page 160 Devi and friends help to mix the white clay for the Dasain *lipnu* of the houses

Naina Singh receiving the Dasain *tika* from Grandmother

Facing page 161 Favourite walk through the woods above the cliffs near Titeng

I

Plans in the air

The heat was like an orange shroud as I walked through the market place in the late afternoon. Ochre-coloured dust cloaked the trees and the grass on the verges. Even the flea-bitten dogs that prowled the bazaar had retreated into the narrow strips of shade beside the buildings. Never had I known a heat like this before.

It was June and we were living in Kasauli, an unlovely cement shanty town of the *terai* – the southern strip of Nepal where the foothills of the Himalayas meet the Ganges Plain. It was a pleasant place to live in the cool season – the flat *terai* had its own peculiar charm – but from the end of March until October a suffocating heat descended and life dragged to a halt. Simple tasks like shopping took twice as long and even talking was an exertion. At night the heat continued. The shop-keepers in the bazaar would carry their beds and mosquito nets into the streets to catch the faint breeze that blew down the gorge, but where we lived the trees blocked the breeze and the heat remained, still and oppressive. When we woke in the mornings the temperature would already be 100°F.

I forced myself to concentrate on my shopping. The sweat trickling down my face was beginning to make my eyes smart and my throbbing headache was growing worse. The heat seemed intensified by the crowds milling around the vacant patch of ground on the edge of town where the market was held. There was no cover of any kind. A few of the permanent stalls had roofs, but most of the fruit and vegetables were laid out in dusty piles on the ground. Some of the vendors had rigged flimsy shades by draping their shawls over stakes, but many were in the open and I wondered how they could stand the glare and heat of the sun for hour after hour.

I checked off the items I had bought – potatoes, onions, tomatoes, bananas, papaya – everything was complete so I picked up my bags to go home. Outside the market the bare backs of the line of rickshaw-wallahs were shiny with sweat as they waited for customers, and the porters carrying sacks of potatoes and rice worked in slow-motion silence. I debated whether to take a rickshaw but it took less energy to walk than to haggle over the correct price.

I took the street leading past the Mini-Bus Stand towards the main road. It was lined with cloth shops, a restaurant with a tatty piece of sacking hanging in the doorway to keep the flies away, and several meat shops (the source of the flies) displaying startling orange goats' heads rubbed with turmeric powder. Inside the shops, fat affluent merchants sat cross-legged on low cloth-covered platforms beside their money-boxes, eyes half-closed, ignoring any customers who entered as if they were totally indifferent to the business of making money. A Taru woman of the *terai* plains passed me by in a bright lime-green sari with heavy silver bangles round her ankles and neck, gracefully swinging her hips so as not to spill the earthenware pot of curd on her head.

Reaching the main road I had to jump smartly out of the way of an oncoming bus. This street was the first flat and straight stretch of road for 150 miles to the north and the buses, freed at last of the twists and inclines of the mountains, would celebrate their arrival by roaring down the street at speeds they were never designed for. I watched as a holy cow narrowly escaped getting its backside grazed, and an unlucky rickshaw, caught between the bus and the edge of the road, was forced to plunge into the ditch. Only the ox-carts could out-bluff the buses. Nothing seemed to shake them from their slow lumbering course.

Another bus passed by, this one chugging slowly and loaded with people returning to the mountains. Not satisfied with the crowds hanging in the doorway and on the rooftop, its conductor boy was calling for yet more passengers. Kasauli seemed to be one vast bus depot. Regardless of the time of day it was always full of buses venting their black choking fumes into the already hazy air. Kasauli lay twelve hours' bus journey south-west of Kathmandu, at the junction of the East-West Highway and the north-south Siddhartha Highway, two of Nepal's four major roads. Dozens of small motor repair shops advertising 'Body Building' had grown up on either side of its wide and squalid main street. I walked past line after line of buses and trucks pulled up outside these shops; some like candy sticks with their baubles and tassles and bright stripy colours, others mere empty shells, stripped of their tyres and submerged to their hubs in mud or dust. Their names bore witness to past days of glory – 'The-

Dhaulagiri-Super-De-Luxe-Bus-Service', or 'The-Jumbo-Jet-One-Day-Kathmandu-Mini-Express'. This was the graveyard for the buses that could no longer make the steep grades of the mountain roads. Some would be given a facelift and continue to serve on the 'retirement run' – a totally flat stretch of road between Kasauli and the Indian border which was notorious for having the slowest buses in the whole of Nepal.

At the end of the Kastha Karyalaya Wood Shop & Works I turned off the main road on to a footpath. Our house lay on the first few undulating feet of the Himalayas, sheltered from the dirt and squalor of the main street but within earshot of the honking horns. The path led across a patch of rather bumpy waste-land, used for grazing animals. During the monsoon season the hollows filled with rain and the buffalo would spend most of the day wallowing up to their scraggy necks in the water. One morning I had crossed the waste-land early and seen hundreds of giant saffron-yellow frogs hopping in and out of the pools like an Old Testament plague. When I returned the next day to confront my husband Duane with the proof of my story, they had vanished without trace. I found it hard to believe that so many frogs, so large and so brilliantly coloured, could disappear so completely, and I wasted many hours searching for them without success. Thereafter whenever we crossed the waste-land Duane could not resist a tease about the phantom frogs.

Beyond the waste-land the path turned up on to dry rocky ground shaded by one or two disfigured trees whose branches had been chopped to feed the ever-hungry buffalo and goats. Scattered amongst the boulders and stumpy trees was our village of 'Kanchi Bazaar', literally meaning 'Little Sister Bazaar' which seemed a nicer term than 'suburb'. It had no shops and the houses were small, some with modern tin roofs and cement walls, but others merely a collection of sticks and stones. Reaching our house which stood rather starkly on its patch of land with no attempt at a garden because of the lack of water, I undid the padlock and opened the front door. Ours was one of the larger homes in the village – two-storey, with traditional mud walls and thatched roof. I had kept the window shutters closed and for the first few seconds the air felt blissfully cool inside the darkened house. Shanti, our housegirl, had 'washed' the walls and floor that morning with a fresh layer of runny mud which helped to cool it down, and the thatched roof shielded us from the worst of the heat.

I put the shopping away and took a shower. Our house consisted of two large rooms, one upstairs and one down, with a side extension which included a kitchen and bathroom with a verandah above. The shower was merely a length of hose running from a barrel of water on the verandah, but it served to cool me down. Still dripping I turned on the fan and lay down. I must have fallen asleep for the next I knew was the clatter of the front door announcing the arrival of my husband.

'You're becoming a proper *Memsahib*,' he said with a grin as he looked at me lying there. 'Listen, how would you like to go to Baglung?'

'What do you mean – for a holiday?' I roused myself from my inertia and opened one eye.

'No, to live and work there.'

'Only if it's cooler than here,' I mumbled, closing my eye again.

'It's bound to be cooler up there in the mountains. The government wants to construct a small hydro-electric power scheme in Baglung and Himal Hydro have got the contract.'

By this time I was wide awake. Himal Hydro was the Nepali construction company for which Duane was working as a civil engineer. Their headquarters were in Kasauli but they specialised in small-scale irrigation and hydro-electric schemes all over the country. We pulled out the maps and started making plans for a preliminary survey visit.

Baglung lay in the Dhaulagiri Zone, 150 miles due west of Kathmandu and about 30 miles west of the Siddhartha Highway – not remote by Nepali standards where villages can lie up to ten or even fifteen days' walk from the nearest road, but still the only way to get there was to walk or take a Twin Otter plane which flew once a week to a small airstrip four hours' walk from Baglung. As Duane had limited time for this first exploratory trip, we decided to take the plane.

We bought tickets for the next flight and a week later took a bus to the airport to await the small Twin Otter. We were accompanied by a friendly Brahmin engineer from the Ministry of Water and Power who called himself B.P. For this survey trip we were pleased to see he had abandoned the formal *daura-saruwal* suit of civil servants, and was dressed in a very unofficial blue denim outfit, complete with matching hat. The temperature was 110°F in the shade, and our fellow passengers – a fat merchant wearing a chequered *dhoti* and shirt and a Gurkha soldier returning on leave from Hong Kong with his family – were gathered in a sweaty circle underneath the only functioning fan. Outside, the dust of the runway shimmered with the rising heat and reflected pools of yellowish sky.

The plane arrived and with few formalities we boarded and were soon bumping down the runway. It was a relief to watch the plane's nose swing upwards and feel the lift under the wings as we took off and left behind the stifling plains. Soon we passed over Kasauli nestling in its sheltered concavity between the plains and the foothills, and hit the powerful thermals that rise up along the edge of the mountains. The plane bounced around and then we were through and flying over the creases of the hills northwards towards the white wall of the Himalayan peaks.

The plane turned up a side river. Clouds swirled past the cabin windows and when we emerged the valley was much narrower and the sheer ice-covered face of Dhaulagiri loomed very close through the cockpit window. We were flying straight towards the peak when suddenly the plane banked sharply against the valley sides and turned a breathtakingly tight bend. The flight time was up and I assumed we had reached our destination. Looking out of the window it didn't seem possible there could be an airfield hidden somewhere in the wrinkled scenery beneath us. There was not a scrap of even remotely flat land. The pilot executed some remarkable aerobatics, dipping low across saddles and turning further sharp bends under the shadow of the mountains. Where was the airfield?

'I think the pilot has turned up the wrong river,' remarked B.P. in his calm, unruffled manner. 'I've made a number of survey trips on foot through this area and I know it quite well. He should go back and take the Kali Gandaki valley.'

Five minutes later we felt the plane turn another tight bend and head back the way we had come only to swing round into a broader valley. It seemed B.P. was right and the pilot *had* taken the wrong turning. But now we were in the right valley and would soon land. It was getting late, and as we flew up the Kali Gandaki river, dwarfed by the high valley walls, the sun sent long shadows shooting across the mountains. I felt very small and insignificant as I saw the miniature shadow of our plane crossing the endless ridges and valleys.

We descended and circled. Still no sign of an airfield. On again to the next bend in the river and a repeat manoeuvre. Our fellow passengers were beginning to look quite agitated, and even my confidence in the pilot was beginning to waver. Contrary to posted signs, many people had unfastened their safety belts and were walking up and down the short aisle peering out of the windows. Several of them crowded round the open cockpit door and began to throw advice at the pilot.

'You haven't gone far enough,' said one.

'You should have turned at the last river valley,' said another.

'Do you want us to fly this plane for you?' joked a third. They were mostly Baglung inhabitants who knew these ridges and valleys like the courtyards of their own homes.

After some more alarming aerobatics we were astonished to see the pilot pull out a footpath map of western Nepal and scrutinise it thoroughly, glancing out the window to compare the topography below. As the map covered a very wide area and had little detail we couldn't believe it would help. We must have been right for soon the pilot announced that he was returning to Kasauli as it was too late in the day to land.

There was an outcry from the cabin and half the passengers charged the cockpit and threatened to take over.

'Keep going! Keep going!' they shouted. 'It's only a bit further!'

But the pilot had had enough of this rugged confusing scenery and headed back to the wide safe plains of Kasauli, anxious to arrive before dark. We stepped out on to the hot dusty airfield once again. 'Better luck next week,' said B.P. with a patient smile as we parted.

A week later at the appointed time we returned to the airport and gathered around the same fan. It was, if possible, even hotter, and we were silent in our mutual discomfort. A fat Newari shop-keeper sitting on bales of merchandise wiped the folds of his face with a large white handkerchief and glanced at his watch. The plane was late—a bad omen. A solitary buffalo wandered on to the runway and the airport policeman dragged himself away from the shade of the building to chase it off. He was still chasing it when the plane droned in. The buffalo took fright and galloped straight down the runway. The policeman ran harder, waving his baton and shouting, but his cumbersome uniform and assorted armaments hampered his movements. At the last possible moment the buffalo turned into the long grass at the side and both were lost to sight in the cloud of dust that rose up as the plane landed.

On boarding we were relieved to see a different pilot at the controls. We took off and crossed the first ridge of hills and were halfway to our elusive destination when a flashing red light appeared on a dial in the cockpit. After an agitated consultation with his assistant, the pilot executed a 180° circle and we found ourselves heading back to Kasauli once more. I was so afraid we were going to crash that I was actually relieved when we stepped out safely into the inferno of the plains once again. A failure in one of the fuel pumps, the pilot informed us. No, the plane was not going on that day.

Frustrated at this second failure, B.P. declined a third attempt and decided that we should walk. As a government official he soon managed to conjure up a jeep that would drive us to Naudara, from where we would continue our journey to Baglung on foot.

By the time we had persuaded the airline authorities that we wanted our money back and not a ticket for next week's flight, it was already 5 pm. To our dismay we found that half the plane passengers were also travelling in the jeep. B.P. was happily ensconced in the front seat beside the driver, so we squeezed our way into the back which was tightly packed with ten passengers and their belongings. Most of them were Baglung traders returning with their merchandise and between them they had several bales of cloth, some sacks of rice and lentils, six chickens with their legs tied together, the entire contents of a vegetable store, and two crates of Khukri rum. Somehow I managed to find a small space at the back with my legs hanging over the end. As the sides and roof of the jeep were of flapping canvas I was soon feeling sick from the exhaust fumes and the bends of the road. The cloth merchant tried to cheer us up by liberally dispensing the liquor man's rum, and the chickens, after initially flapping wildly and smothering us in feathers, discovered a hole in the sack of rice and spent the rest of the journey quietly pecking.

The road climbed slowly but steadily upwards following the Tinau Khola river until we reached a broad basin and crossed the first pass. Speeding up slightly we dropped down in giant looping bends to the next river, only to slow up again as we climbed further squiggles on the other side. The journey seemed never ending. Halfway to Naudara we stopped at a wayside village for a snack of small pieces of curried liver and more glasses of rum, except for B.P. who announced that he was a strict Brahmin and therefore a vegetarian and teetotaller.

It was midnight by the time we reached Naudara, and its inhabitants were asleep with their shops and houses locked and barred. Unperturbed, the cloth merchant knocked up the owners of a lodging house. I was already half-asleep but our companions insisted that the landlady prepare a full-scale meal of rice, lentils, curried vegetables, and chicken. The landlady reluctantly disappeared outside to catch the chicken and fetch the water and firewood. Our lodging house was a simple mud-and-stone building and we sat on straw mats on the floor and watched the woman stoke the fire and stir the bubbling pots of rice and lentils. Finally, having eaten towards 2 am, Duane and I and B.P. lay down to sleep on mats in the upstairs room, but our companions were into the swing of the party and with no sign of fatigue continued to entertain each other with drunken stories.

We were up the next morning at 6 o'clock to search for porters to carry our bags. At first sight Naudara was an unprepossessing collection of huts, but we soon realised it was a major embarkation point, serving the western reaches of Nepal. Behind the façade of tea-shops lining the road were the warehouses, piled with boxes of biscuits, packs of cigarettes, coils of pipe, tins of paraffin, bolts of cloth, and any other goods the remote villages found it worthwhile to import. As we left Naudara, the porters were preparing their burdens for the day, binding up the sacks of rice tightly with string so that they wouldn't burst or slip during their journey. The traditional method of carrying these loads was on the back, sometimes in conical bamboo baskets called *dokos*, with a tump line or *namlo* passing over the forehead for support. Regular porters could carry up to 150 lbs in this way, and even 200 lbs over short distances. We managed to find a young lad who was carrying a 'light' load of just one 60 lb tin of kerosene who was willing to take our rucksacks as well. He balanced them on top of the tin and ran down the path to catch up with the rest of his convoy of porters. Anxious not to lose sight of him so early on, we too had to make a running start to the day.

The path, worn bare to the red rock underneath, led down a short hill to the river from where we followed up the gently winding valley of the Andhi Khola. For the first three hours the valley bottom was wide and flat and the river meandered freely from side to side. So our path, which tried to follow a straight line, crossed the river over twenty times before I gave up counting. There were no bridges. In shallow spots there were stepping stones but in most places we had to wade, and I grew tired of taking my shoes on and off, so I walked much of the way 'empty-footed' as the Nepalis say. Roughly-made irrigation ditches led the river water into the nearby fields where the rice was newly planted, a fresh vibrant green, almost golden as the sunlight shone through the gently waving blades. The river itself was an iridescent kingfisher-blue in the deep pools where its meander brought it against the valley walls. I was tempted to stop for a swim but the rest of our party wanted to make up for lost time so we pressed on.

The path led us in easy stages upwards, through the hard-packed mud of the rice fields, over the rocky spurs and along the river bed itself where the way was rough and stony and strewn with boulders. It made no difference to the barefoot porters who went at the same pace regardless of the terrain. At times walking was strictly single file, but where the land was flat and the fields on either side not yet planted, the path broadened to a six-lane track. There was heavy traffic in both directions. That first day we passed cavalcades of porters, perhaps a thousand or more, travelling westwards with their loads. It was as if we were in Europe six hundred years ago with the highways filled with foot traffic, with pilgrims and peasants and soldiers and holy men, all travelling to their different destinations.

To serve these travellers numerous tea-shops lined the route. Many were temporary huts of bamboo and thatch, pavilion-style with open fronts or sides, and small wood-fuelled mud *chulas* with a couple of kettles puffing away inside. Tea was sweet and milky, brewed in the kettle itself and served in thick glass beakers. But we were grateful for anything as the way was hot and tiring, and the river water not safe to drink. There was very little shade in the valley bottom so the sparse trees around the tea-shops seemed cool and inviting.

'*Namaste*, Sir. Where you go? What is time?' A grinning schoolboy came up to us as we sat in a tea-shop, anxious to practise his few English phrases. It was impossible to feel lonely when trekking in Nepal.

'Where have you come from?' asked the tea-shop owner.

'Naudara.'

'And where are you going?'

'Baglung.'

'Have you eaten rice yet?'

'No, not yet. We'll eat at the top of the pass.'

'You don't mind travelling by our "number eleven bus" then?' He laughed loudly and went off to serve some more customers. Fortunately we had B.P. with us who explained that 'number eleven bus' was their euphemism for travelling on foot, since the number 11 in Devanagri script resembled a pair of legs walking along.

Three hours out from Naudara the path abruptly left the river and we began the real climb up to the village and pass of Karkineta at 6,000 feet. The path took the direct approach and rose endlessly upwards in short steep zigzags. The slope faced due south and even the local people complained of the heat, but to us the occasional breaths of wind seemed wonderfully cool after the heat of Kasauli. At strategic points along the steepest sections of the route, wide-spreading *pipal* and *banyan* trees had been planted, with *chautaras* around their base. These were stone benches specially constructed with a ledge at just the right height so that porters could lean backwards and rest their loads in the shade of the tree. Their builders gained religious merit for making them and often there was a pot of water provided for thirsty travellers.

Gradually the village of Karkineta grew larger and closer. The thought of food when we got there kept us going and when we finally reached the top we were taken aback by the stunning far-reaching views. Despite the hazy air, the whole of the Dhaulagiri and Annapurna ranges could be seen at close hand to the north, and westwards stretched an endless jigsaw of ridges, spurs and valleys. The ridge of Karkineta swung round in a graceful S-curve, encircling a great bowl of rice terraces and cradling the village itself, like a line of children's bricks, in the dip of the pass.

We ate our meal of rice, lentils, and curried vegetables in a white-washed tea-shop trimmed with red mud balanced right on the crest of the ridge. Outside in the courtyard children played with home-made windwheels – two sails of bamboo on a stick which turned with the wind as the children raced across the yard. The tea-shop was run by a Thakhali family – a tribe who came from Thak Khola towards the Tibetan border. Inside it was spotlessly clean with a smooth mud floor and the family's bronze dishes and beakers displayed on a low ledge encircling the room. 'Please come again,' they said as we got up to leave. 'Next time you must stay the night here.'

Regretfully we said goodbye and descended the far side of the ridge, down through arenas of graceful rice terraces curving with the contours.

There were no other foreigners on the route and Duane and I attracted a good deal of comment from passers-by and fellow travellers. With fair hair bleached blond by the sun, neither of us could pass unnoticed in Nepal. Although I was slim and about five foot five in height I was still a good deal taller than the average Nepali woman, and Duane at six foot three seemed like a giant. In addition he had a moustache and beard – quite a contrast to most Nepali men who were smooth skinned. Sometimes when we stopped in a tea-shop children would surreptitiously run their fingers along Duane's arms to make quite sure the hairs were real!

'Is "he" your son or younger brother?' they would ask Duane, pointing to me.

'She's my wife!' Duane would reply. Despite my long hair, they were confused over my sex because I was wearing jeans for the trek. It was only when I shook my arms that they noticed the bangles on my wrists and were convinced I was a woman.

'Why did your parents marry you to such an old man?' they would say, turning to me. The only people who occasionally had beards were old men, so they always thought Duane must be well over fifty.

'We're the same age,' we'd reply.

'No, that's impossible! You're teasing us!'

Halfway down the hill we noticed a trail of dark drops and rounding the corner came across our porter sitting in the middle of the path staring dejectedly at his tin which was leaking a steady trickle of paraffin. We weren't surprised with the reckless way he carried on. But he gave us a pained look – clearly it was the fault of our rucksacks, and what were we going to do? We felt helpless – not even a piece of chewing gum between us. We tried various plugs of leaves and sticks but our efforts were unsuccessful until the cloth merchant caught up with us.

'Use soap,' he said.

'And where will we find soap in the middle of the "jungle"?' countered the porter.

'Foreigners', said the cloth man, as though explaining the habits of a strange new species, '*always* carry soap'.

Fortunately we did indeed have a bar of soap in our rucksack and with this we managed to fix the worst of the leak.

We moved on again, the porter still complaining bitterly at the loss of part of his load. To cheer him up we bought tea and biscuits at the next tea-shop. This one was run by a high-caste Brahmin family, and after drinking his tea I noticed the porter washed his own glass before handing it back to the tea-shop woman who then gave it another thorough wash. As nobody else did this I raised the matter with B.P. who explained that because the porter was low-caste his glass was untouchable to the Brahmins until it had been rinsed. I was quite shocked at such a blatant example of caste distinctions, but the porter himself accepted it as just another fact of life.

At the bottom of the hill we crossed a small river, climbed another low hill, and then followed a curving bamboo-lined gully, finally emerging on a grassy plateau. The town of Kusma, our destination for that day, lay on a similar plateau barely a mile away, but in between lay the cliffs and gorge of the Modi Khola river. Wishing for wings to fly us across we had no choice but to spend the next hour descending several hundred feet to the river and up the other side. As we crossed the Modi Khola on a new steel suspension bridge I looked upstream to the fishtail-shaped mountain of Machapuchare which guarded the entrance to the Annapurna sanctuary – the source of the Modi Khola. Even in the hot dry season the Modi Khola was a turbulent icy-green, fed by the Annapurna glacier.

A friendly local girl fell into conversation as we climbed the other side. As the way became steeper I kept my breath for climbing rather than talking so our conversation became more and more one-sided. Unfortunately she had a rather morbid turn of mind.

'Do you see that landslide scar? Three people were killed when that swept down . . . look over there, that cairn in the river bed marks the spot where a man fell to his death,' she said as the path narrowed to a person's width with no protection to stop one falling over the sheer cliff edge. Not wishing to end up in the same place I hurried on, pursued by the girl already recounting another sad story.

Kusma, when we reached it, reminded me of a Wild West town – a broad main street lined with white-washed shops and houses with wooden verandahs. It seemed deserted. Large flagstones had been laid across the path and in the centre of the town was a small shrine with a bell. The cloth merchant and our porter rang the bell to wake up the sleeping gods and paid their homage to the shrine. At the end of the town a lodging house sign advertised 'coffee and pancakes'. Our mouths watered but when we inquired within they only had the usual sweet tea and curried vegetables. On the recommendation of the cloth merchant we didn't stay the night at Kusma, but continued for another half hour until we reached an open-fronted hut where a woman with a baby strapped tightly to her back prepared us food and spread out mats and quilted cotton *seracs* for us to sleep on. In Nepal it was the custom for any house to offer hospitality to travellers, and no fee was ever charged for sleeping, only for the food. Tired from the day's trek we quickly fell asleep, lulled by the sound of the nearby river.

Early the next morning we crossed the great Kali Gandaki river on a 150-foot-long suspension bridge. Kali Gandaki, the 'Dark One' – named for the black goddess Kali and the grey-black sediment it carries in the rainy season – has a quite remarkable history. Just north of Baglung it forms the deepest gorge in the world where it flows between the towering massifs of Dhaulagiri and Annapurna. These two peaks, both over 26,000 feet high, lie barely 22 miles apart, yet in between them flows the Kali Gandaki at an elevation of only 4,000 feet. Unlike most rivers the Kali Gandaki does not rise in the mountains and flow away from them to the plains. Instead it rises in the Tibetan Plateau to the north at a considerably lower elevation and flows *towards* the mountains. The reason for this phenomenon is that the Kali Gandaki river is far older than the Himalayan mountains themselves. While they were still unformed layers of sediment on the ocean floor, the Kali Gandaki was already flowing along its present-day course. When the drifting continental plate of India rammed into the rest of Asia, the force of the collision lifted the layers of sediment off the ocean floor to form the Himalayas. As the mountains were thrust upwards to their present height the Kali Gandaki, like a gigantic saw, cut down through 22,000 feet of rock, keeping pace with the uplift to maintain its original course.

Not surprisingly the Kali Gandaki valley forms an ancient trading route from Tibet and Central Asia through to the plains of India. We followed this route as far as the cliffs at the foot of Baglung, sometimes down on the valley floor picking our way through banks of boulders left behind by the floods of the last rainy season, and sometimes climbing up the valley walls to round a rocky pro-montory which blew spray in our faces from the force of the waters thudding against it. The river was almost 200 feet wide in places and swift flowing.

After wading across the Kathe Khola tributary our path abruptly left the Kali Gandaki and we started climbing up the cliff face. The path had been cut out of the rock itself and was so steep that in places it required the use of both hands and feet, and I had to be careful not to kick the person following on the head. As if to mock us an eagle glided effortlessly past on the up-currents of air along the cliff edge, rising and falling by an imperceptible shifting of its wings. Far below the blue-green waters of the Kali Gandaki snaked their way to India and the Bay of Bengal.

At the top of the cliffs we entered a small wooded knoll lying on a narrow peninsula between the Kali Gandaki and the Kathe Khola. The *sal* trees grew tall and silent on either side, the sunlight barely able to pierce their thick leafy canopies. Our porter placed an offering at a small wayside shrine. 'This is a holy wood,' he explained, 'protected by the goddess Devi. That's why the trees must not be cut down for firewood.'

We left the wood and once more in the bright sunlight picked our way across the flat plateau, through the chequerboard of fields dotted with tiny ochre-coloured houses, towards the town of Baglung. At the final tea-shop the cloth merchant put down his bags and announced that he was spending the night there. We were surprised as there were several hours before dark and his home was in Baglung, only a further ten minutes' walk.

'It's Tuesday,' he said, in answer to our questioning looks. We were still mystified, so he laughed and explained that on Wednesday, Thursday, Friday, Saturday, Sunday and Monday you could arrive home unharmed, but if you arrived on a Tuesday, well . . . . He raised his palms upwards and rolled his eyes to convey the consequences you could expect. Had the plane flown according to schedule he explained, he should have arrived on a Sunday, but now it was Tuesday and he would have to spend the night here and go to his house in the morning. The rest of his companions continued with us, apparently unconcerned about the dangers of returning home on a Tuesday.

On the highest corner of the plateau lay the surprisingly large town of Baglung. It was the headquarters for the Dhaulagiri Zone, one of thirteen zones into which Nepal was divided, and its administrative function was reflected in the numerous offices that displayed the red and white government signboards. Newly erected three- and four-storey brick buildings had spread their way across the fertile plateau, but the old part of the town huddled in the furthest corner, edged on one side by dangerously eroding cliffs, and on the other by the rising mountain slope. We passed through its narrow cobbled streets with their hotchpotch of houses and shops growing untidily on either side and booked ourselves into an inn fancifully called the Rhododendron Hotel, whose signboard advertised 'Fooding and Lodging'.

The next day while Duane and B.P. went off to survey the hydro-electric site, I began my search for a house to rent. There were many suitable large brick houses owned by the shop-keepers and money-lenders for rent in Baglung, but we were looking for a simpler house, less ostentatious, and preferably in a village where we could become part of a natural community and not remain apart. It had been our idea for some time that we wanted to get closer to the local people and we felt that one way to break down barriers was to live with them and follow their lifestyle rather than our own.

I looked all morning but found nothing close to Baglung. In the afternoon however I noticed a small village across the Kathe Khola river. It hugged the contours of the mountainside on land so steep it seemed the houses must have roots to stay there. The compactness of the village and the simple unadorned houses suggested it was a Magar village. I hoped so. We had met people of the Magar tribe in Kasauli and they had impressed us with their friendliness. We knew they had a strong sense of community, with fewer caste restrictions than the high–caste Brahmins.

I crossed the river and paid a visit to the village.

Magar girls

2

Village on the mountainside

My first impressions were not encouraging. The village resembled a giant fungoid growth. Lumpy walls, the same colour as the red earth, erupted from the rock and were capped by a tangled mop of thatch. Low doorways and punch-holes that hardly qualified as windows were set haphazardly in the walls. Roofs and verandahs protruded at strange angles and larger houses had sprouted smaller ones out of their sides. It had just been raining and the paths and courtyards were muddy and filthy and filled with families of small black pigs whose bellies scraped the ground as they snuffled through the accumulated debris. On the verandah of one house a small boy squatted, quite naked, clutching at a post for support. Two hens pecked avidly at the yellowish stream that flowed from his bare behind.

My convictions about living simply slipped away and in their place I began to list all the reasons why it would be foolish to live here. It was too extreme, too simple. We would get sick and our friends would say 'I told you so', or worse still accuse us of 'going native'. Was it really necessary to go to such lengths in order to make friends. Surely keeping an 'open home' was more important than the style of the home, and having possessions was all right so long as we were willing to share them?

Apart from the small boy and the myna birds chattering noisily on the sparse trees, the place appeared deserted.

I wandered on through a confusing web of footpaths undecided, and found myself in a curving row of 'terraced' houses, each one a different shape and size. The path traversed their narrow courtyards, the houses on one side and a series of sunken pig pens on the other. At the far end a woman and a young girl were emptying a bucket of pig swill into a wooden trough. They were dressed in faded black with maroon headscarves and heavy red bangles on their wrists. I approached slowly but in the noise of their work they didn't hear me until I spoke.

'*Namaste*, sisters! Can you tell me the name of this village?'

Startled, the young girl let out a stifled scream and fled. The bucket clattered down the stone wall into the pen where it was quickly surrounded by hungry black snouts. The older woman turned round, mouth open wide in surprise. I squatted down to be on her level and began talking about anything in an attempt to reassure her that I was human.

'We're staying in Baglung and I came for a walk up the Kathe Khola. I saw this village from the other side and I had to come and have a look. Do you live here?'

'Yes,' she said warily.

'What's the name of this place? I thought it might be a Magar village and I wanted to meet some Magar people.'

'Yes. We're Magars. This is the village of Titeng.' Her village accent was so strong that at first I half-thought she was speaking a tribal tongue and not the Nepali language in which I had addressed her. She disappeared inside the nearest house, and when she emerged with a small circular mat and motioned me to sit down, I knew the initial breakthrough had been made.

Curiosity overcoming her fear, the young girl crept back and eyed me from the safety of the verandah, half-hidden by the supporting post, and another older woman appeared from inside the house. I explained the reason why we had come to Baglung and they looked at me disbelievingly.

'Electricity? Here on our river?' they exclaimed.

We chatted about this for a while and finally I was able to slip in the question I had been wanting to ask from the beginning.

'Would it be all right if two foreigners came to live in your village?' I said, half-hoping, half-expecting the answer would be a negative one.

'They would never live here; they would live in the bazaar,' they answered, pointing to Baglung.

'We don't want to live in Baglung, we want to live in a village,' I said.

The women were silent as they thought about this. Then the younger one smiled and said: 'Of course it would be all right. We're foreigners too, we're not Nepalis.'

Their casual acceptance was encouraging but their remark that they were foreigners puzzled me, for Magars were Nepalis, just as much as the other tribes and castes.

Not much is known of the history of the Magars, but they are of
Mongolian stock and believed to be one of the earliest tribes to
descend from the north and settle the fertile middle hills of Nepal.
Later the Aryan groups of the Brahmins and Chhettris pushed
northwards into Nepal from India, following the Moghul invasion.
They brought with them their Hindu religion with its complex caste
system, and the low-caste artisans, a people whose slightly darker
skins and curlier hair probably came from the pre-Aryan Dravidian
race. They imposed their Hindu beliefs on to the pre-existing
animistic culture of Nepal. The Magars and other tribal groups were
given a caste status somewhere between the high-caste Brahmins and
the low-caste artisans. The Brahmins being more aggressive and
better educated slowly took over the prime farming land in the valleys
and the Magars were pushed higher up the slopes where the land was
steeper and less fertile. The Brahmins and Chhettris also took over the
political leadership of the country following the victories of the
Chhettri King from Corkha – Prithvi Narayan Shah. Thus it may
have been that the Magars viewed themselves as foreigners, outsiders,
a belief reinforced by their different customs and different language
which they had retained in most areas, though not as it happened in
Titeng itself.

I asked the women if there were any empty houses that we could
rent and received the inevitable answer that I must talk with the men. I
waited on, but at 7 pm they had still not come so I left. On my way
back to Baglung, I met them returning home. Alcohol fumes mingled
with the fresh night air as they staggered past me. Even had I waited it
was doubtful I could have got much sense out of them.

If it had been left to me our idea might not have gone any further. I
gave Duane as accurate an account of the village as I could, including
details of the mud, the pigs, and the small houses with no windows.
When I had finished my fairly negative account, Duane did not
hesitate. 'Wonderful!' he said. 'Sounds just the place we're looking
for. Let's go there early tomorrow and talk with the men.'

As I had too much pride to be the one to back down, I found myself
climbing the steep hill to the village the next morning with Duane. We
met the village headman – a venerable grey-haired elder – who told us
there were no empty houses to rent but there was a *goth* belonging to a
certain Naina Singh which might be suitable for our purposes.

A *goth* may be loosely translated as a barn or stable. In Titeng they
were similar in design to the houses, and indeed many of their houses
had started out as *goths*, the difference being merely the degree of

finishing. As a family's wealth increased, they might add additional storeys to their *goth*, construct doors and windows and give the outside a plaster of red mud. The basic superstructure was wood and the walls were stone held together by mud mortar and topped by a thatched roof. The ground floor of a *goth* provided shelter for the family's buffalo and was walled on three sides only, whilst the upper floor provided storage for grain or straw, and perhaps extra sleeping space for members of a large family.

Naina Singh's *goth* was a solid unpretentious two–storey barn, filled with straw and goats and manure. Not a very promising habitation, but I was delighted that instead of the miniature windows of the houses, the walls had large gaps that stretched from the roof to the floor, so my fears of living in a dark hovel vanished. Duane and Naina Singh squatted down on one of his terraced fields to draw up a contract which Naina Singh signed with his thumbprint. We were to pay him Rs.20(£1) a month.

We agreed to rent only half of the *goth* for various members of Naina Singh's family were already living there. His goats lived in a small room at one end and the oldest son's family occupied a room of similar size at the other end. Another son and his wife occupied a small area of the upper storey which had been partitioned by a shoulder–height mud wall. We were to have what was left. This consisted of most of the upper floor where Naina kept his straw, and a small stable on the ground floor lacking a front wall, and currently occupied by a nanny-goat and her two kids.

We arranged for the goat family to vacate this and a proper front wall with a door and window to be constructed. The upper floor however, which was the bulk of our new home and was reached by going outside and up a bamboo ladder at the side of the *goth*, we decided to leave as it was. This meant that one end of the room had no real wall or door, only a large triangular opening looking out to the sky and the bamboos and the rooftops of the surrounding houses.

We concluded our agreement with Naina Singh. We were happy that as part of the arrangement we would eat our evening meal with his family, and felt this would be an important step towards integrating into village life.

From as early as I can remember I had wanted to travel, even though my first trip to France at the age of three caused me to hold my nose much of the time because of the unpleasant state of the French drains. Whether this travel itch came from my father with his stories of crossing the Atlantic seven times by the age of eight and the oranges and lemons that grew in his California garden, or my grandfather and great grandfather who had both been naval captains and left a house stuffed with curios from around the world, or my grandmother who had grown up in Palestine, it was hard to say, but compared to their stories my life in south London and Sevenoaks where I grew up seemed very mundane and the weather cold and miserable. As I grew older and learned that life overseas was not always filled with 'oranges and lemons', my desire to travel took on a new focus and purpose. With modern-day communications and the tremendous problems facing Third World countries, it seemed to me that a Christian's responsibility towards his neighbours extended beyond national boundaries, and I waited for an opportunity to work in a developing country.

I was single when I first went to Nepal, and the businessman I sat next to on the Delhi-Kathmandu flight, learning that this was my first trip to the Himalayan Kingdom, insisted on changing places to give me the window seat. I looked out and my first sight of the country lived up to all its Shangri-La reputation. It was the land of my imagination, temptingly green and lush, creased with ridge after ridge of mountains on which tiny hamlets grew and narrow paths curled around, and above everything, even the aeroplane, the peaks of the Himalayas. At ground level in Kathmandu it was a land of smiling people; the immigration officer smiled, the taxi driver smiled, the hotel manager smiled, the children who accosted me in the street to sell me postcards or play 'Alouette' on a squeaky violin smiled, even the beggars – and they were not many – sometimes smiled. With such a welcome it was easy to dismiss or overlook the poverty, but behind the smiling faces and beneath the icing sugar of the Himalayas were the statistics: Nepal was one of the ten poorest countries in the world, per capita income was around £75 a year, and one in seven children died before the age of five.

For those who are willing to leave the security of the hotel compound and the tour bus and explore the narrow medieval streets of Kathmandu, the first shock is not the poverty but the dirt and filth that is everywhere. Kathmandu when I first arrived was still waiting for a sewer system, and flies buzzed around the meat and fruit markets, around my glass of milky tea, and in the wake of the dirt and flies came the diseases – everything from sores, skin infections and worms, to dysentery, typhoid and tuberculosis.

I spent the next two years working as a secretary in a hospital at Tansen, just off the Siddhartha Highway some 200 miles by bus south-west of Kathmandu. Tansen was my introduction to Nepal. There I

Top right: A heavily-laden porter rests his load on the route to Baglung
Below: Kali Gandaki river on the walk from Naudara to Baglung

Above: The children *(left to right)* Top row: friend, Laute, Kali
Bottom row: Bhakhu, Devi, Gophle
Below left: Grandmother spinning in the courtyard

learnt something of the language and assimilated as much of the culture as I could whilst living a pseudo-western lifestyle. It was not quite like life in safe suburban Sevenoaks; the water ran out of the taps a cold muddy brown and was rationed during the dry season, the electricity sparked intermittently for a few hours each evening, and I shared the four walls of my house with a plague of white ants and other insects. But still it was relatively comfortable and insulated.

My job was mundane but useful. I typed records for the hospital, wrote letters, and coordinated a private mailbag to and from Kathmandu. My office was within the main hospital building, and a small crowd of the more ambulant patients would peer through the doorway. I liked having them there; they reminded me that I was helping them, even though I was not combating poverty and disease directly. There was no lack of patients. With only one doctor for every 100,000 people in the rural areas, very few people had access to adequate medical care. Some patients walked for up to ten days to reach the hospital, the severely ill being carried on stretchers or in bamboo baskets strapped to a porter's back, for there were no roads in the western half of Nepal.

Work at the hospital was enjoyable. I found the Nepali people friendly and open and easy to talk to. But somehow there was a barrier to a deeper friendship. It was a barrier not only of language, but of lifestyle, wealth and differing cultures.

While I was working at Tansen I met Duane, a civil engineer from the United States who had arrived to finish the construction of an additional wing to the hospital. Our first words to each other were exchanged in Nepali, for we met at a language practice group. It happened to be my turn to lead and I told a short story in Nepali about my black cat, Rum-Tum-Tugger. Duane must have been impressed for he became a frequent visitor to my office where I made good use of his talent for fixing things. My typewriter, like most of the hospital's equipment, was old and rundown and needed constant attention.

Duane came from the mid west of the U.S.A. where his father's job as as Lutheran pastor had seen the family move frequently – living in rural farming communities where the towns rarely had a population of more than a few hundred. Duane was tall, blond-haired and bearded, and I was amused to discover that his Nepali work-mates had given him the nickname 'Lam-khutta', which was their word for mosquito, but literally meant 'Long-legs'. It seemed a most appropriate name for the length of his legs and the speed with which he moved around on them. Duane was full of enthusiasm for Nepal and, like me,

loved trekking. Entertainment in Tansen was limited, so on our days
off we walked. We trekked to Ranighat, a splendid ruined Rana palace
on the banks of the Kali Gandaki, visited Bhairabsthan, the old capital
of the ancient Malla kingdom where there was a temple dedicated to
Bhairab, the god of terror, and made a pilgrimage to Satya Batti (True
Light), a lake on the top of a remote jungle-clad mountain between
Tansen and Kasauli. On the right night a goddess was believed to
appear out of the lake and grant pilgrims fulfilment of their wishes.
We visited it on the wrong night and the lake was soggy and
disappointing, strewn with tattered strips of red cloth and leaf bowls
discarded by previous pilgrims. But still my wish seemed to come true
and a year later Duane and I were married.

The house in Kanchi Bazaar, Kasauli, was our first married home,
for by this time Duane had left Tansen and was working for Himal
Hydro. In Kasauli, as in Tansen, although we had many Nepali
acquaintances amongst the people with whom we worked, we found
it hard to develop a deeper friendship with them. We knew only one
side of them; they told us about their families and the villages they
came from, but it was a side of their lives we couldn't see and therefore
couldn't understand. Most were immigrants from the mountains,
people who had lost their farms or been forced to leave them and seek
employment in the towns. Kanchi Bazaar was not a real community
or village, but a shanty town of fractured and dislocated families, none
of whom was still farming. We got to know these people but never
became really intimate with them. There were too many foreigners
working in Kasauli, and the Nepalis tended to identify us as one large
rather intimidating group, and we ourselves found that if given a
choice it was much less effort to talk with our fellow expatriates than
struggle with the language and communicate with our neighbours.
They in turn were over-awed by our lifestyle, our 'fine' house and its
furnishings, and their visits were awkward, rather formal occasions.

Shanti, our housegirl, was the exception to this, and I looked on her
more as a friend than a servant. But even Shanti had a mysterious other
side to her. I remember going to visit her home for the first time and
being shocked. It was no more than a shack, put together with scraps
of wood and old tin sheets scavenged from the streets, with gaping
holes in the walls and roof through which the rain poured in. But I did
not have to see her home every day, and when Shanti came to work
she was always neatly dressed and smiling, although she did arrive one
day with black eyes and bruises and a story of how her husband had
drunk too much and beaten her.

Duane and I had many discussions as to how we could achieve a better understanding and relationship with our Nepali neighbours. We felt that the more we exposed ourselves to their way of life and communicated at their level, the better we would understand them and their problems, and the better they would understand us and our problems, our motivation for working in Nepal, and the ideas that we were trying to share. We were well aware of the great disparities between the 'haves' and 'have-nots' and the injustices of such things as world trade and even 'aid', and as Christians felt called upon to share what we had to do our very small part towards correcting the imbalance. To achieve this we were convinced we had to change our western lifestyle with its emphasis on possessions and money, and spend more time with the village people, living alongside them. More than ninety per cent of Nepal's population were subsistence farmers living in traditional communities in the mountains, and if development programmes were to be effective these were the people they must help.

Back in Kasauli after the survey trip we began making preparations for our move to Titeng. I told our next-door neighbours that we would be going to live in Baglung District. They were a family of seven – squatters – who lived in a hut walled with branches. They had lost their land in the mountains through debt, and moved to Kasauli in the hope of finding work and a place to live. The father's high-caste status barred him from menial work so the family survived on the small sums he earned as a consultant astrologer, and on the goats and calves they fattened up for sale to their neighbours. With this background you expected the children to be backward and deprived. But they were smiling, friendly and well-mannered, regularly coming top of their class at school.

'Life is so much easier here than in the mountains,' said the mother when she heard we were going. 'We don't have to carry water or firewood far, or do heavy field work. The children can go to a proper school, there's plenty of food in the bazaar. Everything would be fine if my husband wasn't so lazy.'

I realised then how little I understood about life in Nepal.

3

First encounters with pigs and patukas

It was winter when we returned to live in Titeng, and the fields around us lay in barren tiers, red upon brown, except where the mustard bloomed in narrow strips and cast its luminous lemon shadow. As we emerged on the cliffs at Baglung I threw a quick glance upwards to check that Titeng was still rooted to its steep mountainside, and reassured, hurried on down the stone-flagged path.

After our previous experience with the planes, we had decided that walking was less hazardous than flying. Glancing back at our porters, I felt quite proud of the way we had reduced our luggage. We had sold or passed on most belongings from our house in Kasauli, and what remained was packed into six porter loads – two suitcases, one tin trunk, one canvas bag, one bedding roll, one guitar, and two *dokos* (bamboo baskets) filled with miscellaneous items.

If Duane had had his way we would have brought far less, but I found it easy to rationalise why we needed the extra items – cooking utensils and dishes in case we wanted to entertain guests or cook our own food, guitar and art materials to fill spare moments, camera and notebooks to record the life around us, engineering books for Duane, and a radio-tape-recorder to keep in touch with the rest of the world. Most were things that did not belong in a village home and therefore by rights should not have come. Would they prevent us seeking our entertainment in the village culture? It was hard to know. We were unaware at the time of the amount of mental baggage we had brought, but the longer we stayed in Titeng the more we realised how our opinions and attitudes had been coloured by our western upbringing.

We crossed the Kathe Khola river on a small rickety suspension bridge, its two cables swung from stone cairns on either bank, and as the heavily-laden porters followed, its wooden planks rippled like waves on a beach. On the far side we followed the river bed upstream for a hundred yards and then began the climb. Conversation dropped and breath came in short sharp pants. At a *chilaaune* tree on the curve of a switchback we stopped for a rest and measured our progress against the opposing hillside. Halfway there.

Leaving the main path we took the 'direct ascent' route to Titeng. The final incline was so steep that the village disappeared from view and the path deteriorated to shallow toe-holds cut in the vertical ledges of the terraced fields. Shafts of golden dust slanted across the slopes from the evening sun and the bare fields glowed the colour of red brick. In the distance we could hear the excited cries of the children; a welcoming committee was gathering. I wished, not for the first time, that we could arrive inconspicuously and wondered if we would ever achieve the distinction of being undistinguished. As we emerged over the rim of the hillside, the children erupted into shouts and hoots of laughter.

'Look Seti! One, two, three, four, five, *six* porters! They must be very rich!'

'What's in that strange long container? Must be a cooking pot of some kind.'

'Bhakhu! Feel this mattress. Isn't it soft? Fancy having so much stuff you need six porters to carry it all!'

So much for travelling light! Our illusions shattered, we directed the porters to set down their loads and went to inspect our new living quarters.

'Come this way,' said Naina Singh our landlord. 'I have had everything prepared.'

But as we had half-expected, it was not ready. The straw was still stuffed to the rafters of the upper room, and although a rough wall with a door and window had been constructed in the lower room, the floor was oozing with soft red mud. We stared at the room and wondered what to do. We had to stay somewhere that night but didn't want to upset Naina Singh by complaining on the very first day.

'It's not ready. We can't sleep here tonight. It's too wet.'

'But Sahib? What do you mean? Everything is ready! Just put your beds on the floor – they won't be harmed by a little mud.'

'We don't have any beds. We sleep on the floor like you.'

'No beds? You sleep on the floor?' he asked unbelievingly. We could see the other villagers shaking their heads and thinking what fools these foreigners were. But they agreed we could not sleep on the wet mud.

Retiring to the courtyard they discussed the matter at leisure, puffing on clay pipes and repeating the facts of the situation over and over again. Clearly we were to blame for not bringing beds. It was dark now and in faith we paid the porters off and let them go back to Baglung to find shelter for the night. Eventually the headman came shuffling up to us with their conclusion. He was an elderly man with close-cropped greying hair and a happy-sad face whose eyebrows were permanently raised in perplexity at the problems he had to deal with.

'We must move the straw out of the upper room,' he announced.

'But I haven't got anywhere to put it,' whined Naina Singh. 'If you put it outside and it rains I shall be ruined!'

Things were not going well. We hadn't even moved in and we were apparently on the verge of ruining our landlord. Dismayed at being responsible for such a disaster we were about to tear up the contract when the other men stepped in and started throwing the bundles of straw out of the upper room.

'Don't take any notice of Naina Singh,' they said. 'He's always like that. Look at us – we all keep our straw outside.'

'He only does it to make you give him more money,' whispered the headman in Duane's ear.

Village life had more politics than we had expected. We hesitated, but in the end allowed the men to clear a space for us on the upper floor. Naina Singh had disappeared, but his wife called us to come and eat, and we felt the family could not be too upset if they were offering food.

We bent over double to get in through the low carved doorway of their house, and it was like entering a cave. Inside was a single room, smoky and dark, except for the dull red glow of burning embers from a pit in the middle of the floor. The roof was low, the walls bulged, and over the years the covering of red mud had become so thick that there was no longer an angle between the walls and the floor, only a smooth continuous curve. As our eyes became accustomed to the poor light we could see long strings of soot dripping from the blackened timbers of the roof. Along one wall copper water pots glinted in the firelight, three or four large ones in a row, followed by a collection of smaller brass bowls. On the shelf above were two small pots filled with flowers and a row of dubious-looking bottles. Beyond the pots an old heavy chest, some straw mats and more copper bowls, these ones large enough for a child to fit inside. Wedged into spaces in the rafters were a collection of hoes, scythes and plough-heads, and various rolled rice-paper documents. Apart from the chest there was no furniture, no plastic utensils, and probably the only articles to have been manufactured outside the area were the glass bottles.

We sat down cross-legged on a mat along one wall and Naina's wife handed us heavy brass plates filled with rice and lentils and brass bowls of hot milk with unidentifiable black lumps floating on the surface and a strong burnt taste. We ate eagerly and then noticed that the other members of the family were eating a heavy black porridge made from millet flour boiled in water. This porridge we were to find out was the staple of the villagers, rice being eaten only by the wealthy or on special occasions.

'Did you cook rice just for us?' we asked. 'Please can we try some of your millet too?'

'You don't want to eat our millet porridge. It's bitter and hard to swallow. It'll make your stomachs swell up,' the landlord's wife replied.

Gently we insisted and she heaved us out a ladleful of the heavy sticky porridge which we ate with our fingers. She was right. It had an unusual bitter flavour and it filled us up very quickly.

'Thank you. We like your millet porridge just as much as the rice. We don't often eat rice where we come from.'

'You don't eat rice! How can you live without rice?'

'We eat meat and potatoes and bread.'

'Potatoes? Bread?' they asked with scorn. 'What sort of food are those? You don't eat rice? Truly? What a strange caste!'

The meal over, we washed our hands over a large copper bowl and returned to our *goth*. The men had moved half of the straw and there was now room to spread out our mattresses and covers and go to sleep. The open design of the room gave us curtains of sky as we lay on the floor and it was reassuring to see the moon and stars return our stare. A breeze rustled the bamboos and filled the room with the scent of straw and earth and dung. In the distance a buffalo moaned. Then there was silence.

We were woken up before dawn next morning by the crowing cocks and the rhythmic ka-chung, ka-chung of the *dhiki* which hulled the rice. The villagers' work had already started, but we lay in bed and watched the sky grow slowly lighter. From our house Dhaulagiri was hidden by a mountain ridge but we could see the peaks of Annapurna. When she was shrouded in cloud we learnt to expect bad weather. This morning however she was clear, an icy blue outline against the sky, until she was caught in the sun's rays and turned first rose and then golden. Slowly the sun crept down the surrounding mountainsides and touched the rooftops of Titeng, and the shadows retreated into the deeper clefts and gorges.

Still in our sleeping-bags we rolled over and looked down into Naina Singh's courtyard below. It was the meeting point for the men of the village for it was the first place in Titeng to receive the morning sun. The courtyard was of beaten red mud, roughly rectangular in shape, its long axis lying east-west along the contour of the mountainside, and our barn stood on its southern boundary, raised on a dry walled terrace about four feet high. At its eastern end the courtyard was bounded by a small circular house, and at its western end by Naina Singh's main house, but on its northern side the land fell steeply away in great terraced steps to the river, so that from our upper-floor windows we viewed not only the courtyard and its inhabitants, but the whole of the opposing valley as well – the cliffs by the river, the sinuous green lines of the terraces, the zig-zag red lines of the footpaths, the gullies filled with bamboo, the brown and white splashes of the houses, the rough steep pasture land above, and finally the rocky outcrops and bluish outline of the forest on the summit.

If we craned our necks and looked east towards Baglung, the view was even more spectacular. Purplish-orange pillars of sandstone rose out of the gorge and supported the perfectly flat table-top of the Baglung plateau. The base of the cliffs was strewn with huge boulders the size of houses, and it seemed as if a giant had come by with his scissors and set-square and levelled off the mountain, tossing the unwanted shapes into the river. Beyond this the Kali Gandaki river flowed, and above it rose the mountain ridge that culminated in the peaks of Annapurna.

The sun was just striking the courtyard and the men had dragged a mat into the sun and were absorbing its warm rays after the chill winter night when the temperature had fallen to near-freezing. To keep themselves warm they lit up a short straight-stemmed clay pipe which they wedged between their middle finger joints, close to the knuckles, wrapping their forefinger and thumb around its base to form a funnel so their lips did not actually touch it and make it unclean for someone else. Sucking in their cheeks they took deep puffs, finally releasing the pipe with a loud kissing sound before tossing it to the next in line.

All had the traditional Mongolian features – broad faces, slanting almost slit-like eyes, high cheekbones, and short stocky bodies.

Amongst other castes the Magars had a reputation for being slow-witted and simple-minded but extremely honest. Their nickname was *sojhai*, meaning the 'straight ones'. So far they had been little touched by development or western influences, still keeping to their old traditions and living out their lives as they had for hundreds of years.

From time to time they got up to stamp their feet and wave their arms or let out a bellow into the clear morning air, delighting in the sound which echoed across the valley. Although their heads and shoulders were swathed in blankets, and scarves wrapped turban-style, their legs and feet were bare. The headman was conversing in his high-pitched rather hoarse voice to nobody in particular:

'They are putting the roof on the new school today and the *Pradhan Panch* says that every village must send volunteers, and Titeng must send two carpenters and three stone masons.'

His cheekbones gleamed in the morning sun where the skin was stretched tightly over them, and his mouth and eyes were a web of deeply creased smile marks. He had a delightfully mischievous face with small black eyes that shone in the deep hollows between his cheeks and brow. He was wearing traditional clothes – a length of coarse-weave undyed cloth wrapped round his waist like a skirt, a tie-string shirt of the same material, and a black cotton waistcoat, somewhat tattered. Over this another length of cloth was knotted across his shoulders so that it fell down his back forming a bag for carrying miscellaneous items. Some of the young men preferred western style shorts and T-shirts, but both young and old wore the traditional cloth cap *topi* on their heads.

'Who is going to go?' the headman continued. 'We must have five volunteers. The *Pradhan* said they must be there directly after rice-time, so they should have left an hour ago.'

The men listened impassively behind their cocoon of blankets. Obviously not enthusiastic. The headman repeated his plea at a higher pitch.

'We must send five volunteers. Five volunteers! Last year we forgot to send volunteers to work on the town gaol and the *Pradhan* said we wouldn't get away with that another time.'

Our attention was distracted by the children who were playing a game. They leapt off the dry wall into the courtyard and bounced around like frogs until they fell over exhausted, the winner being the one who lasted longest. It must have served to keep them warm for they were dressed in the flimsiest of cotton shirts and shorts, the younger ones with bare behinds.

In another corner a group of girls had scratched lines for a game of hopscotch. I was intrigued that so many thousands of miles apart they were playing the same game that school children in England played. But here each girl had a baby strapped to her back, and as she jumped the baby's head rocked up and down in time to her bounces. The girls were dressed like the women in short tie-string blouses and long skirts called *lungis* held up by rolls of *patuka* bundled around their waists. The *patuka* was a curious garment that caused all the women to appear pregnant and thus disguised those who actually were. It was a length of material about three feet wide and five yards long, and its main purpose was to support the back and provide padding for the heavy loads they carried. Besides this it kept up their skirts and served as a hold-all for personal belongings: money, keys, pipe, tobacco, and snacks of popcorn all found their way into the folds of their *patukas* and retrieving these in public could pose quite a problem.

Naina Singh's wife had quietly appeared at the top of our ladder bearing a tray of minuscule popcorn.

'For you,' she said, placing it on the floor.

'What is it? Maize?'

'No, it's roast millet. Don't you like it?'

'We've never had it before.'

'Try it. It's good,' she said, disappearing down the ladder.

We picked up the bowl of roast millet and it was then we noticed the row of disembodied faces with scruffy hair and runny noses. The children must have been standing on tiptoe on the chicken pen beneath our room so that their heads just showed above the level of our floor. As we looked the faces popped down out of sight and muffled laughter issued through the slats of the chicken pen. Turning our attention back to the millet the faces reappeared, only to pop down as soon as we looked up. This game of jack-in-the-box continued until we decided to get up which caused panic on the chicken coop as the children scrambled to get away with screams of 'They're coming!' I rolled up our bedding and went to inspect our downstairs room. In the courtyard the headman had finally given up and was shuffling off on his bent legs to exhort a different part of the village.

The lower room was still very wet and in this cold weather would take several weeks to dry out, so I organised a makeshift kitchen area amongst the bedding and straw upstairs. We had brought two small kerosene burners for cooking and I was careful to set these up as far as possible from the straw. I started to put a kettle on to boil and stopped. No taps, no water. Poking my head through the wall I called to the people in the courtyard.

'Where do you get your water from?'

'The spring we use is that way,' they said, pointing past the house next door. 'But there's a better spring above the village. That has *good* water. In winter it comes out hot and in summer cold!' They paused, waiting to see my reaction to this miracle, and then went on: 'Go to the spring below the village – it's too far to carry from the upper spring.'

'Is it good water there? Can we drink it?'

'Yes, it's good water. Come with me,' said a woman. 'I'm going there myself.'

I took our kettle, which was the largest container we had, and followed her down the path, past a small gully filled with bamboo, and down through dry terraced fields. In the middle of the terraces a small poinsettia tree bent low and spread its painted fingers over a cleft in the ground from which water poured forth through a wooden spout. The area around the spring had been neatly lined with stones and a small low wall. A hubbub of noise rose through the poinsettia tree. If the courtyard was the meeting place for the men, this was the meeting place of the women. They were gathered around in various stages of undress, washing their clothes and their children, and filling their large water pots that gleamed a coppery gold in the morning sun.

They had not seen me approaching. I stood on the stone steps enjoying the scene but too shy to confront such a large group. A woman turned to leave with her full water pot, saw me, and let out a cry. Silence fell on the group. Recovering her composure she burst into a loud screechy speech: 'Oh Sister! I wasn't expecting to see you. You gave me such a fright! I thought you were a ghost. Have you come to fill your pot? Come on down. Make room for her.'

'After you. I've only just come. I'll wait my turn.' I felt uncomfortable to be pushed to the head of the queue. These women had more work than I to get through and if I wanted to be treated as one of them I had better insist on equal terms from the first day.

But the women were adamant. 'No. *You* go first. Look at our big pots. We'll be here all day. You've only got a small one.'

Reluctantly I rolled up the legs of my jeans and stepped down into the stone-flagged basin beneath the spring. I had worn jeans for the trek the day before and had not yet unpacked the rest of my clothes.

'Why do you wear trousers?' asked the woman with the screechy voice. 'Aren't they hard to sit down in?'

'No. They're easy for walking in the mountains. How do you manage in your long skirts? Don't you fall over them?'

'No. We lift them up like this.' She hitched up her skirts into her *patuka* and danced a couple of turns around the spring.

'But I don't have a *patuka*,' I said, laughing.

'You must get one,' she insisted. 'You would only need a small one as you don't carry heavy loads. Five yards should be enough.'

Still curious, she moved closer and tugged the material of my jeans. 'Very strong. But what do you do when you're untouchable?'

I stared at her blankly.

'When You Can Not Be Touched,' she repeated, enunciating each word loudly and clearly, and giving me a knowing nod. I still didn't understand. There were some stifled giggles behind me. The woman had one last try:

'Once a month, you know, No Touching,' she said, becoming as specific as she dared. 'Look, this is what we use.' She smiled at me and bundled up her layers of rags that served as a petticoat.

'I, er, have some special things,' I said rather lamely, taken aback by their directness and wondering how I could possibly describe a tampon and its uses. 'Come to our house later on and I'll show you.'

'Ah, she has some special things,' the women echoed, apparently satisfied with my answer.

Back at the house, I put the kettle on to boil. That first day we were on show and were not left alone for long. Soon the ladder creaked and three men appeared. They balanced awkwardly on the ladder until our insistent pleas persuaded them to come inside and sit down. They introduced themselves as Ratna Bahadur, Lal Bahadur, and Prithvi Lal, Bahadur being a common suffix that meant 'the brave'. After the customary small talk they inquired whether there was any chance of finding work on the electricity project. They were all stone-masons and carpenters and claimed they were the only men in Baglung district who knew how to work with cement. They had learnt the technique from some Indian workmen who had come to Baglung a few years ago, and since then were always employed when important work had to be done. They had built the gaol and the high school buildings in Baglung. We didn't inquire whether they should at that moment have been putting the new roof on the school as the headman had requested – perhaps we were the cause of the lack of volunteers.

Duane was delighted to find men such as these so close at hand and explained where and how to apply for jobs. We invited them to stay and handed them glasses of coffee. They had never tasted it before and sipped it cautiously.

'It's good. What kind of tea is this?'

'It's a special kind of tea called coffee.'

'Ka-phi, kaphi?'

And so began their taste for coffee. Thereafter they knew just the right time to drop in for a chat, and developed an acute ear for the sound of the kettle boiling and the chink of glasses. Unfortunately the first woman we offered coffee complained it was so strong it made her dizzy, so the rest of the women were too frightened to try our 'strong liquor' and we had to be content with serving them tea. But this too was a luxury which they didn't normally keep in their homes, and even the headman would come to us to beg a few tea leaves when important guests turned up.

In the afternoon I set out to explore the village and find a family who could supply us with milk each day. Ratna Bahadur had told me to try Keshu Ram who lived in a house above us and owned several buffalo.

I climbed carefully down our ladder – some of its struts were missing and others held in place by wedges of straw – and took the path above our house. Its steep uneven steps had been carved out of the rock itself and worn smooth by countless feet. Since no part of the hillside was actually flat, the village was of necessity built on several rising layers. Our house was on the lowest level. Later I discovered there were two main paths, an upper and a lower one, with occasional offshoots, but that first day it was very confusing. The houses were tightly clustered together, the customary layout in a Magar village where the inhabitants were closely related and where land was too valuable to spare for building purposes. 'We're all one family,' was a comment we were to hear frequently in Titeng.

All the houses followed the same basic design, but no two were exactly alike. Some had had extensions added, others had been divided and subdivided. Each told its own story, reflecting its owner's whims and fortunes, the rise and decline of his household. They were of stone or bamboo on a wooden frame, liberally coated inside and out with red mud mixed with cow dung for cohesion, some with slate roofs but most with thatch. The older houses were oval-shaped, but even the newer houses had few vertical or horizontal lines in them. Not that their builders were ignorant of the skills needed to construct a good house; they knew by sight the exact pitch a thatched roof must have so that the rain would not leak through. More importantly they built in harmony with their surroundings so that the houses, painted in their red ochre, merged into the landscape and it was impossible to say where the rock ended and the houses began.

Every house, whether circular or square, had a verandah on the ground floor covered by a thatched roof that abutted the main wall of the house. This was where the men could rest during the day, where babies were slung from the rafters in hessian hammocks, and where guests were entertained. This verandah had to be freshly plastered each day with mud and cow dung to keep it clean. In Kasauli my Brahmin neighbour had told me it was done to purify the house so that the 'faithful' could enter. The Magars were not so devout, but still they followed the custom. The mud they prized was a deep red colour and only found in certain locations so the women carried it from two or three hours' walk distant and always kept an extra supply in a trough inside their houses. Set into the base of each verandah was a small pen, simply a hollowed-out space with a wooden trapdoor, and this was the coop for the chickens that scavenged freely during the daylight hours.

I stopped at Keshu's house. It was circular, with a thatched roof in need of a haircut. Built on two tiers, the thatch of the upper roof was so long and shaggy that it touched the thatch of the verandah roof and almost obscured the black eyes of the small windows set into the wall. The curved verandah was set high off the ground and when I looked closely I realised its wall was the rock itself, covered with a thick coating of mud, and the uneven steps leading into the house had been hewn out of the rock. On the verandah was a grinding stone and hanging from the roof a line of tattered blankets and quilts that were more patches than material. Beside these and attached to the wall itself was a section of tree trunk covered at either end with pieces of cactus. It was easy to identify once I spotted the bees passing in and out of the hole in its centre.

Keshu's family were sitting in their courtyard. A woman in a purple blouse and flowery red scarf had hammered wooden stakes into the ground and was weaving a straw mat. She sat very upright with her legs splayed wide and straight. Beside her a younger woman, dressed in black, massaged her baby with mustard oil – a custom they believed kept the child's skin fair.

'*Good mara–ning!*' shouted a well-groomed young man as if issuing a command to a regiment of soldiers. He was dressed in a holey khaki sweater and a watch, far too big, hung slackly on his wrist – prestige symbols of a Gurkha soldier. On his lap he cradled an enormous wide-eyed baby.

'Good morning. Does Keshu Ram live here?' I asked in English. The young man smiled and nodded his head: 'Yes.'

'Where is he?'

'Yes.' He smiled and nodded, and I tried again but he had apparently exhausted his few words of spoken English. We switched to Nepali and he introduced himself as Kanchha, Keshu's youngest son. He was a Gurkha soldier with the Indian army and temporarily home on leave. His baby was the fattest I had seen for its age in Nepal, easily outstripping the two-and three-year-olds that were gathered round, though it was only six months old. Kanchha told me it had been born in the Gurkha Camp Hospital in India and only recently returned to the village.

'So your wife was with you in India?'

'Yes. But next time she'll stay in the village. My parents need her to work in the fields.'

'And what do you do in the army? Do you like being a soldier?'

'Nothing much,' said Kanchha with a wry smile. 'We learn how to parade and play with guns. The life's all right though – we get meat once a day and a ration of rum in the evenings. But it's not as good as being in the British army – there you get to go to Hong Kong and England.'

'*I* was in the British army,' said his father Keshu Ram who had just arrived and was still wearing *his* old khaki shirt. 'I fought in the Forty War – served in Hong Kong, Malaya, Singapore, Burma. Fifteen years I spent in the army, but then my pension was cooked and now I'm eating it.'

Keshu agreed to supply us with a pint of buffalo milk a day, at two rupees a pint. This was a fair price, about the same as it cost in Baglung where it was invariably watered down.

'We're not like the Brahmins. They give you half a pint from the four-legged buffalo and half a pint from the two-legged!' said Keshu, meaning that they added water.

I hoped that getting it straight from the udder, we would not have that problem. In Nepal the cattle were small and produced little milk. They were kept to work in the fields and supply manure and it was the water buffalo who were the main milk producers. These large ungainly creatures looked like relics from prehistoric times. They had bony almost hairless black bodies, elongated necks and heads, and a wild, possessed look in their eyes. They were untamed and unpredictable and I hated meeting them on a narrow path for they had the unnerving habit of swinging their great horned heads just as I was going by, and I had heard stories of villagers knocked over the cliffs by their own buffalo. In view of these stories I would forget my pride and scramble into the nearest field when a buffalo appeared. To the Nepalis however, the buffalo was a highly prized animal. A full grown milker was worth a year's labour, so a man would take greater care of his buffalo than his children; if a child died he could always father another, but if his buffalo died, his whole family might starve.

A man's wealth could be measured by his fields, his copper pots, and his buffalo. Titeng was fairly prosperous for a Magar village – most families had one or even two buffalo. Part of their wealth came from their proximity to Baglung which in recent years had expanded considerably and provided the villagers with building work during the slack winter season, so they had a cash income which was lacking in most villages.

I concluded the agreement with Keshu who promised to bring the milk down in the morning. 'Please go well,' he said, giving the traditional farewell greeting. 'Please sit well,' I replied.

I continued up the path which twisted and turned as if avoiding an unseen enemy, until I came to the 'terrace row' I had encountered on my first visit to the village. Some women were washing dishes outside in the courtyard, squatting on the edge of the path so that the waste water and scraps of food ran down into the pig pens below. Each house in Titeng had its pig pen, for the Magars were fond of pork, a meat forbidden to most other castes. The pens were sunk into the ground and walled by slabs of slate turned up on end, and contained a trap-door leading to an underground hideout where the pigs were locked up at night. But, like the chickens, the pigs seemed to spend more time outside the pens than in. The women stopped their work and greeted me.

'Do you like our village?' they asked.

'Yes, of course I do.'

'No, you don't *really*, do you? It's not as nice as where you come from.'

'Yes, I do. I like it better.' I could tell they were pleased. They fingered my clothes, my fair hair and my skin, but my hands caused the biggest exclamations. One woman after another squeezed them and wrung them and sucked in her breath with surprise.

'How soft, how soft,' each one said. 'You've never had to work, have you?'

'Of course I have to work,' I declared indignantly. 'I use my hands just like you do.'

But after I had lived in Titeng some months I realised they were right. I had never used my hands as they did – sweeping the mud over the rough floors, clearing out the buffalo manure, picking up stones from the fields, lifting the weeds, wielding their hoes and their scythes. *Their* hands were pitted and scarred and their skin so tough they could lift burning coals out of the fire to light their pipes.

At the western end of the village I reached the cliff and the main path coming from Baglung and leading on up the mountain to villages beyond. Two large *pipal* and *banyan* trees guarded the entrance to the village, and I sat down on the stone ledge at their base. Bamboo on the cliff edge waved gently in the breeze, creaking their stems, and through their fronds I looked down to the terraced fields across the valley. From this height the river was just a small blue trickle, glistening in its boulder-strewn bed. I wondered what sort of impression we had made on our first day, and hoped it was good.

As I sat there, people passed by, exchanged greetings, and continued upwards to their villages. In this way word slowly disseminated across the whole mountainside that two foreigners had come to live in Titeng.

Later that evening as Duane and I were relaxing in our upper room, two women plucked up courage to climb our ladder and peer in. They were surprised by what they saw.

'Not cooking? Not working?' they enquired, puzzled. 'Just sitting?'

Shamefacedly we admitted our guilt.

4

We're all one family

Naina Singh's family had sixteen members when we arrived and seventeen by the time we left. They were the first people we got to know and remained our guides and closest friends throughout the year.

The family owned two houses besides the barn that we were living in. From our upper room we looked down on to their main house which was just to the right and a little below us. It was two-storeyed, not very big, with a thatched roof and a thatched verandah. Their second house was a single storey circular one at the opposite end of the courtyard. If we wanted to go to the spring we had to pass in front of their main house, and if we wanted to go to Baglung we had to pass their round house, so the family kept a close tab on our comings and goings.

It took at least a month to figure out who was who in this extended family. The Magars lived in and out of each other's homes so we never knew who belonged and who was merely visiting. The situation was further confused by the lack of names. Nepalis did not call each other by name but by relationship, for example younger brother, older sister, or by their position in the family, Second Son, Third Daughter, and so on. There were special names for all of these. The oldest son of a family was Jetha, then came Maila, Saila, Kaila, Raila, Thaila, and Kanchha. If there were more than seven sons they added a Big Kanchha and Little Kanchha, but after that they gave up; eight sons was probably the survival limit. The daughters were similarly named Jethi, Maili, Saili, and so on. This meant that in a village such as Titeng there were many Mailas and Sailas, and it was impossible to work out who was related to whom, and indeed they all claimed to be brothers and sisters. Quite often the women and children did not know their real names and besides, it was irreverent to call a person, especially one's own husband, by name. Instead they referred to him as 'Our

Master', or if they were feeling less courteous 'That Old One', or more commonly with just a jerk of the head.

The family's day began around five in the winter and as early as three in the summer, which was when we heard Devi's Mother who lived in the room below us, get up and start her grinding stone. Preparing enough flour to feed the family took considerable time and energy and Devi's Mother spent two or three hours every morning turning the small grinding stone round on its grooved base. She was married to Naina Singh's oldest son Jetha who had gone off to look for work in India. Naina Singh said he was in the Indian Army, but as the soldiers had regular leave every one or two years and Jetha had not been home for four years, the other villagers whispered that he would not be coming back now – perhaps he had died or gone off with another woman.

Naina Singh's family

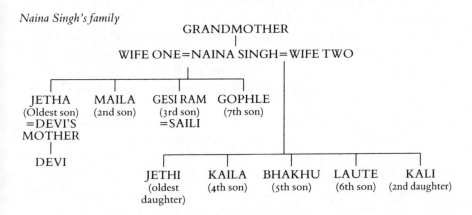

Devi's Mother did not know her own name or age. As she had a four-year-old daughter called Devi, she was known throughout the village as Devi's Mother and addressed in this way. I felt sorry for her; both her parents had died and now her husband had deserted her and she was left with no choice but to stay on with her parents-in-law, doing the most menial tasks, for daughters-in-law occupied the lowest rank in the family hierarchy. Her one claim to respect was Devi, Naina's only grandchild; an attractive and lovable little girl who was consequently spoilt by all. With no husband to buy her new clothes or jewellery Devi's Mother appeared quite shabby although she was young and had a kind, attractive face. I found her easy to get along with; she was a very humble person, often laughing at herself and saying she wasn't clever, but with a natural sensitivity and sympathy for people. She lived close to us so we saw each other a lot and she was the first person with whom I became good friends. I would try to get her in for a glass of tea some mornings, but she was always wary that Naina Singh would see her, so I took to slipping the tea inside her room and she drank it as she bent at the grinding stone.

As soon as dawn broke we would hear the clink of copper pots and see Wife One, with her youngest son in a bamboo basket on her back, disappear into the misty gloom to collect water from the spring.

Naina Singh had two wives and during the whole year in the village we never learnt their names, so they became known to us as Wife One and Wife Two. Theirs was an easy-going relationship based on a mutual respect and a division of roles. Wife One as the senior wife was in charge of the housekeeping and usually stayed close to the home. She prepared all the meals, put the grain out to dry each day, carried the water, cared for the younger children, and did the washing. Wife Two sometimes helped with these chores, but her place was in the fields.

I was intrigued by their relationship when I first arrived, and since Nepalis were not so reticent on these matters I decided to plunge in and ask: 'How do you get on with each other? Don't you ever quarrel?'

'No, not any more,' they replied. 'Sometimes we used to when we were younger, but what's there to quarrel about?'

Wife One was one of the kindest, most considerate people I have met. I never heard her raise her voice to anyone, not even to the children. She put us to shame in the way she lived her life, always ready to listen or sympathise and help in whatever way she could. She could see an unmentioned need, and several times I would return at the end of a busy day to find our water barrel filled up, or our floor freshly swept and 'mudded'. Whenever she prepared special foods she would bring a plate for us to sample, and frequently in the mornings we were woken up by her bringing us a plate of freshly popped millet or sorghum. She was quiet and retiring by nature, a worried frown hovered on her forehead, and she dressed plainly in black or homespun cloth. But in many ways she was the keystone of the family, the person they turned to with problems.

When we first arrived she called us *Sahib* and *Memsahib*, terms which though widely used seemed to have overtones of colonialism, and we disliked them.

'Please don't call us *Sahib*,' we begged. 'We're your friends. Can't you call us Brother and Sister?'

Wife One thought for a moment. 'No,' she said. 'You're the same age as my children. I will call you *Nani* (child).'

So thereafter she called us Big Child and Little Child, and we were touched by the love that was implicit in these names.

The family's water requirements were modest and they managed to get by on about twenty gallons a day. This water had to be carried by hand so each woman did at least one trip a day to the spring, and often two or three.

Wife Two shared in the water carrying. In contrast to Wife One, she was always laughing. She carried her pipe and tobacco leaves in the front pouch of her blouse so that they were close to hand, and we rarely saw her sitting down without a small clay pipe in her mouth. She had strong Tibetan-type features with sagging eyelids that almost obscured her eyes. In spite of this I managed to confuse her with Keshu Ram's wife on account of their rings. Nepali women rarely wore rings on their fingers, but Wife Two had a distinctive one on the third finger of her left hand. It was triangular-shaped, of red and turquoise enamel, and I used it as an identification mark at the beginning when I was confused by all the people. Unfortunately Keshu Ram's wife had one exactly the same, and as she lived in the next house and was of similar age and build to Wife Two, for a long time I thought they were the same person.

This was Wife Two's second marriage. Her previous husband had died, leaving her with one child, and her parents had then given her to Naina Singh as his second wife. We were not sure why Naina had taken two wives, and we never summoned up the courage to ask him outright. It was quite acceptable, though not common. The usual reason for a second wife, or even a third or fourth, was lack of children or male heirs, but this was not the case with Naina. Grandmother told me that her husband had died shortly after Naina, their first child, was born. Consequently their land was not divided and Naina had inherited all, so perhaps he took two wives to produce a large family and share the burden of childrearing so that at least one wife was free to work in the fields until the children were bigger. Between them the two wives had managed to raise seven sons and two daughters; the three oldest sons and the youngest were Wife One's, and the rest were Wife Two's, but they were treated equally by the two women.

Whilst the two wives were carrying water, Saili and Devi's Mother would put handfuls of crumbly red clay into a wooden trough, add water, and mix it to the consistency of a runny porridge. This was for doing the *lipnu* – the layer of mud which they smeared with their hands over the verandah and entrance to the houses each morning. Where the edges had been broken up they worked in fresh green cow dung to bind the mud together. When Devi's Mother did the *lipnu*, she always included our doorway as well, but if it was Saili's turn, she was much too shy to approach this close on her own.

Saili was Naina Singh's other daughter-in-law, married to his third son, Gesi Ram. They had only been married for three months when we arrived and they slept at the far end of our upper room, behind a shoulder height mud partition. Saili was a shy oriental beauty, with wide prominent cheekbones, slanting dark eyes, delicately curved eyebrows, and a small nose almost hidden by the jewelled ornaments that pierced it. She had a high girlish voice and was given to blushing and fits of giggles. Duane had only to look at her and she would dissolve behind her shawl shaking with laughter.

The women didn't seem to work to a pre-arranged schedule, but each knew what had to be done and quietly did whatever was needed. Sometimes Wife One would do the *lipnu*, and Devi's Mother would mind the children, and often all the women would be involved in water carrying.

When the family's five water pots were full, Wife One would go inside the main house to prepare the first meal of the day. Not long after this we would see a line of animated haystacks and bushes file across the courtyard and disappear into the buffalo stable. It was hard to identify who was underneath these mounds of fodder for all we could see were their legs and feet. If these were large and dirty and proceeded at a steady plodding pace towards the buffalo shed, it was probably Wife Two or Gesi Ram, but if they were skinny and dirty and the haystack bounced along scattering leaves and stalks in its wake, we knew it was Bhakhu.

Bhakhu was son number five and my favourite. He had caught my attention on our first visit to the village and this image remained in my mind. He had been leaning against the courtyard wall of Naina Singh's house puffing on the stub of a cigarette, *topi* cocked forward on his head, eyes half-closed to two slanting black slits, looking like a tough young Gurkha who has just demolished the enemy single-handed. When he saw me looking at him the image dissolved; his face cracked into a wide grin and he became just another child with a head that was too big for his skinny neck and body. He was thirteen, but like most Nepali children appeared younger because of his small size.

Bhakhu didn't allow the problems of life to get him down. He would stride through the village with his head in the air looking more like a young *raja* than a goatherd, smiling at the world with his row of perfectly formed teeth. Bhakhu had experimented with school, but after three years when he learnt nothing more than how to scrawl his name, he had given up and started working fulltime in the fields. He was at the awkward stage when he didn't know to which group he belonged. One day he would be playing five stones in the dust with his younger brothers Laute and Gophle, and the next day he would tie a red kerchief round his neck and be off with the young men to watch girls in the bazaar.

Feeding the water buffalo, like the water-carrying, was a never-ending task, and one that had to be done every day, no matter whether the family were busy or sick or had a wedding or a funeral to attend. If the buffalo were hungry their agonising moans pierced the thickest of mud walls and drowned the loudest of children's screams. Each buffalo needed at least two man-loads of grass or other fodder a day, but this was a bare minimum.

'They'll eat whatever amount we give them,' said Wife Two.

'Water and grass. That's our life,' said Devi's Mother, speaking for the women. 'That's all we know about.'

The buffalo in the village were kept tied up to protect the crops and children, and this meant that all their fodder had to be gathered by hand. In the summer months there was plenty of lush green grass, but in the winter when no rain fell every blade shrivelled and the buffalo were dependent on straw from last year's crops and the leaves of the trees. Gesi Ram or Bhakhu would climb to the tops of the trees and balance precariously whilst they lopped off every branch and leaf until the tree was completely shorn except for a topknot of one or two thin branches that were always left. It was dangerous work but even the women did it in their long skirts.

The buffalo knew the timetable and waited expectantly in the mornings. As soon as the first load of grass appeared, each buffalo set up a chorus of groans hoping the grass would be unloaded into *its* feeding trough. They were extremely temperamental and it was only possible to milk them when their attention was diverted by a mound of fresh fodder. Even so the family's buffalo gave their milk only for Naina Singh, and we secretly thought this most appropriate for there was no doubt that our landlord was himself a very temperamental person.

Naina Singh was the only person in the village who was not immediately friendly and welcoming to us, and in the course of our stay, particularly early on, we had a number of disagreements with him. He was not a person with whom we could strike up a casual conversation; often silent and morose, given to muttering to himself, he rarely joined in the courtyard conversations. But with time, we learnt how to handle him and to ignore his strange touchy ways.

His sons were his main cause of melancholy.

'They have no common sense!' he moaned to us one day. 'No intelligence, not one of them. Why do I have such stupid sons?'

'But Gesi Ram – he's smart,' we objected, trying to cheer him up.

'Gesi Ram? No! He's just as dumb as the rest.'

His womenfolk also caused him considerable irritation. They were never quite quick enough to jump to his command and in his opinion spent too much time gossiping and not enough time working. Admittedly he did have a real cause for anxiety in providing for his large family. Of his seven sons, two had left home to seek their fortunes elsewhere, one was physically and mentally handicapped, and three were too young to work in the fields. This meant that Naina had only Gesi Ram to help him, and a lot of hungry mouths to feed. He was fond of pointing this out and at times would almost grovel before us and say what a poor man he was. Perhaps he hoped to get some extra money from us in this way, though he never actually asked for it outright. Nobody else in the village ever presumed upon our wealth or commented on it except in a light-hearted manner. They respected the things we had and if they borrowed an item such as kerosene, they returned it in full measure.

Naina Singh could be annoyingly obsequious at times. Whilst other people called us Brother or Sister, Naina addressed us as *Sahib*, and when we passed by would cuff one of his young sons and make him say '*Namaste Sahib*'. This embarrassed us but we found the best course was to ignore it, and in time we established a good relationship with him.

In the winter months once the buffalo were fed and milked, the men could relax in the courtyard until Wife One called them to eat their morning meal, but in the summer months both the men and the women put in two to three hours in the fields before returning for food. They ate two meals a day, the first between 8 and 10 o'clock in the morning, and the second in the evening.

After the morning meal, courtyard life quietened down. Bhakhu would take the goats out to graze and the rest of the family would disperse to work in the fields or whatever task was on hand. The family's goats were Bhakhu's responsibility. Every day he let them out of the pen beside our downstairs room and guided them out to forage along the cliffsides and down by the river. Often the boys of the village would band their flocks together and this gave them more freedom to talk to each other or splash about in the river. One time this had disastrous results. We knew something was the matter when we saw Naina Singh pacing the courtyard, muttering to himself and glowering at everybody. We stayed out of his way and soon we saw Gesi Ram bearing a dead goat on his back and Bhakhu following, for once his shoulders sagging and his jaunty impudent smile missing. The goat had fallen over the cliff.

The men burned the hair off the goat and cut it up right there in the courtyard. Thanks to Bhakhu we enjoyed an unseasonal meal of goat meat. Naina Singh called at our room later on when we were drinking coffee. 'Can I come in?' he asked, having first checked that the time was right for a drink. We invited him in and offered him one of our two bamboo stools to sit on and a glass of coffee.

'What would you do?' he asked, turning to Duane. 'Such a family I have! My son Bhakhu! He lets my goats fall down the cliff. I've been out all day working hard cutting grass, and now I come back home very tired and what do I find? – My goat has fallen over the cliff and my wives haven't lit the fire yet – they haven't *even lit the fire!*' His voice squeaked higher than usual in his frustration. 'Such sons! Such a family! My women don't obey or respect me as they ought.'

'Yes, I know,' sympathised Duane, with a sidelong glance and smile at me. 'My wife is just the same. No obedience, no respect!'

'Women!' said Naina, shaking his head and making a face. 'They have no intelligence.'

When Bhakhu was busy in the fields, his younger brother Laute would take care of the goats, but on other days Laute went to school. He was eight and in class two and could already write his own name, which was more than his father could do.

The younger children, Kali, Gophle, and Devi, had no specific tasks, and spent their day playing in the courtyard with the neighbours' children, or tagging Wife One around as she did the chores. Kali, the youngest daughter, was six, and Gophle at five years of age was the seventh and youngest son. Wife One would potter around the courtyard feeding the pigs and chickens, cleaning out the buffalo stall, and laying out the family's grain store to dry in the sun. This was a chore that had to be done almost every day to prevent mould growing, as the bamboo storage containers were not airtight. She would sift through the grains discarding any black or mouldy ones, and get rid of the dirt and stones by deftly tossing the grains into the air on a round bamboo tray.

'*We're all one family*' was the motto of Titeng. There were no rules or regulations, no precise boundaries or fences delineating where one family's territory ended and another's began. Frequently Wife One would have another's baby strapped to her back as she pottered about in the yard, or Mati Lal's wife would come down to sit with Gophle and Grandmother if Wife One had to go out to the fields. At times I would see six-year-old Kali grinding corn with Prithvi Lal's wife, or Bhakhu helping to plough Lal Bahadur's fields. Theirs was an informal, tolerant society. Their children were rarely disciplined; until the age of seven or eight they were allowed to run wild, but after that they had to work. By this age they had connected work with food, and that seemed to be all the discipline that was required.

As soon as the sun was really strong in the courtyard, Grandmother would appear. She was the oldest person in the village, a good many years past seventy though she did not know her exact age. She had high status in the family, second only to her son Naina Singh, and in the village, where she was known simply as 'Grandmother'. We always knew where to find her; a corner of the open buffalo stable attached to the house was reserved for her, and here she had her straw mat, her coarse rough blanket for sleeping, and her basket of rough unspun goat's wool. Day in, day out, we would find her sitting on her mat, one knee drawn up under her armpit, the other leg tucked beneath her, plying the greasy tangled wool through her fingers till it became smooth and soft, then spinning it into a coarse thread on her wooden drop spindle. We felt sorry that in her weakened old age she was relegated to the buffalo stable where the chilly winds of winter blew straight through, but the family saw it in practical terms: 'It's too difficult to carry her in and out of the house', they said.

Grandmother could no longer walk. Her joints had stiffened and now her knees were permanently locked into a bent position. She claimed they gave her no pain, but maybe she was just tough. Her spirit, as if to make up for her physical weakness, was extra sharp, and we would frequently hear the strident tones of her voice ringing out across the yard as she scolded one of her many grandchildren or daughters-in-law.

During the sunny winter days when we first arrived, Grandmother would leave her stable to sit in the yard outside. It was the job of Maila, the handicapped son, to carry her in and out, and we nicknamed him the 'granny carriage'. They made an odd pair with their combined disabilities. It often developed into a battle of wills, for Maila's thoughts were prone to stray from the job on hand, and with Grandmother on his back, he would stop to stare in through our windows to check on what we were doing. Grandmother would storm and yell at him, but she was helpless in his hands, and Maila knew it. He would act deaf and all Grandmother's shouts and threats were in vain until he chose to move on again.

Once deposited on her mat in the sun, with the basket and spindle beside her, Grandmother would proceed to strip off her blouses and *patuka* and expose her sagging wrinkled breasts. Inspecting her clothes she would extract the fleas and bugs, occasionally breaking off to scratch her body with her long clawing fingernails. Her hands were gnarled and twisted, the large swollen knuckles locked into a tight grip, yet this did not prevent her spinning.

'See? Tease the wool and gently pull out the thread as you turn the spindle. It's not hard. I taught Wife One how to spin. I tried to teach my granddaughters-in-law, but they weren't interested. Look, when you have a length of thread like this, wind it up on the spindle and start again.'

Wife One brought me out a hand-carved spindle and Grandmother started me off. I tried and got a lumpy yarn that became too thin and broke.

'You have to keep it even. Don't do it too fast. The wool isn't good. It's coarse and short, but it's all we can get. Years ago we used to get fine long hair.'

I watched in admiration as her deformed hands drew out a fine even thread from the tangled wool. In no small measure this contributed to her sense of fulfilment; Grandmother was still a useful and functioning member of the family despite her age and disabilities.

Grandmother was our self-appointed time-keeper, always anxious to know where we were going and why. If she was not in the yard, she would peer round the end of the stable to check on our arrival or departure, and nothing escaped her sharp eyes. We soon learned to report to her when we came and went. Used to our own independence this could be irksome, especially when we wanted to leave in a hurry, but it also gave us a wonderful feeling of belonging and being missed. At first she rather disapproved of us and scolded me several times for not locking our lower room door or removing our ladder when we went out. In those days I avoided her and was careful not to annoy, but as time passed Grandmother visibly softened till at the end she was one of our staunchest friends.

As relations eased I would always stop and chat with her when I returned from the bazaar and give her a report of what I had done. Her favourite topic of conversation was agriculture. She would comment on who had planted their crops and who was late doing so, who had repaired their irrigation channels and who had not, and she loved to point out some fields high up across the valley where the lucky farmers managed to grow two crops of rice a year. As she talked she would break off to utter a raucous ha! ha! ha! to the chickens who had strayed too near the grain spread out to dry, or to hawk and spit into the conveniently situated pigpen just below the courtyard.

One day as I was sitting with her watching the valley and its life, her head stiffened. 'Three have gone by today,' she said. I followed the direction of her eyes and saw a funeral procession wending its way down the valley. The corpse, wrapped in white and carried on a bamboo stretcher, was preceded by a group of musicians wailing on their long horns, and followed by a procession of relatives and friends. They were on their way to the Kali Gandaki river, a sacred tributary of the Ganges, where there were cremation *ghats*. So Grandmother sat there, day by day, keeping a tally of the bodies, knowing that her turn would soon come.

When there was a break in her chores, Wife One would get out her weaving. She hammered pegs for one end into the courtyard wall and supported the other end by a leather strap which passed round her back. She always sat bolt upright, legs straight, her balls of grey and dark brown wool on one side, and her smoothly polished wooden shuttles on the other. While most families in Titeng wove lengths of cotton material, Naina Singh's family wove woollen blankets, because only they had Grandmother with the time and patience to spin into wool the fleeces, which they bought from itinerant Tibetan traders. Grandmother sorted the hairs into boxes of white, black, brown, and grey, before spinning, and Wife One wove these into thick coarse blankets and shawls for the winter months.

'They used to bring us sheep's wool,' said Wife One. 'But now we can only get goat's. It's not so good – the wool is coarse and breaks easily.'

Maila, after depositing Grandmother in the sun, would stand and stare until she lost her temper.

'Get on with you! Be off! Go and do some work for a change,' Grandmother would say, and he would grin and slowly wander off in his stumbling gait. Maila was Naina Singh's second son and the most endearing of people. When we first arrived he was our most regular and faithful visitor, our shadow in everything we did. When we got up in the morning, Maila was there. He would stare at us with an intense child-like curiosity while we made our breakfast and frequently shared a cup of coffee, and when we finally went to bed he was often still there. We got used to his presence and quite missed him later on when the work in the fields increased and Maila's visits became less frequent.

The family declared that he was *laato*, unable to talk, a term applied indiscriminately to deaf people and anyone who was not normal. Maila suffered from a combination of disabilities: he was partially deaf, mildly mentally handicapped, and physically uncoordinated so that he walked with a drunken stagger. In spite of this he was extremely strong, and we discovered that he was not so deaf that he could not hear, nor so dumb that he could not turn this partial deafness to his own advantage.

'Maila!' Wife One would call. 'Go take the cows out.' Maila would turn a conveniently deaf ear. We knew he could hear and understand, because often he was up in our room and he would glance at us with a conspiratorial grin on his face. So Maila was a lazy, affectionate *laato*, scoldings poured off him like water, and though Naina Singh and the rest of the family yelled at him, they could not shake Maila from his complacency.

'Poor Maila,' Wife One said one day. 'He should be married by now but we can't find a girl who'll have him.'

'Maila? What good is he?' said Naina Singh. 'He can't even plough!'

But Maila did not worry about his lack of accomplishments and was one of the happiest people in the village. He had an irresistible grin and a loud uncontrolled laugh. He was the butt of many jokes, but never seemed to mind, and would laugh good-naturedly at them. But in spite of their jokes the family and villagers treated him with a great deal of tolerance, made allowance for his weakness, and probably showed him more love and acceptance than most disabled people receive.

In winter the sun left the courtyard by 3 o'clock, for Titeng faced north. Grandmother would pull little Devi inside her shawl and wait for Wife One to put the grain away and carry them both inside. Darkness fell around 6 pm and, as the rest of the family returned tired and hungry from their day's work with baskets of fodder on their backs, the buffalo set up their evening demand for food. From every house smoke curled through the thatch or slates to blend with the approaching night.

Evening was often the only time we would see Gesi Ram, Naina's third son. Like his father he was not a great one for joining in the courtyard conversations that the other men enjoyed so much, so we found him hard to get to know. But he was a hard, steady worker. We never met his younger brother Kaila, the fourth son who was working as a carpenter in Rukum, eight days' trek west of Titeng. As each festival approached the family talked of the possibility that Kaila or the oldest son Jetha might return, but each time their hopes were dashed, and we never met either of them. We did, however, meet their oldest daughter Jethi who was already married and lived with her husband's family up the valley. As she visited Titeng frequently and stayed for weeks at a time she was very much part of the family still. Like her mother Wife Two, Jethi was outgoing and full of fun, constantly laughing and joking.

When the evening meal was eaten, the day was over. There were no lights and it was expensive to keep the fire burning, so the family retired to sleep on their rice-straw mats on the floor. Wife Two and the younger children stayed where they were and slept in the main house warmed by the fire, Gesi Ram and Saili climbed the notched pole to their partition on the upper floor of our barn, and Devi and her mother retired to their room on the lower floor. Wife One crossed the courtyard to the small oval house, and Maila and Bhakhu wrapped themselves up in blankets on the verandah.

Naina Singh, for a reason he kept to himself, slept in a haystack in the nearest field.

5

Lighting the lamp in Titeng

Our lower room had dried out and we began to unpack the rest of our belongings and move them downstairs. We had been living in a cramped space amongst the straw in the attic of the barn which was now becoming inadequate for entertaining the great influx of visitors who daily climbed our ladder. We decided to make the lower room our kitchen as Naina Singh was unhappy for us to cook upstairs near the straw and the thatched roof.

This straw was a source of contention. Naina Singh now claimed we had agreed to rent only *half* the attic and therefore he would retain his straw in the other half. We produced the contract document, fortunately thumb-printed by Naina Singh and countersigned by Gesi Ram, which stated we had agreed to rent the whole room up to the partition.

Naina Singh took the document warily as if it might explode, turned it over several times in his hands, scrutinised the writing and then told us quite rightly what he thought of contracts and their makers. The rest of the village sat on their verandahs and listened carefully, enjoying every minute. In Nepal business is transacted in the open and this particular discussion took place in Naina Singh's courtyard, easily audible in the other houses. Naina continued to be difficult and finally stalked off leaving the matter unresolved.

We looked for Gesi Ram who had read the contract and who we hoped might persuade his father to stick to it. But Gesi Ram had wisely disappeared. To our surprise though, the other villagers including the headman were on our side and promised to talk to Naina Singh.

'Be patient,' said the headman diplomatically. 'Naina Singh doesn't mean to be difficult but he's getting old and doesn't understand these things too well. You're paying a good price so we'll talk to him about it.'

We were sorry to have caused a quarrel so early in our stay, and felt rather guilty because the space we wanted, though small, would normally have housed a family of six, not two. To salve our consciences we explained it was our custom to have separate places for cooking and sleeping. They nodded their heads gravely and promised to help but the straw remained, covering a good two-thirds of the attic floor.

In our lower room Duane made some wooden shelves and Devi's Mother helped me reorganise our things. To our way of thinking we had not brought much – our clothes, some books and files, two paraffin lamps, a stove, a radio, guitar, camera, some cushions and mattresses, a plastic water barrel, and a variety of cooking utensils including some Tupperware containers for storing food, two stoneware pots, a couple of pans, three Nepali brass plates and an assortment of knives and forks in case we entertained people who were not accustomed to using their fingers. As Devi's Mother and I scrambled up and down the ladder carrying the kitchen equipment, the crowd of onlookers grew larger and larger. I didn't mind, except they would position themselves on the ladder itself so that each trip required a gymnast's balance as I passed them with my hands full. Their whispered comments half-amused and half-annoyed me.

'So much stuff for just two people. She must be starting a shop. Look at all those things on the shelves.'

My frustration grew and my self-consciousness increased as I saw our possessions littered around the floor. I wished I had chosen a more private time of day to move them. But happily they provided the onlookers with much entertainment.

'What's that tyack tyack?' asked Wife Two. I picked up our clock and gave a quick demonstration of how it worked. She was fascinated, having never seen one before, but Bhakhu, the Class Three drop-out, was able to show her how to tell the time.

Our radio caused a lot of excitement, particularly to Maila the handicapped son who couldn't leave it alone and sat for hours pushing all the knobs and buttons, bending his good ear down to listen to the music. The 'black box' they named it, but after initial excitement expressed their disappointment that it didn't speak their language. I searched for Radio Nepal, but Titeng was so hemmed in by mountains it was impossible to hear their weak signal; only the Chinese and Russian propaganda stations came over loud and clear. The radio was in fact a combination tape-recorder, but since we used it mostly for playing pre-recorded cassettes, it was some months before the villagers discovered the full magic of the 'black box'.

Above: The fields of Titeng
Below: Our 'house', on the day we arrived. Straw still in upper room
– new door and window frames at our request in lower room

Above left: Tiring work. Wife One and Wife Two working the rice dhiki
Above right: Children on the ladder leading to our upper room
Below: Preparing the evening meal inside their house. *Left to right*: Wife One, Wife Two, Mail

Their interest in the radio was not surprising, but they were equally intrigued by our paraffin lamps. We had two, one of which was a graceful tall-stemmed Aladdin lamp that gave off quite a powerful light. Its fame soon spread around the mountainside.

'I know where you live,' said an old man on the other side of the valley. 'Every morning I sit on my verandah and look across to your bright light. It used to be dark in Titeng but now it shines.'

'We've heard about the bright light in Titeng and we've come to see it,' visitors from distant villages would announce, balancing themselves on our ladder so that just their heads were visible. 'How it shines! We don't need a bright light like this – we can't read or write. We just eat and go to sleep at night.'

Laute and Gophle loved to watch the ritual lighting of the Aladdin lamp, particularly the moment when once the wick was flaring properly I replaced the tall cylindrical glass bulb and the mantle burst into a white glow.

With the extra space we made ourselves comfortable. The downstairs room which was small but had a proper door and window with shutters became our kitchen, pantry and dining-room. We didn't spend much time in this room, only going there to cook and eat, because it was dark and rather damp as one wall abutted the mountainside. But it was a useful storage room, and when visitors came they could sleep here in privacy. Duane obtained a large slab of stone from the quarry above Baglung and we laid this on the floor and put our two paraffin stoves on top. As a concession to comfort we had two bamboo stools. We really should have squatted, with our knees spread wide apart behind our armpits and our feet flat on the ground, which is the way Nepalis do their cooking, but it was impossible. I could squat on my toes for a limited time, but if I put my feet flat on the floor I fell over backwards, to the amusement of anyone watching.

The upstairs room with its ever-open windows was our lounge, study and bedroom. We laid straw mats over the floor and alongside the two-tone mud walls placed our cotton mattresses covered with a red flower-flecked cloth particularly liked by the Magars. These mattresses served as beds by night and armchair and sofa by day.

In the corner nearest the doorway I hung a curtain of the same flowery material and behind this we hung our clothes from a small bamboo bar. Towels and underwear we stuffed in a *doko*. These conical baskets made of interwoven slats of bamboo were versatile containers and we kept a ready supply of them. The villagers used them for carrying loads, for chicken coops, and as cribs for their babies; *we* used them as cupboards, laundry baskets, rubbish bins, and upside down as seats.

The tops of the walls at shoulder height formed a convenient shelf running the length of the upper room. From these the roof slanted upwards to its peak in the centre, supported on unplaned beams of wood and heavy bamboo. Two vertical posts in the middle of the room and at each end added their support. Because the barn was built into the slope the overhang of the roof touched the ground at the back. Duane particularly liked this room which gave him the freedom to walk around without bumping his head; downstairs he could only stand upright between the supporting beams. The vertical posts were a hazard in the dark but we pitted them with nails for hangers and Duane constructed a couple more shelves for odds and ends. Finally we hung some pictures on the uneven walls and the villagers found this concept of decoration strange but nice.

Living on the floor our mattresses and clothes quickly became dusty, and our knees got much practice at bending. As we normally sat in the upper room this was where visitors called, so to serve them tea we had to go outside via the bamboo ladder to the kitchen. But Duane, being tall, was able to stand outside the kitchen and pass the tea glasses in through the upstairs window, and our house became renowned for this dumb-waiter service.

Another problem was the wild life that shared our house. I used to pride myself on my coolness – I could pick up a spider with my hands and let a mouse run across the room without jumping for a chair – but in Titeng the problems were magnified by the straw. We not only had ants, spiders, scorpions, cockroaches, flies, and mosquitoes, but some very sizeable rats who made their nests deep in the straw, and the family's chickens who had the habit of flying up to peck through it, often upsetting our belongings and once sending our precious Aladdin lamp crashing to the floor. I was dismayed to find that the rats chewed holes in our books and underwear and even through the Tupperware containers to extract the sugar and flour inside.

I unpacked a rat-size trap made in the U.S.A. which a thoughtful friend had provided as a farewell gift. It had a strong spring which almost amputated my fingers the first time I tried to set it. I positioned it on the floor near the straw. When I came back later in the day there was no rat but a bundle of feathers. To my horror it proved to be one of the family's chickens that must have flown up and pecked at the scrap of food on the trap. It was dead. Regretfully I took it over to Wife One and offered to pay. 'Don't worry,' she said. 'It was only a young one.' We had a delicious chicken stew for supper that night. Later in the year when food was strictly rationed we were tempted to arrange another 'accident'.

At my second attempt I placed the trap on the shelf formed where the low walls met the thatched roof. Judging from the droppings along it, this was the rats' highway from the straw to the foodstuff. Unwisely we lay down to sleep right underneath this bit of wall, and in the middle of the night there was a loud snap, a squeal, and a monstrous rat with a necklace of trap landed on me, dripping blood. It was still alive – the American designers of the trap had obviously not been familiar with the size and stamina of Nepali rats – and began to run in circles round the room. I screamed loudly and shook Duane awake. He cordonned the rat in a corner and gave it a death blow.

'What happened in the night?' said Saili, next morning. 'We could hear you screaming through the partition.' I told her the story and she shook her head with amusement. 'You can't do anything with those rats. They eat one part in ten of our grain.'

On a bleak cold morning around 5.30 Naina Singh appeared in our room. Duane was away in Kasauli ordering supplies, and I was still sleeping.

'I must move the straw out today,' Naina muttered. 'Must move my straw out.' He always repeated his sentences at least twice. Delighted at this unexpected move, I raised no objection to the inconvenient hour. I struggled into my clothes as best I could inside my sleeping-bag, for Naina, being unfamiliar with our foreign custom of dressing and undressing at night, had decided to squat in one corner of the room. Quickly I carried downstairs our more valuable things and covered up our clothes. Then for a couple of hours Naina, Maila, Bhakhu, and myself struggled back and forth with the bundles of straw. When we had finished it seemed as if a hurricane had blown through the room, but with the straw gone, we said goodbye with much relief to the rats.

The villagers tolerated the rats but were concerned about the larger beasts, both real and imaginary, that roamed outside. One night we were woken by an uproar from the villagers: '*Kira ayo!* A beast has come!' Their calls echoed across the valley and up the mountain and were taken up by one village after another until the whole mountainside was resounding with cries. Then they started beating the drums. We sat in the darkness listening, but the beat was hypnotic and we soon fell asleep again. The village was full of talk the next morning.

'A *kira* stole two of Lal Bahadur's pigs last night,' said Wife One.

'What kind of *kira*?'

'A large animal with spots. A caste that eats meat not grain. It lives in the forest at the top or in the cliffs by the river. On full moon nights it comes looking for food. We shout and beat the drums to frighten it away.'

It sounded like a leopard. I knew that they were found in Nepal but hadn't expected them to hunt so close to habitation. The following night I heard some deep leopard-like grunts right outside our room. I was very excited and tried to shine the torch to get a glimpse of the animal, but it must have slipped away at the first sign of disturbance. The drum-beating and yelling started again and went on for several hours. Duane remained sceptical of my story but next morning the evidence was there – two young goats from Keshu Ram's house just above ours had been taken. The leopard continued to harass the village throughout the winter months but disappointingly we never caught sight of it.

Now that our house was organised there was one thing we still lacked – a toilet. The village 'toilet' was a grove of bamboo set in a small gully at the eastern end of the village – an area that had to be approached with great care. Not only was it unpleasant and inconvenient as there was no cover in the daylight hours, but it was full of flies and a source of disease. Throughout Nepal there was a lack of sanitation and little understanding about the causes of disease. As in Titeng they generally assigned an unproductive area outside the village – a pathway or a gully – to be used as the toilet area, and in the monsoon the run-off from these areas caused pollution of the rivers and other water sources, so that dysentery was very common. We decided to build ourselves a proper pit latrine. It would give us some privacy and lessen the risk of infection, and we hoped would provide a practical demonstration of good hygiene.

Constructing the latrine was not easy. Naina Singh wouldn't allow it to be close to the houses because it was unclean and would pollute them, so we agreed to build it on the second terrace field below the courtyard. Maila and another fellow helped to dig the pit and as Duane was at work I was left to supervise. 'Make sure the pit's no less than four feet deep. Otherwise it'll flood in the rainy season,' Duane told me.

Communicating with Maila was quite a problem, and with his friend was not much easier. The villagers said they both had 'deep minds' which puzzled me as neither of them seemed to be the intellectual type, but I soon learned it meant 'deep' like a well, taking a long time for the penny to drop and instructions to sink in. They stared at their spades, circled the spot, and finally began to dig. Who could blame them their confusion? To them it was a mysterious useless hole and to make matters worse, when the hole was deep enough I told them to cover it over with large flat stones.

'Used to make us build those in the army,' shouted Keshu Ram who kept an eye on everything from his courtyard which overlooked ours. 'Never understood why – dirty habit always going in the same place. Most unclean.'

The latrine was finally finished to our satisfaction and we built a bamboo shelter over it and opened it for public inspection. 'Very fine,' said the villagers as they filed in one by one. But nobody started to build their own. Its main drawback was the distance from our house. To reach it we had to descend our ladder and the steps into the courtyard, cross the courtyard, go down a notched pole on to the first terraced field and finally down some very wobbly stone ledges on to the second terrace and the toilet – a hazardous route at any time but especially in the dark.

For the first week the children lined up along the courtyard whenever we visited the little hut and tried to peer through its bamboo slats, but the novelty soon wore off and they left us to use it in peace. To our knowledge nobody else used our latrine or built their own, preferring their customary spot among the bamboo. Reluctantly we had to admit our first public health effort had failed, and we had much to learn about communicating effectively.

When I was next in Baglung I was dismayed to see what a landmark we had created. The latrine stood like a lone sentinel against the barren fields – a folly of western culture. I hurried home and planted the site with Morning Glory seeds and by the summer the latrine was covered with a profusion of purple and blue flowers.

These early days were full and busy as we settled down and learnt to cope with our new lifestyle. The everyday chores took so much time that the day passed quickly leaving me with little sense of achievement. Living without electricity we used the daylight hours more efficiently, getting up and going to bed earlier than usual. Our day began at 6 am when the general level of noise and sunlight flooding through the openings made sleep or even comfortable dozing impossible. We got up, threw our sleeping covers into a *doko* and went down the ladder to make breakfast. Breakfast was a bonus meal that the rest of the village did without. We had tried to do the same but found we became too hungry. Unlike the villagers we couldn't eat the enormous helpings of rice or millet that they managed at one sitting, so we compromised and started our day in true English style with breakfast. This was usually porridge, but sometimes muesli if we had bought some on the last trip to Kathmandu. We missed having bread. There was none available in the bazaar and without an oven we could only make *roti*.

After breakfast we made a trip to the spring to fetch water. The spring was situated just half a mile downhill from the village, but on the uphill return with a full water pot the half-mile seemed to grow longer and longer. The village women carried their water pots in bamboo *dokos* on their backs, supported by a *namlo* (tumpline) that passed over their foreheads. After one or two futile attempts to balance the water pot on my hips, I took a tip from them and fitted myself with a *doko* and *namlo*. On the first attempt I heaved the full water pot into the *doko*, adjusted the *namlo* to what I hoped was the right angle on my head, and strained to get up. Nothing happened. I tried again. My knees simply wouldn't straighten and I toppled sideways.

'Put it on the ledge. It's too hard to start from the ground,' said the women.

I took a deep breath and heaved the *doko* and water pot on to the ledge, splashing myself in the process. This time I was able to get up without my knees buckling but it took all my strength and stamina to balance along the narrow muddy path back to the village. On the steeper sections the weight of the water reduced my stride to tiny mincing steps. To make matters worse the *doko* bounced around as I walked, rubbing a sore spot and spilling a steady stream of water down my back and legs. By the time I reached our house the lower part of me was drenched and the water pot half-empty. Again I studied their method and discovered they used short squat *dokos* that were more stable on their backs. But still water was spilled and each woman wore a piece of sacking over her back to save her clothes from becoming soaked. Despite further practice my performance didn't improve, so Duane usually carried our water, holding the pot in one hand by its flattened out rim. Water-carrying was not normally a man's job, but Duane had already broken their customs, to Grandmother's horror, by taking his turn at washing our dishes in the courtyard. My sense of failure was further rubbed in when one day I met Wife One, who was smaller and older than me, returning from the spring with two full pots and Gophle her five-year-old balanced on her shoulders, a load that must have been over 100 lbs and more than her own weight.

We soon learnt to conserve water, and our 8-gallon barrel could last for two days. Like our neighbours we used the water we carried only for drinking, cooking, and doing the dishes, and if I wanted to wash our clothes or wash myself I went to the spring or the river. The river had the advantage that it was never crowded and there was unlimited water and plenty of rocks on which to dry the clothes. It was directly below the village and the path descended in steep zig-zags through the terraced fields.

The floods of past rainy seasons had brought down many boulders, damming the river into a series of deep pools and cataracts. On the south bank, growing out of fissures between the boulders, three sacred *swami* trees spread their massive branches low across the water. When I needed to escape this was my favourite place, for it was quiet and only the goats and cows came down to graze. I loved to sit on the high boulders in the shade of the *swami* trees and watch the river rushing past and the white-capped river chats playing in its spray. From time to time a dipper would hurry upstream, wingtips just flicking the surface of the water, or a magnificent white-breasted kingfisher would plunge into one of the foaming pools.

Tucked in amongst the boulders and *swami* trees were three tumbledown stables where some buffalo were kept. During the day they were turned loose to graze. Being unused to humans they always panicked at my arrival, and so did I. They would snort and buck and attempt a suicidal jump from the boulders to the river. With my heart thumping, I would creep past them and then they would calm down again.

My washing spot was a wide flat stone in the river that made the ideal scrubbing-board. 'You aren't doing it right,' Mati Lal's wife yelled across the water one day. 'Look, your soap is flowing down the river.'

She produced a hard cake of brown soap and proceeded to scrub my clothes, occasionally slapping them against the rock. It seemed a good way to get them clean under the circumstances so I followed her example, and after a few months our clothes were reduced to rags, just like the villagers'. Theirs were patched and darned so many times it was often impossible to find more than a scrap of the original material.

I would spread the clothes to dry across the boulders. Even on winter days they dried quickly in the sun, and regardless of their original bright colours, bleached to a light greyish-brown. I had to keep an eye on the goats who found that Marks and Spencer's underwear made a tasty supplement to their normally frugal diet of grass and leaves. I grew to enjoy washing days and would sometimes take a quick dip in the icy water. Washing myself presented a problem for unless the river was totally deserted it had to be done with my clothes on, or at least a long petticoat or *lungi* tied under my armpits, so as not to cause offence. It took me some months to perfect the technique of getting myself clean underneath this outfit.

Food consumed a remarkable proportion of my day – obtaining it, preparing it, or just thinking about it. The time spent on these things grew in inverse proportion to the availability of food. In the early monsoon when the food situation was at its worst, Duane developed an annoying habit of reciting every restaurant he had ever visited, and recalling his favourite dishes at each. As the Magars consumed all they produced and didn't have any excess to sell, we were lucky that Baglung bazaar with its shops was within walking distance.

It took less than an hour but it was a strenuous walk. We had to descend all the way to the Kathe Khola, cross the river, and ascend the steep path up to Baglung spread on the plateau above the cliffs. The final climb just before entering the town was the most taxing. It was a landslide area, steep and slippery, with an overpowering stench that forced me to hold my breath. This was the communal toilet area for half the town. If I took the path in the early morning the scree area to either side would be covered with squatting figures. In the summer hot breaths of fetid air wafted up the slope to the row of tea-shops that balanced at the top to greet the weary traveller. Each year the rains had removed more and more of their foundations so that now they seemed poised to plunge into the filth below. On cold days when the wind was in the reverse direction I would stop at the first tea-shop, and a woman with an enormous goitre hanging from her throat would serve me tea and ladle out a greasy ring-bread from her pan on the fire. She made these by scooping up the batter in her bare hands and letting it dribble into the hot fat through the gap between her thumb and forefinger. Refreshed, I would be ready to begin the hunt for food.

The term *bazaar* in Nepal refers to any town large enough to have a row of shops, and Baglung had several such rows, most owned and run by the Newar caste. It was like a medieval town; the streets were narrow and cobbled, the houses crowded closely together, and there was no system of sewers, only a gully in the streets where the rain had created its own drainage channel.

From the tea-shops the main path divided into three. The right fork followed round the curve of the cliffs, quickly leading out of the town past more houses precariously balanced on the edge. The middle path continued more or less straight on, towards a small square with a shrine and red-daubed statues, and then lost its identity in a maze of narrow twisting streets. The third path turned left and led into the main street of Baglung and this was the route I usually chose. It was paved with large flagstones and shops lined it tightly on both sides. These were terraced in the sense that they adjoined each other but like the houses in Titeng no two were the same. They were made from stone or locally fired bricks with mud mortar, and were three or even four storeys high which emphasised the feeling of containment. They were built in traditional style with verandahs and a plaster of red and white mud, and the roofs were of thatch or slate, although a few had corrugated tin or flattened-out paraffin-can roofs. In the morning the merchants opened up their wide shop-front doorways by hooking the small wooden flaps to the ceiling and removing the wooden slats from the grooves in the lower half of the supporting posts. The front face of the shop was then open to the street and shop-keepers retired for the day to their cloth-covered platforms and money-boxes.

Beyond the compact area of the bazaar proper stretched the beginnings of 'modern' Baglung – a development which had grown up amongst the rice fields within the past five years. It consisted of some rather ugly brick houses, four or five storeys high to avoid wasting the valuable rice land, with perhaps an ornate balustrade of cement if the owner was particularly affluent. These were rented for government offices, and in this area was the Police headquarters, the fifteen-bed hospital, the post office, and the telegraph office.

We were fortunate that in the bazaar the major necessities could be bought – rice, flour, sugar, lentils, and paraffin – though all were subject to 'shortages' from time to time, which meant that the shop-keepers hoarded the item in their back rooms and sold small amounts for double the price. Fresh fruit and vegetables were more difficult to obtain. They weren't usually sold in the shops but were brought into the bazaar by village folk who would squat in the streets and sell their produce straight from their *dokos*. It was a matter of being in the right spot at the right time and it was hard to anticipate where that would be. A *doko*-load of spinach could easily be sold in five minutes, such was the demand for fresh vegetables, and if I happened to miss those five minutes it might be two weeks before another supply appeared. Seeing the demand it puzzled us why local farmers didn't produce more vegetables for sale, but after we had been in Titeng a while we realised that their time and land was totally committed to grain production, the bulk food that would fill their stomachs, and vegetables were a luxury for the rich.

There were just three types of shop – cloth shops, copper-pot shops, and rice shops. The cloth shops were by far the most numerous and were colourful but sold nothing but cloth, and each shop had an almost identical selection. The merchants never tired of pulling down the bolts from their shelves, displaying yards of material with a flick of their wrists, and finally cutting off a length with their huge scissors. Outside each shop would be a tailor with an ancient Singer sewing-machine, ready to sew the cloth into blouses, skirts and trousers.

The copper-pot shops sold every kind of metal utensil – copper and brass water pots, cast bronze drinking vessels with spouts, aluminium kettles and pans, heavy iron woks, copper *puja* trays and vases, and boxes of rusty nails. One or two of the more progressive might have some shiny stainless steel plates which were expensive but becoming popular with the wealthy, stainless steel being stronger than brass or copper and not breakable like bronze.

The rice shops were the most interesting because I never knew what I might find. Their merchandise was displayed on shelves or in a network of wooden boxes on the floor that contained anything from coriander and cumin seeds to globs of sticky black tobacco, sugar, flour, half a dozen different types of lentil, and strange brown balls that were sometimes dried coconuts, sometimes lumps of brown sugar, and sometimes cakes of hard soap. The rice itself, four or five different kinds ranging from Basmati the most expensive to Kanika the broken rice used for brewing *rakshi*, would be in large sacks at the back of the shop. Mixed up with these things would be tins of paraffin, school exercise-books, pens, inks, bangles, rubber flip-flops, cigarettes, jars of mouth-scorching chilli sweets, hair ribbons, combs, biscuits, towels, plastic funnels, and bottles of coconut oil for the skin which showed a picture of a ravishing south Indian girl with bluish skin and brilliant pink lips and cheeks. In some shops a large pair of scales hung from a beam, but the loose items were mostly sold by volume, the bronze *pathi* and *mana* containers being the units of measure, and I got as much as I could heap on to them. Even the potatoes, which were the size of nuts, were measured in this way, so the amount I received depended on my skill in balancing them round the rim of the container.

I usually stopped at a small rice shop in the middle of the main street, where I could buy rice and lentils and potatoes, and if I was lucky there might be a tray of tiny green tomatoes the size of cherries, or a bunch of mottled bananas hanging from a string above the shop front. The shop-keeper was a Newar with a little finger nail two inches long – a status symbol that showed he was not a manual worker. Contrary to my expectations there was little bargaining for the goods for sale, and only with the fresh vegetables and fruit was it sometimes possible to lower the price.

We had arranged to eat most of our evening meals with Naina Singh's family and the rest which we cooked ourselves soon settled down to a rotation of pancakes, potato soup, and fried rice. Although the choice was limited, the enjoyment we got from food was just as high, and the discovery of a *doko*-load of tangerines leaning against the town tapstand, or a couple of shrivelled aubergines hiding in the murky interior of a tea-shop, would send us into ecstasies. Since Naina Singh's family didn't have much fresh food I bought them gifts of vegetables whenever I could.

We didn't eat much meat. The only kind that was regularly available was chicken or goat meat and both were highly priced and mostly bone. The chickens were sold alive and for us the few shreds of meat to be found on their bones were never worth the physical and emotional effort required to kill, pluck, and gut them. Goats were sold in quarters or eighths, and a goat would be walked round the town until enough buyers had been lined up to make it worth butchering. Then the meat was strictly divided up: one leg each, complete with skin and hoof, one quarter of the liver, one quarter of the heart and kidneys, one quarter of the guts, one quarter of all the other bones in the body and their accompanying meat and skin, except the head which was sold as a separate lot.

Buffalo meat, pork, and eggs were forbidden to high-caste Hindu Nepalis, but were secretly consumed under the euphemisms 'big goat', 'fatty goat', and 'white potatoes'.

'They're killing a "big goat" by the cliff on Saturday,' a woman would whisper to me, and so word passed around. Nobody liked to admit they ate buffalo meat and it went for a quarter the cost of chicken and half the cost of goat meat. We caused some surprise in the bazaar when we admitted we ate buffalo meat, but it was not often available and for most of the year we became vegetarians. Eggs were on sale from time to time, and sometimes the villagers brought us theirs as gifts – three or four the size of walnuts carefully tucked inside a *patuka*.

During the barren months because of the difficulty of finding food we began to eat some of our meals out. Duane went off to work at 8 am and didn't come home at midday, so at least once or twice a week we ate our morning meal at Prasad's place in Baglung. Prasad's place was the classy eating establishment. It had no tables or chairs and gave no outward sign of being anything other than a private home. We were taken the first time by a young Nepali friend who was a government official, and quickly discovered that the food was the best in Baglung. The rice was always of the highest Basmati quality, light and fluffy, and there were usually two types of vegetable curry as well as a spicy chutney and glasses of thick *moi* – the liquid produced from churning the milk. Prasad was a Newar who had taken two Thakali wives, a tribe renowned for their fine tea-shops. Even when the fields were bare and the bazaar devoid of vegetables, Prasad's place managed to serve up fresh spinach or bamboo shoots, and we suspected he must own a secret garden high up in the mountains.

The shortage of vegetables spurred me to start a garden on the spare ground beyond our toilet. The bedrock was not far below the surface and the narrow field was full of stones. But the biggest problem was water for these winter months were dry, so now we had to carry two pots of water a day – one for ourselves, and one for our garden. I planted a variety of vegetable seeds and Maila helped me put a fence around the plot.

Whenever I was free I liked to spend the time with the villagers, joining in their conversations and sharing their tasks. There was much to be learned and they made patient teachers, enjoying the interest I showed in their work. In the winter months there was less field work and the women spent long periods of the day weaving new straw mats for the coming year. Through watching and helping I learnt to weave these, to cut grass, to work the rice *dhiki*, and to grind corn.

The rice *dhiki* consisted of a long beam balanced on a fulcrum like a see-saw, with a wooden peg capped with iron on one end. The women worked the short end with their feet and the long end with the iron peg pounded into a hollow in the ground where the rice was dropped and slowly dehusked. This method left the pinkish layer of bran round the grain so it was more nutritious than the machine-hulled rice available in the bazaar.

I disliked the grinding wheel. It appeared deceptively easy, watching the women swing the stone round by its wooden peg, and when I tried I was surprised at how lightly and smoothly it turned on its stone base. I spun it round at a brisk pace but after seven or eight rotations it seemed to stick and became harder and harder. I tried changing hands but that was no better. Then I thought I had put too much grain in at one time and tried clearing it out. But the truth was my muscles were weak.

'Give up,' said Wife Two who was sitting beside me laughing. 'It's too hard for you. Here, let me continue.'

'No,' I replied stubbornly, determined to finish the small bowl of maize she had given me.

I changed hands again, then tried with both hands, much more slowly. The hardest part was pushing the wooden peg away from me to the furthest point on its revolution. I found if I pulled it towards me fast enough it would continue partway on its own, but the last few inches really put a strain on my back and stomach muscles. Foolishly I continued until the bowl of maize was finished, and found myself laid up with a bad back for the next two days.

Grass-cutting was more fun for we went to the woods and along the edges of the fields and there was always a chance of seeing a pair of blue magpies with their long tails floating behind them like streamers on a kite, or a flock of white-crested laughing thrushes.

On afternoons when I stayed at home I was never alone, for a constant stream of visitors called. With no doors to our upper room, people could look straight in and every day new faces appeared on our ladder anxious to view the foreigners and their belongings. These were the times when I became most aware of the gulf between us. They would gaze open-mouthed at the things in our room. They had never seen mattresses and cushions before. As for our straw mats, they refused to sit on them.

'No, Sister!' they said when I insisted. 'We'll spoil your mats with our dirty feet. They're too fine for us.'

'But they're only straw like yours. After all, you made them!' I replied.

'Yes. But these are so clean and new. We'll sit on the floor.'

It was impossible to convey to them the relative lack of value to us of a straw mat, without appearing to be condemning their things. Their attitude left us full of questions, and wondering whether we should have brought the Axminster after all.

The problem of rubbish disposal raised similar feelings of unease. In one sense there was no problem; the pigs devoured any edible remains and the rest we carried outside and allowed the children to pick through. They dived for the paper, particularly any coloured pictures such as postcards. Old tins and bottles they also treasured and used batteries were torn open and the black paste inside taken to decorate doors and window frames. Whatever was left, if anything, we burnt.

But one day I automatically poured some bad milk away and Devi's Mother saw me. 'What are you doing?' she asked, horrified. I explained that it had gone off.

'But the children would have drunk it,' she replied. She dropped her voice to a whisper, 'If you ever have some more, don't tell the others. Bring it here. My Devi needs it.' I felt ashamed at my lack of thought and the incident brought home to me the level of their need.

Disposing of the gifts of food they brought us – *roti*, roast corn or millet, and bowls of cold congealed pork, nine parts fat – was an even greater dilemma. We always thanked them profusely for these offerings, but sometimes they were stale and cold and, apart from the roast millet, frequently unappetising. To refuse their gifts was rude; to accept them and throw them away seemed immoral. We never resolved this problem completely. Instead we compromised, tried to eat as much as we could and then served the remains to the pigs when nobody was looking.

The high point of our day was the evening meal with Naina Singh's family. Wife One already cooked for fourteen people so to cook for two more was very little trouble. In the winter we ate around 7 pm but in the summer as late as 8 or 9 o'clock. Usually Bhakhu or Laute came to call us and we would turn down our Aladdin lamp and descend the ladder. Outside their house we picked up a small bronze pot of water and washed our right hands, the hand used for eating. Then we took off our shoes and stepped inside.

'*Namaste!*'

'*Namaste*. Maila, move out of their way. Bhakhu, give them a mat to sit on.'

The scene was already familiar. Wife One was sitting beside the pit-fire, its flames reflected in her eyes, watery from the smoke. Surrounding her, steaming cauldrons contained the evening meal. She was always calm as she served out the food, even when Gophle lay on her lap trying to suck milk. It was not unusual for a five-year-old to be breast-fed still, especially if a younger sibling had not usurped his place.

Satisfied that we were seated comfortably Wife One dug into the largest cauldron with a heavy brass spatula and heaved a sticky glob of millet porridge on to each plate. She added a spoonful of rice from a smaller brass pan and then ladled the *tun* into separate small bowls –

brass ones for us, but aluminium ones for the rest of the family. *Tun*
consisted of anything that would make the millet more palatable.
Often it was boiled lentils or soya beans, with spinach, stinging
nettles, fern tips, bamboo shoots, or the leaves of the mustard plants
according to season. At a special festival it included meat.

'Bhakhu, take this one out to Grandmother. Big Child and Little
Child, here are yours.'

'You've given us too much. Take a little off – we only have small
stomachs.'

'You eat so little. We have to fatten you up. You must eat plenty of
rice and *ghiu* and milk.'

We picked up the bowls of *tun* and poured a little of the watery sauce
over the millet and began to eat. It was hot, and I burnt my hand and
had to wait for it to cool down. By now the children had theirs, served
in an assortment of bowls and tin plates, and were squatting happily in
the corners gobbling down the millet. They were always hungry.

Sometimes we talked or listened to their conversations, but on the
whole mealtimes were for eating, not speaking. Unfortunately Titeng
cuisine was not the most appetising and I had to be truly hungry to
swallow it down. One or two meals were not so bad, but the
monotony of the diet took away my appetite. The family were too
poor to use oil or spice, and the most we could hope for would be one
large chilli floating in the *tun*. In the dark I sometimes swallowed this
chilli by mistake and it would leave me speechless, ears tingling and
eyes and nose streaming.

We soon developed our own list of favourite menus: Duane liked
the millet, but I preferred the wheat or maize porridge. I liked the soya
beans, the spinach, and the fern shoots, and he preferred the stinging
nettles and bamboo shoots. Many times the *tun* felt and tasted like
green pond slime, and we didn't ask what had gone into it that day.

'It's delicious,' we would bravely say, forcing ourselves to swallow
it.

'It's only poor food,' Wife One would reply. 'Why do you like to
eat here when you can get good food in the bazaar? Would you like
some more rice or *tun*?'

Wife One continued to sit by the fire, stirring the embers. She
would not eat until all the family had finished. Then she would have
the scrapings. As the children finished eating they lay down right
where they were and fell asleep and we had to be careful not to trip
over their bodies in the dark.

After the meal was finished we would relax and chat for a while. If

Naina Singh was present we would discuss the state of his crops and any other gloomy subjects he could think of; if he wasn't there the mealtimes would be even more relaxed, with much teasing and joking amongst the family. Finally we would rinse off our hands and rise to leave. At first I used to offer to wash our dishes, but the family became so upset that after a bit I willingly left it to them. Saili would take them outside and scrub them with ashes from the fire.

'Goodnight. Thank you,' we said as we left, and Wife Two laughed and said thank you back, mimicking us. This was a joke because the word 'thank you' was reserved for very special occasions and great honours, and was never used for so small an offering as a plate of millet porridge. But we had been well brought up and found it hard to drop the habit, so we said thank you every night and that gave them one more thing to laugh about.

Slowly we adjusted to our new life and situation. Our legs became stronger and our appetites increased. We could now recognise most villagers by sight, though one or two still confused us, and we had given up hope of ever learning their real names. They were much more at ease with us now, and Saili had even got to the point of bashfully stuttering a few words to Duane.

One particularly busy day I had callers all day long. Finally they left and I shooed the children out and settled down to write some letters in peace and quiet when three more women appeared. They squatted on the floor and peered round the room commenting loudly on everything they saw. After a long conversation they showed no signs of going away, and my patience wore thin. I started to make hints that I had some work to do. There was no response so I repeated my request more bluntly, suggesting they could come back when I was less busy. Still no reaction. Did they understand me, I asked.

'Yes, Sister, we understand,' said one of the women. 'But we *won't* go away. This room is so wonderful we *have* to stay!'

6

An invitation to a wedding

The wheat was planted and already a few green shoots were poking through the earth, relieving the monotony of the brown dusty landscape.

It was Phagun,* the eleventh month of the Nepali year, and Hindu astrologers had deemed this an auspicious month for getting married. Nearly every day a wedding was celebrated in the bazaar with much festivity; forests of banana palms were uprooted and the merchants did a lucrative business in yards of red cloth.

Even Titeng was not immune from the wedding fever. One evening when we went to eat supper, Wife One was not in her customary place beside the steaming cauldrons, and the familiar tranquil atmosphere of the evening hours had been replaced with a bustle of activity. The focus of this was the fireplace in the centre where an enormous clay pot and a copper pan were heating on the roaring fire.

We coughed and choked and shielded our faces from the intense heat. It was hard to make out anything in the smoke-laden atmosphere.

'Come and sit over here,' called Wife One, a disembodied voice, from the far end of the room. We stumbled our way over and lay down with our mouths close to the floor where the air was slightly clearer.

'What's going on?'

'*Rakshi*! We're brewing *rakshi*,' answered Wife One.

'There's going to be a wedding,' broke in Devi's Mother. 'Our cousin is getting married. You know – the one who lives above the village in the All-Alone-House. It's going to be a big wedding – everyone from the bride and bridegroom's villages will be going – five or six hundred people. We'll never brew enough *rakshi*!'

*Phagun = mid–February—mid–March

'You're invited too. You *must* come,' said Wife One.

Saili arrived with a pot of water, panting heavily. As the youngest daughter-in-law, she had been delegated the task of keeping the clay pot filled with cold water, and this involved many back-breaking trips to and from the spring. The *rakshi* spirit was distilled by heating fermented millet juice in a broad shallow copper pan. Inside the pan a small bowl was placed on a tripod in the centre above the millet juice; on top of the copper pan, completely covering it, balanced the clay pot filled with cold water. As the millet juice was heated, the alcohol evaporated and then condensed as it came in contact with the cold bottom of the clay pot, and dripped down into the small bowl. From time to time the water in the clay pot became too warm and had to be exchanged with fresh cold water. Once collected the spirit was reheated to purify it.

'It takes three hours to make four or five pints,' said Wife One.

'How much grain does it take?'

'Five or six *mana* of grain make one *mana* of *rakshi*.' Wife One shook her head with a wry smile. 'We can't afford to make it but we still do. Every day the men waste their money drinking *rakshi* in the bazaar. What to do? It is our custom.'

Wife One handed us small glasses to taste. It was coarse with an earthy flavour and burned our throats.

'Are you going to the wedding?' Grandmother called out the next day from the yard as she picked the fleas from her blouse. 'It'll be such fun. Everyone will go. There'll be singing and dancing, and a big feast.'

'Are you going?'

'How can I?' she said a little sadly. 'Someone has to stay in the village to watch the houses. Don't worry – they'll send me down some food from the feast.'

'Come and help us make the wedding plates,' invited Wife Two. The women were sitting around a mound of shiny *sal* leaves, suitable for making leaf plates when they were not devoured by the buffalo. 'We had to go all the way across the big river to get these leaves. They don't grow around here.'

I sat down and the women showed me how to fold the leaves making a double thickness, and 'sew' them together with thin slivers of bamboo into neat leaf plates with rims. These disposable plates were sufficiently watertight to hold liquids and were used at festivals or whenever large numbers of people gathered for a meal. As we worked they admired my new glass bangles bought in the bazaar for a few rupees. Jethi, the married daughter, wanted to try them, so we swapped bangles and exchanged compliments. They preferred heavy red ones that were tough and didn't break so easily when they were doing field work.

'They're so fine and delicate these bangles,' said Jethi. 'But they don't look nice on my dark skin. Look at Saili. Isn't she beautiful? She's so pale she looks like a white person.'

'I like dark skin. At home we buy special oils to make our skin darker.'

'You want to be dark and we want to be fair,' sighed Jethi.

Each woman also wore thick circular earrings covered with gold, and two nose rings – a flower-shaped one through the left nostril, and another hung like a pendant from the nasal septum. The latter looked particularly uncomfortable as it obscured their lips, and when the women were drinking they sometimes flipped it up with one hand so that it didn't dangle in their drink. Jethi unclipped her nose ring and passed it across. 'Sister, you must get your nose pierced, then you can wear a ring like this.'

It was heart-shaped and had a small red stone set in the middle.

'Doesn't it hurt?'

'Only a little. They rub your nose with a special leaf so it's not too bad. Then they stick the needle through.'

The idea did not appeal. I excused myself, saying it was not our custom to pierce our noses. They were quite satisfied with this rather inadequate answer. '*We don't have the custom*' explained and excused everything, for the basis of their social code was honouring the customs and traditions of their ancestors.

We continued in a close bond of common purpose. 'Fold, pin, cut,' jangled the bangles and nose rings, and the stack of leaf plates grew higher as the sun crept towards the horizon. Duane arrived home and I waved to him and continued with the leaf plates. 'Fold, pin, cut,' I muttered. Devi's Mother looked at me puzzled. 'Your Master has come home,' she said anxiously. 'Don't you have to go and make his tea?'

I looked at her and the warm feeling of oneness slipped away as I was reminded of the gulf between us. As a woman I had no rights of my own unless my husband gave them to me; I had been given to him and he owned me. This was especially true for the Brahmin women, but the Magars were not totally subservient. They didn't hesitate to tease or scold their husbands, and when I saw Gesi Ram and Saili working side by side in the fields laughing and joking together, there

was little sign of this male domination. But on important matters such
as buying or selling land, or negotiating a loan, it was the men who
made the decisions. At festival times it was the men who gathered
together to talk or drink or play cards all night long. The women
never participated in these informal gatherings, even when a discussion of village affairs took place; at the very most they might sit on the
edge of the group and listen quietly.

When we first arrived I did not hesitate to sit down with the men
and join in their conversations. But after a few months I became more
self-conscious of my place as a woman.

'Don't worry,' said Devi's Mother. 'It's all right for you. You're
educated. Look at all the reading and writing you do. Look at all the
places you've travelled. You can talk with the men, but we can't. Our
tongues are thick enough, but our brains are thin and weak.'

On the day of the wedding the village was quiet for the women and
children had gone to the bride's house to help with the preparations.
We joined the men who were sitting in their habitual place in the sun
beside Naina's round house, discussing weddings and marriages.

'It's our job to arrange a suitable match for our children,' said Keshu
Ram our milkman, who was something of a philosopher and loved to
talk. 'The boy's father must visit the surrounding villages to ask if
there are any girls of the right age. It's not good for the girl's parents to
go out hunting; they must wait till someone comes to them. If the
boy's father discovers a suitable girl then he talks with her father and
together they agree on a price and a date for the wedding. Usually we
go to nearby villages, but sometimes we marry people from the other
end of the valley. You know Saili and Devi's Mother? They come
from a village five or six hours away.'

'Can you marry people of a different caste?'

'No, never someone of a higher or lower caste. That's not allowed.
It's possible to marry a Newar or a Gurung, but nobody has done so.'

'How do you decide if the couple are suited?'

'That's up to the girl's father. He must send out messengers to check
whether the suitor is an honest man. Are there any bad rumours about
him?'

'Do they demand a high bride price?'

'Sometimes. If they know you are rich, or the girl is particularly fine
or well-educated. Once a headman's daughter ran away with a soldier,
and her parents demanded 17,000 lentil cakes and 10 paraffin cans of
rakshi before they would sanction the marriage.'

'Don't you ever marry people in your own village?'

'No. Usually we don't marry within our own villages,' answered Lal Bahadur, a muscular young man who lived in the house next to Keshu. 'But my family can marry with the headman's. That's because they're not originally from Titeng but came just two generations ago from Raato Maato across the valley. All the rest of us are descended from two brothers who came down from the north, from Muktinath, so long ago nobody can remember when. Myself, Keshu Ram, Naina Singh, and Mati Lal are descended from the older brother, and the other families from the younger.'

'What happens if the couple don't like each other – do they have to stay married?'

'We're not strict about that, unlike some castes. If the couple don't get on, or if the husband takes another wife, the woman may run away with another man. Sometimes a man fancies another's wife, and he'll capture her in the night and carry her off.'

'Won't her husband be very angry?'

'Maybe. But he can go to the headman and arrange to get his money back. So long as he gets his money back it's all right.'

'What about you?' asked Lal Bahadur. 'Did your parents arrange your marriage?'

'No. We arranged it ourselves. In our countries you can choose who you want to marry. We fell in love with each other and decided to get married.'

'Ah!' said another man who lived at the far end of the village. 'That happens here too, but those kind of marriages never last. Look at my worthless son Damar – he always was a disobedient boy! As soon as he was fifteen he ran away to India to seek his fortune. Couldn't find a job, so he came back, borrowed some more money and went to Rukum, west of here. There he fell in love and married this girl. I tried my hardest to dissuade him, but he wouldn't heed my advice. I paid out 400 rupees for her gold earrings so they could be married. What happened? They didn't live together two years before she ran away and left him! I paid 400 rupees for those earrings! I could tell she was a no-good type from the beginning.'

We wondered what they made of our marriage and our respective roles within it. None of their men helped with the household chores as Duane did, and none of the women wandered round on their own as I did. Whether they secretly approved or disapproved of us we never knew; they did not analyse things, and when they spoke or questioned us it was always of facts and rarely of feelings. But they were aware of the differences. We would see them nudge each other and point in our direction when Duane did something out of keeping with his role as husband.

'Your men don't do this sort of work, do they?' I would call out, treating it as a joke.

'No,' they replied. 'They don't know how to!'

It was a great help to have Duane sharing in the household chores which took so much longer without any modern conveniences. But as the year went on I slowly acquired their norms and felt increasingly guilty that I wasn't slaving from dawn to dusk for my husband's well-being. Moreover I could not thank him with a hug and a kiss. They never showed affection in public and out of respect for their feelings we tried to do the same. But once in a while we broke the rule and risked a brief hug. We were rewarded by some smothered laughs and knowing looks. Even holding hands was taboo, but there was little opportunity for this on the narrow paths where walking was strictly single file.

'Do you quarrel as much as we do?' I asked.

Keshu Ram let out a long laugh. 'Of course! But you know how the proverb goes: "The quarrel between a husband and wife is like a fire of straw. It flares up quickly and dies down quickly."'

While talking we had produced a few of our wedding photos for them to see, and they showed great interest in these.

'Didn't you have a band?' asked Keshu Ram. 'How many people were at the wedding feast? Only fifty?'

'This photo is the best,' said Lal Bahadur, pointing to a very posed photo where Duane and I were gazing lovingly into each other's eyes behind some blurred flowers.

'Ah!' said the ex-Gurkha soldiers among them. 'Just like the Hindi films we used to see in India!'

At midday it was time to go to the wedding feast. We made our way up the steep path to the bride's house above the village. There was no problem finding the way for everyone was going – the women in velvet shawls and jewels, and the men in clean white loincloths and blankets.

The bride's house was a typical mud and thatch building, but standing apart like a lonely marker on its own fields. On this particular day it was far from lonely, and in the seething motion of its swarms of people reminded me of a disorganised beehive. Men had gathered in clusters round the bottles of *rakshi*, becoming more vociferous as the minutes slipped away and the bottles emptied. In the cowshed women stoked the cooking fires and yelled instructions to the teams of water carriers and fuel gatherers who formed a steady procession across the courtyard. Young girls on the verandah, faces flushed with anticipation, whispered and tossed their jewelled heads and bangled arms as they waited sadly to say farewell to their friend. Children screamed and rushed round the courtyard with excitement; buffalo, chicken, pigs, goats and dogs added their voices to the discord, and in the midst of this the headman, shuffling feebly in circles, issued his high-pitched squeaky commands to anyone who would listen.

Feeling very drab in my faded wrap-around skirt and lack of jewellery, I pushed my way through the mêlée towards the cowshed where the crowd was thickest. It had been temporarily turned into a kitchen and three fires were blazing. Cooking rice for five hundred people was not easy, but the villagers had set about it with characteristic fervour. Against the wall a line of bamboo *dokos* waited like empty honey cells to receive the fluffy steaming rice. Some had already been filled and capped with a folded banana leaf to hold the heat. In the corner a buffalo chewed the cud, neanderthal nose in the air, disdaining the surrounding turmoil. Through the smoke and people I caught sight of Wife Two bending over a vast cauldron of rice. I shouted a greeting and she gave the rice a stir with a branch and made her way over. She was wearing her best black blouse and skirt, with a length of starry blue material knotted over one shoulder.

'We've been at it since early morning and still not finished,' she said with a sweaty smile. 'We've got to cook three and a half *muris* of rice.'

I expressed my incredulity. A *muri* was about 160 pounds, so this was more than 500 pounds altogether. Wife Two laughed. 'What good is a wedding if you can't eat as much as you want?'

Amid all the bustle it took me a while to realise that somebody was missing. 'Where are the bride and bridegroom?' I asked.

'The bridegroom hasn't come yet. But the bride's here. She's inside the house, and full of sorrow at her fate. Can't you hear her?' answered Wife Two, dropping her voice to a whisper. I pressed my ear close to the black carved window and the sound of sobbing struck a discordant note in the otherwise happy drama.

By late afternoon the headman managed to organise everyone to sit down in long straight rows around the courtyard, and the feast was served on the leaf plates I had helped to make. Besides mountains of rice, there was a cauldron of boiled maize and pig's innards, and the inevitable pan of pork. As guests of honour we were also handed several very cold ring-*roti* that tasted like boiled leather. We munched our way through these with a smile on our faces, anxious not to offend, and we must have succeeded for they smiled back and gave us several more. But the maize and pig's innards were delicious. As for the pork, that was the usual village cut – three-quarters fat, and one-quarter skin, with a thin seam of meat at the end. We ate our way through three helpings before they were convinced we were full. The headman shook his head and lamented our lack of appetite.

By the time everyone had been fed and their stomachs stretched to full capacity, with one or two spare cubes of pork fat secreted in their *patukas* in case of sudden hunger pangs, it was late. Suddenly out of the dusk we heard the wailing of horns.

"The Bridegroom's coming! The Bridegroom's coming!'

We rushed to take up grandstand positions on the rice terraces overlooking the courtyard, and peered along the hillside.

On the nearest ridge, silhouetted against the evening sky, the minstrels were the first to appear – a roguish-looking band who might have stepped straight out of a medieval manuscript. As they came closer we could see their faces shining with the strain of their non-stop performance and the thousand-foot climb from the bridegroom's house. Their instruments were various. Several carried six-foot-long horns made from a collection of tubes, bamboo and empty tin cans, which produced a chilling wail, while other members of the ensemble beat out the rhythm on drums and tambourines. At intervals they paused on their journey to perform a short comical dance.

Behind the band came the guests from the bridegroom's village, shouting and clapping their hands, and in the thick of them, the bridegroom himself. He was sitting upright in a cloth sling stretched from a bamboo pole held aloft on the shoulders of four friends, one hand clutching the pole and the other an unfurled umbrella. We held our breath as the stretcher-bearers negotiated a particularly tricky bend in the steep path directly above a ravine, and for a moment the bridegroom hung between imminent bliss and imminent death. But all was well; the procession continued and as darkness gathered they lit flaming torches. We followed the blaze of lights as they wove in and out of the trees on the far side of the ravine, disappeared from view, and finally reappeared just below the courtyard of the bride's house.

There was a flurry from the band who had formed ranks at one end of the courtyard. As the stretcher entered, the attendants closed around it like armour-bearers, shielding the bridegroom behind their black umbrellas. Then accompanied by a long blast from the horns but with a distinct lack of dignity, the bride finally made her entrance – piggy-back style on her brother's back. One bare foot and the hem of an embroidered red *sari* peeped out, but otherwise she was covered from head to toe in the folds of a fringed red shawl. She was carried three times round the bridegroom's group before penetrating the screen of umbrellas.

We waited in tense silence. This was a crucial moment when the bridegroom for the first time saw the bride chosen for him, and had to pronounce his approval or disapproval. What was going on behind the umbrellas? Was it a look? Or an embrace? Or merely a cool-headed assessment of the strength of her back for work and the width of her hips for childbearing? It was to remain a mystery, but he must have approved for the band's overture rose to a climax and suddenly we were all clapping our hands and throwing rice over the couple. The parents and close relatives stepped forward and gave their blessing and consent with a *tika* mark of rice and curds smeared over the foreheads of the bride and bridegroom. Then without more ado, still on her brother's back but with her red shawl lowered to expose her head and *tika* mark, the bride was whisked back inside the house once more. The armour-bearers lowered their umbrellas and the bridegroom stepped forth from the bamboo sling.

He was dressed to our astonishment in the latest style of long black trousers, a pink and lime-green flowery shirt, platform shoes, and a traditional patterned *topi* and dark glasses. He took his place of honour on the only chair, and more bottles of *rakshi* were opened and passed round.

While the bridegroom and his party were being feasted, the band continued to entertain us. I studied a young boy playing a gently curved horn of beaten copper about a foot long. By storing air in his bulging cheeks he was able to blow the horn at the same time as breathing in, thus producing a continuous blood-curdling wail. But as time went on the effort took its toll and his eyes bulged wider as the sweat rolled down his cheeks.

To our disappointment the bride never made a second appearance. Perhaps she was too overcome with grief to face the jubilation outside. As the night wore on, the bottles of *rakshi* passed from hand to hand and the tempo of the band increased. They were paid 15 rupees each plus as much food and *rakshi* as they could consume, the young boy minstrel told me. One or two men started to dance and the crowd clapped their hands and laughed at the antics of the dancers. We watched for a while and then regretfully, overcome with tiredness, stumbled down the path back to the village.

As for the bride, her fate was sealed. The next day we witnessed her 'carrying off' to the new home in the same bamboo sling in which the bridegroom had arrived. She was still dressed in her red *sari*, shawl pulled over her head, but we were just able to catch the shine of something gold beneath – the huge saucer-shaped earrings given by the groom as a seal of their marriage. The band led the way, somewhat the worse for their drunken carousel of the night before, relatives and guests carried the wedding gifts of copper and brass plates, then came the bride in the bamboo sling, and finally the bridegroom walking proudly behind his latest acquisition.

'Come and see us, we live higher up the mountain,' the wedding minstrels had told me as they waved farewell. We had been in Titeng for several weeks and I was eager to explore further afield, so one morning I forced myself out of bed even earlier than usual and set off.

A community of villages extended upwards from Titeng at 3,000 feet to the summit of the mountain at 9,000. Although I couldn't see the other villages, their names excited my curiosity – Aatmuri, Kumaldara, Damaigaon – and I had met some of their inhabitants on the path to the bazaar. From Baglung I could glance across and see Titeng in its true perspective, a minute pimple on the face of the mountain, whose shadowy purple forehead beckoned from the skyline.

I didn't know the way but I knew I had to go up, so I took the shortest most direct route. It was a never-ending flight of uneven steps, some slanting up some down, some steep, some shallow, so I had to watch my feet and not the scenery. The morning was cold and crisp for the sun had not reached this side of the valley, but I quickly warmed up. Within ten minutes I passed through the village of Upper Titeng. Familiar sounds were issuing from the houses – the crowing of the roosters, the thud, thud of the *dhiki* and the low moans of the buffalo.

'Where are you going?' the inhabitants asked me.

'To Damaigaon and the top of the mountain.'

'Why? Have you come to bring us medicines?'

'No. I'm just going for a walk to see the scenery.'

'Just to walk and see? No other reason?' They shook their heads in perplexity and went back to work. A woman handed me three large lemons and I thanked her and dropped them in my bag.

As I climbed so Annapurna and Dhaulagiri exposed more and more of their ice-covered faces above the surrounding mountains. I stopped frequently to look back at the view. A group of boys raced past me with their bags and *topis* on their way to the high school at Baglung. 'We'll be there in less than an hour,' they told me, 'but it's twice as long coming back'. After two hours I reached the village of Dhungabari, its ochre-red houses scattered like sun-burned freckles on the cheeks of the mountain. In the neighbouring fields enormous boulders sprouted like mushrooms. As I climbed the final hump to the village, the last flowers of the poinsettia formed an avenue of scarlet.

Dhungabari was not compact like Titeng. Solid two-storey houses belonging to the higher castes stood alone on their respective fields, some with new corrugated tin roofs. I turned around and gazed down our valley to the wider but still deeply incised valley of the Kali Gandaki. Baglung appeared dwarfed, but with each detail still clearly visible, like a map between the two rivers. I picked out the wooded peninsula, the town gaol, the high school, and the bazaar itself. Surrounding Baglung on all sides the mountains, broken by steeply terraced V-shaped valleys, rose to their uneven summits.

For the first time I was able to see the upper reaches of the Kathe Khola. Shaped like a cradle, the valley lay serene between the encircling ridges. Steep shoulders of land rose up between the tentacles of river twisting towards each other. Except where rocks or the scar of a landslide broke the pattern, each slope was carved into countless sinuous lines of terraces which flowed with a rhythm of their own forming new-moon and half-moon crescents. Every spur carried the mellow mud imprints of village houses, their courtyards and barns and interlacing paths. Nowhere was land wasted that could be used.

I was taken aback by the sense of cohesion and the beauty of its form. But the inhabitants were not impressed.

'We work hard. We suffer,' said an elderly man I met on the path. 'The land is too steep – there's not enough water. Farming is a struggle. Our women spend their days carrying water and fodder, and then landslides come and sweep our fields away. Is it true in your country the land is flat and life is easy?'

'Well, yes. The land is flat. And we don't have to carry water. But we still find plenty of things to complain about!'

At the top of Dhungabari was a huddle of sorry-looking huts, dilapidated and unkempt, with small misshapen doors and windows. Scraps of material littered every pathway and scraggy bush, and in the sunny courtyards a row of tailors squatted sewing, one of them flicking the wheel of a battered sewing-machine. This was Damaigaon – the Village of the Tailors. It was still common for people to live according to their castes and occupations. So whereas Titeng was

Magar caste or tribe, Damaigaon was the Damai caste, and Salbot, to the west, was Brahmin.

'*Namaste!* So you came,' one of the tailors called out. I looked at him and realised he was a minstrel from the wedding band.

'But I thought this was the Village of the Tailors?' I said.

'It is! Didn't you know that the tailors are the musicians?' He laughed at my puzzled look. 'In the daytime we do sewing, but whenever there's a wedding or some other festival we have to go and play our instruments. Sometimes we play all night.'

'Do you all play something?'

'Yes. Everyone plays an instrument here. Not the women of course – they can't play – but everyone else.'

It was easy to tell that the tailors were low-caste. There were large numbers of children standing around with hardly a scrap of clothing despite the coldness of the weather and the occupation of their parents. Their houses were smaller and more poorly maintained than those of Titeng, and their dress and general demeanour showed their physical deprivation and lack of self-esteem. Their faces were old and tired; their expressions told they were not used to being noticed. As low castes they were not allowed to eat with other castes or enter their homes, and in some cases were not allowed to use the same water source. All the low-caste groups in Nepal were artisans. Besides the tailors there were blacksmiths, goldsmiths, cobblers, potters, and ferry-men. Even within them they had their own hierarchy of which it was generally agreed the cobblers were the lowest because they dealt in cow hide and cow meat which was considered sinful by Hindus.

I tried to imagine being born into an occupation. What if you hated sewing? What if you had no aptitude for music? What if you were born low-caste and poor, with no hope of changing? The caste system was probably the single most important aspect of Nepali society that disturbed me. On the surface there was little apparent friction, for Hinduism, which taught discrimination according to caste, also taught a blind acceptance of one's fate and position in society. I never heard a low caste utter a word of hate or bitterness against the higher castes. They were not actively unhappy and to the casual tourist there was nothing amiss, but a study of their lives quickly showed their relative poverty and lack of opportunities. The government had taken steps to outlaw the caste system, but it was impossible to change through laws alone the attitudes of centuries. The low castes had migrated with the Aryan Brahmins and Chettris, and were said to be of South Indian Dravidian origin, hence their generally darker skin

which was possibly the cause of the original prejudice. Low castes
were generally poor because they owned little land, but caste was not
directly linked to wealth. Sometimes a Brahmin would be the poorest
in a village, because without land to farm he had no skill to fall back
on, and occasionally a goldsmith would amass great wealth, but the
caste rules still applied.

'Sit down! Sit down and eat!' A woman brought me a glass of
milkless tea spiced with black pepper, and a plate of popcorn. Nearby
was a pile of recently cut sugar cane and a press which two boys were
turning. The press consisted of a long beam fixed to an upright post
that revolved in another block of wood. As the woman thrust the
canes into the central post the boys pushed on the outer extremity of
the beam which swung round in a wide arc crushing the canes. The
juice trickled through a hole in the block of wood and was collected in
a copper bowl.

'Sometimes we cook rice or millet in the juice and make a delicious
sweet *roti*,' she explained, squatting in the centre. 'And sometimes we
boil it for a long time and make round balls of sugar which we sell in
the bazaar.'

Knowing they were poor I offered to pay for what I had eaten. The
woman refused my proffered coins but pointed to the large lemons in
my bag. 'They don't grow up here,' she said sadly. 'It's too cold. Let
me give you some spinach in exchange for a lemon.' She ran off and
returned with a large handful of spinach leaves and sugar canes. I
waved goodbye to the Village of the Tailors and continued on my
way, munching the crisp stems of cane and letting the sweet juice
trickle down my throat.

The fields became sparser and stonier, and the forest closer. Off to
my right a steady tap, tap, tap, and the clang of metal identified the
nearby houses as the Village of the Blacksmiths.

'Where's the path to the top?' I called out.

'The path goes to the left, to the Deorali,' they shouted back,
pointing to a dip between the two knuckles of the mountain.

'No, I want to go to the top, not the pass,' I persisted.

There was a pause, and then the answer came floating across on the
clear mountain air: 'Nobody goes to the top; the ghosts live there.'

I should have known. Nepalis never ventured into jungles or
uninhabited areas if they could avoid it. Their paths led from village to
village, crossing a ridge at its lowest point, and the only paths that
ventured into forest were ill-defined 'cow-grazing' and 'fodder-
gathering' paths. I picked one of these which led in the right general

direction, but it soon petered out. As the forest was not thick I persevered, picking my way through twisted stumpy trees covered with dangling moss and ferns and the speckled leaves of orchids. There was a beautiful stillness all around; only the mocking calls of the laughing-thrushes disturbed the silence. Huge rhododendron trees towered above me, branch tips weighed down with blossom of crimson and crushed strawberry-pink. This was their native home, high on the moist slopes of the Himalayas.

The lack of oxygen was beginning to take effect and I stopped for a rest on a lichen-encrusted fallen oak. But the eerie silence and sleep-inducing spell of the forest left me ill at ease and I soon pressed on. The trees became smaller and more misshapen and the sweet-smelling white flowers of the Daphne shrub began to appear. I tried to pick them but the stems were extremely fibrous and I understood why the local people gathered these to make their traditional 'rice' paper. After a number of false summits I finally reached the 9,000-foot peak. Even at this height it was still forested with stunted trees, but through a clearing I had a view to the mysterious other side.

Infinite folds of rock and earth, ridge and forest stretched into the hazy blue distance. As I turned slowly around, the high Himalayas rose majestically above the lower mountains – Gangapurna, Machapuchare, Annapurna, Dhaulagiri, Gurja, and Churen Himal – filling the skyline from east to west. Only where the Kali Gandaki river cut its gorge between the walls of Annapurna and Dhaulagiri was there a break in their line of defence. It was a giant abstract jig-saw of shapes – trapezoids, pyramids, cones and triangles. Feeling very small I walked down the ridge to Deorali, the place of the pass. The forest was broken here, and the open grassy ridge-top gave a feeling of immense freedom. I lay down in a sun-trapped hollow and fell asleep.

Waking with alarm I realised the weather had changed and hurriedly began my descent. I reached our house just as the rain started. After unpacking the assortment of fruits and vegetables I had been given on the walk – lemons, beans, sugar cane, spinach and cassava – I went upstairs to put on a sweater and socks and wrap myself in my down sleeping-bag. Winters were generally dry but there could be occasional days of rain such as this one. I woke the next morning to see Annapurna and the lower mountains shrouded in a fresh fall of glistening snow. Deorali's warm grassy slopes where I had walked the day before were remote and forbidding in their new purity.

7

New developments

A new sound had entered the world of the Kathe Khola valley; at nine every morning and again at 5.30 in the evening, a gong resounded. It was not a harmonious ring, but a harsh clang made by beating a stick against a sheet of metal hung from a tree almost on a level with Titeng on the opposite side of the valley. Its vibrations carried from Raato Maato and Baglung on the north side, across to Titeng, Aatmuri, Kumaldara, and Charkigaon on the southern slopes.

To a people not generally acquainted with time and its regulations, it was another change marking the steady encroachment of western civilisation, its culture and norms, on the Nepali way of life.

As the last echoes of the gong died away, the men from these villages put away their clay pipes, rose from their verandahs, and in single file made their way down the zig-zag path to the Kathe Khola. Without a break in their pace they waded the river, climbed the steep cliff on the other side and gathered round the tree with the makeshift gong. A few yards back from the cliff stood a crudely built shed of bare stones and mud mortar, with a thatched roof. This was Himal Hydro's site office for the Baglung hydro-electric project where Duane worked.

On this south-facing slope the air was already warm as the workers gathered to receive their instructions for the day. Work on the project was in full swing and over forty workers were on the payroll including several from Titeng. To Duane and his colleague Ed Kramer, a Dutch engineer who lived in Baglung with his family, the work was both challenging and frustrating. Their training and experience as engineers in their home countries counted for little in Nepal; everything had to be relearned. Duane had worked the previous year on the Tinau hydro-electric scheme near Kasauli, but prior to that his main engineering experience was working on the construction of a tower block in Minneapolis – a far cry from Nepal. How do you begin a hydro-electric project, even a very small one, with no skilled workforce, no power of any kind, no machinery, limited capital, and thirty miles of mountainous terrain between the site and the nearest road?

The answer was appropriate technology. Where it would normally take one man with one machine a day to excavate a trench, in Baglung it took ten men with hand shovels three days. Instead of 'ready-to-use' cement delivered to the site in a giant mixer, a team of porters carried the sacks of cement four days from the nearest road. This labour intensive method made the best use of limited money, provided employment to a greater number of people, and did not require the importing of sophisticated machinery.

There were plenty of people looking for jobs. Land holdings were no longer sufficient to feed families the whole year through, and local employment was preferable to going to India. During our first month in Titeng many visitors arrived bearing gifts of eggs or milk or vegetables. It took me some time to realise that the pickled bamboo shoots or the limp spinach leaves carried a little more significance than first appearance suggested.

'You don't happen to have a job for us?' the visitors would ask on the point of leaving, after I had naïvely accepted their gifts. It was impossible to refuse all the offerings because some were genuine and had no such strings attached.

'Go to the site office across the river and talk to the men,' I would say.

'But please, *you* speak to your husband for us. Tell him what good workers we are.'

'My husband doesn't listen to what I say.'

'That's what you say, but we don't believe you.'

'Really – he doesn't listen to me!'

But still they kept coming. One of the first workers needed was an office clerk and general assistant. 'Sahib!' announced one man to Duane, not bothering with the preliminary vegetables. 'You *must* employ my son.' They commonly spoke in this emphatic way.

'What can he do? What education does he have?'

'He has his school leaving certificate, he's very good at maths, he can keep accounts – in fact, he can do everything!'

'Can he read technical drawings?'

'Sahib, he is *excellent* at technical drawings!'

'Send him for an interview tomorrow then.'

'I can't believe we've found somebody so well qualified in Baglung,' said Duane, turning to me. 'He can even read technical drawings.'

But the next day he came home with a gloomy face. 'The office clerk turned out to be a twelve-year-old boy. He couldn't keep accounts and he'd never seen a technical drawing in his life. We'll have to train somebody from scratch.'

The first job for the newly hired workforce was to clear a site by the river for the small power house, and dig a trench down the cliff where the penstock would be buried. The scheme was a 'run-of-the-river' design, small and simple, requiring no dam or tunnel. Three miles upstream water would be diverted from the Kathe Khola into a canal by means of a rough barrage. This was known as the 'head-race' canal. It would run more or less horizontally for three miles following the contours of the hillside until it reached the site of the Project Office beside the cliff. Since the Kathe Khola was a swift-flowing mountain river it had meanwhile lost height and at this point at the foot of the same cliff was some 180 feet lower than the canal. The difference in height, known in engineering terms as 'head', provided the hydro-electric potential. By dropping the water from the canal vertically down the cliff in a steel pipe known as the 'penstock', the force would be sufficient to turn two turbines at the bottom, thus generating electricity. The water would then flow back into the river through a short canal known as the 'tail-race'.

The men set to work with picks and shovels and chiselled their way through the rock and huge sandstone boulders by pounding stakes into them. They worked two to a shovel, one holding the handle and scooping up the earth, and the other pulling on a rope tied to the blade, thus lifting and emptying it out. For special tasks such as carrying stones for building the power house extra labourers were hired, and many women and children came from Titeng to earn some extra rupees. Constant supervision was the key to getting things done quickly and correctly. Duane registered their names and gave them each a stick exactly a yard long and told them to build their stones into stacks a yard square so that he could easily measure how many they had carried. They would be paid 9 Rs. for each cubic yard of stones gathered from the river bed. This could be earned in a day and was the standard wage for Baglung. As far as possible the Project kept to local rates so as not to fuel inflation or tempt workers from other sites. At the end of the day when Duane inspected the stacks, hoping for an easy job of calculation, there were hundreds of small piles of stones, very few of them a yard square. It turned out the original workers had brought in their relatives saying 'Cut a stick from that tree there and build your stack of stones according to the size of your stick.' Naturally the sticks had become smaller and smaller.

Learning from their mistakes Duane and Ed had to adapt to a slower pace of work. Things didn't happen as planned, orders were misunderstood, and instructions carried out two or three days late. Some workers were not familiar with even the simplest labour-saving device such as the wheelbarrow. When they wanted to turn right, they pushed their hands to the right and were surprised to see the barrow shoot to the left and fall down. But they came up with their own ingenious solution: turn the wheelbarrow round and pull rather than push. When they were excavating the small tail-race tunnel leading from the power house to the river, Duane brought in a small diesel-operated hand pump to dredge out the water. It was much quicker than the aluminium pans they had been using. He showed them how to operate it, but as soon as he left they resorted to the hand pans again.

'I've come to realise that sometimes their method is best,' Duane said. 'It may be slower, but it's a more efficient use of resources. The pump uses up diesel which has to be imported and paid for with foreign exchange.'

Bringing in supplies for the project proved to be much harder than finding workers. All tools, cement, and other equipment had to be ordered from Kathmandu or India, brought to Naudara (the road-head) by truck, and then carried to Baglung by porters. A professional porter could carry 150 lbs on his back, but with this heavy a load the trip from Naudara to Baglung, in the course of which they had to cross and recross the river and ascend the 6,000-foot Karkineta ridge, took four to five days, and even longer in the rainy season when the rivers were swollen.

The metal penstock presented a special problem. It was over 450 feet long with a diameter of 2 feet. Butwal Engineering Works constructed it in 90 segments, each piece about 5 feet long and weighing 150 lbs, so they could be carried by porters and reassembled on the site. When the porters at Naudara first saw the sections they shook their heads, 'We can't carry these – they're the wrong shape!' Fortunately the promise of extra *bakshish* persuaded them to change their minds.

The Project hired an agent called Dipak who they thought was trustworthy to oversee the storage of supplies in Naudara until porters could be found to carry them to Baglung. Cement was in short supply that year, commanding high prices and therefore liable to be highjacked whilst on its journey. Luckily as a government project the

Baglung scheme was able to buy cement at a regulated price of
Rs. 45 a sack compared to Rs. 100 on the black market. 100 sacks of
cement were stored in Dipak's warehouse in Naudara until they were
needed. When the time came, Duane sent a message asking Dipak to
send the cement by porter to Baglung. No cement arrived that week
or the next. Duane sent another runner to Naudara who came back
with the message that the warehouse was empty – all the cement had
been stolen. Annoyed, Duane made a trip to Naudara to talk with
Dipak where it transpired that Dipak himself had 'borrowed' the
cement and sold it on the black market. He had gambled that the
cement would not be needed and therefore not missed until the price
had fallen when he would replace it with cement bought at a lower
price, thus making a handsome profit for himself. We didn't know
what other 'businesses' Dipak was running on the side, but he was
probably quite a crook for we later heard that he had been murdered
in Darjeeling.

Having replaced the lost cement the problem was finding porters,
for it was by now planting time and most had left to plant their
fields. The few who remained demanded high rates, so Duane struck
what he thought was a good bargain with a man who had a mule
train. The man promised to deliver the cement right to the site office
on the cliff top. Unfortunately when the mules arrived at Baglung
and tried to follow the narrow path to the site office, local farmers
barred their way claiming the mules would devour their crops. No
amount of talking would persuade them to change their minds, so
the mules had to backtrack and approach the site along the river bed.
They were then unable to negotiate the steep path up the cliff face so
porters had to be hired to carry the cement the last few feet of its
journey, and the whole episode ended up costing more than if
porters had been hired all the way from Naudara. But at least the
cement had arrived.

At the Baglung end Duane hired a night watchman called Dil
Bahadur to guard the cement and equipment stored at the site office.
After a few nights on the job Dil Bahadur came to Duane, 'Sahib! I
can't stay any longer. They bother me all night long!'

'Who bothers you?'

'It's like this. Last night I was lying on the floor across the
doorway. It was dark and nobody was around – ' He paused to make
sure he had the full attention of his audience.

'Yes, yes, go on!' said the crowd of workers who had gathered
round, happy to put off work a moment longer to enjoy the tale.

'I was lying there, doing nothing, when I heard a strange sound outside. Suddenly, whoosh! There was a rush of *fre-eezing* cold air. It made me shiver. I got up, went outside, and walked round the shed. Nothing! So I lay down again. Then a few minutes later, whoosh! *Fre-eezing* cold air blew through the shed again. It's no good – I can't stay any longer.'

'It's the bad spirits,' said the crowd of workers, and they began suggesting ways to exorcise them, but in the end Duane persuaded the nervous Dil Bahadur to try again for another night. To help him overcome the spirits he gave him a small paraffin lamp. But the next morning Dil Bahadur had a large black eye and was trembling all over. The spirits had not only caused the strange sounds and rushes of freezing cold air, but they had blown out the lamp and Dil Bahadur in his terror had fallen down the hillside as he tried to run away. Nothing would persuade him to try another night, so Dil Bahadur resigned and old Mati Lal who lived above our house took his place.

'Don't worry about me,' said Mati Lal. 'I'll be all right.'

'Did the spirits come?' we asked the next day.

'They came, but they didn't trouble me,' he said. 'They know I'm used to sleeping on my own in the buffalo shed by the river.' So Mati Lal stayed on as night watchman, and the spirits relaxed their antics.

Nepal was becoming development-conscious. At the high schools pupils studied 'development' in their lessons, and in the villages the word 'development' entered the vocabulary. Progressive farmers talked about 'development' chicken and goats, and 'development' vegetables (improved strains), and even 'development' manure (fertilizer). Nothing was worth while unless it had 'development' tacked on to it. The *Pradhan Panch* and village headmen were called into their district headquarters and harangued about the need to instigate 'development' in their areas. The aims and intentions were excellent but in being passed down the line of command from the Ministries to the villages, 'development' became associated with structures and institutions – roads, bridges, schools – rather than with people. 'How can we worry about "development" when our stomachs are empty?' one village headman said to me. It was hard to find the right balance between infrastructure development and people-oriented development.

The Baglung Project was one of several small-scale hydro-electric schemes being constructed by the government in remote areas of Nepal as a spur to development, but it had a unique genesis.

King Birendra of Nepal was as interested in development as his subjects. Each winter he went on a 'development' camp when he and his advisers set up their headquarters in tents in one of the regional centres of Nepal. From there they travelled out to remote areas to meet the people, hear about their problems and needs, and visit local development projects. The previous year the King had set up camp in Pokhara and during the course of his stay paid a visit to Baglung by helicopter. After listening to many speeches and visiting the various offices, the schools, and the hospital, the King sat down in a specially built pavilion on the plateau with Dhaulagiri as a back-cloth, and a delegation of townspeople and merchants came before him with a petition: 'Your Majesty, please give us electricity!'

The King looked favourably on the idea and back in Pokhara a phone call to the Development and Consulting Services at Kasauli set the wheels turning, with the result that a design for a 100kw hydro-electric scheme was drawn up, approved and funded by the government as an official project, with the contract for construction going to Himal Hydro. The electricity generated would be used for lighting in the evenings and small industrial plant by day.

Himal Hydro had been started with the aim of giving training and employment to a pool of skilled workers and encouraging development of Nepal's number one resource – water power. All profits made were ploughed back into the company which was jointly owned by the Nepal government and the United Mission to Nepal (UMN). The UMN was a rather unusual organisation representing people from many different countries and different denominations of the Christian faith. Convinced that God was concerned with people's material well-being as well as their spiritual, the UMN had become involved in such diverse things as rural cooperatives, reforestation and erosion control, an industrial training school, and smallscale hydro-electric schemes, as well as more conventional medical and educational work.

In Titeng the villagers looked on the electricity scheme with a certain amount of scepticism. 'How's the work across the river going?' asked the headman one evening. 'Will we have electricity before we all die?'

'In less than a year if all goes well.'

'The electricity is for Baglung – it won't come to our village, will it?'

'The plan is to take a line to Baglung first and then make lines to the surrounding villages. The government is in charge of the distribution.'

'How much does our government pay you for working here?'

'We're not working for the Nepal government. We only have a contract with them.'

'Who pays you then? Your own government?'

'No, we're paid by a Christian organisation. They're a group of people who follow the same religion as we do, and want to help other people who are less fortunate than themselves.'

'Aah! So you do this for *dharma* then?'

This was always a sticky question for it was difficult to know what they understood by the word *dharma*. It was a Sanskrit word that the dictionary translated as 'religion', but we had found that they used it most frequently in reference to the system of merit points by which Hindus could earn their salvation. A pot of water for thirsty travellers, a pilgrimage to a sacred-shrine, a priest employed to chant prayers at a festival, all earned the devotee religious points and the chance for a better afterlife. But although these acts were performed with dedication and sincerity, there seemed to be little real love or concern for people behind them. So in explaining our motivation for going to Nepal, we didn't want the villagers to feel that *they*, as people, were not important to us.

'Yes, you could say we do it for *dharma*. But our *dharma* is different from yours. We believe we can't earn God's favour because he offers his love to us freely. We came to Nepal because we don't think it's fair that in our countries we have so much more than we need, and here your lives are so difficult. If everybody in the world cared for one another, and those who have shared with those who haven't, nobody would be poor.'

We felt rather hypocritical saying this for we were aware that we had given up very little and still had far more than they. But the headman picked up this last idea and kept repeating it over and over. 'Yes,' he said emphatically, 'if everybody did that, things would be all right.'

Work on the project continued. The alignment of the head-race canal was surveyed and digging commenced. The land for this had to be bought from the local farmers who like the people of Titeng were sceptical of the benefits that electricity would bring. But they agreed to cooperate when they heard that excess water from the canal would be used to irrigate their fields.

When the work was well underway Duane took me on a tour of the project.

'What use *is* this electricity if you're a villager from Titeng? Is it only the wealthy who'll benefit?' I asked Duane as we climbed the steep cliff from the power house site by the river up to the office and canal. The trench had been dug and now the men were preparing to lay the penstock sections and weld them in place. These would carry water from the canal down to the turbines.

'Well, so far it's the poorest people who've benefited the most,' said Duane, pointing to some Magars and low-caste blacksmiths who were lifting a section of penstock. 'They've gained work.'

'But that will end when the job is finished.'

'Yes, but they've gained new skills and training that hopefully will get them a better job in the future. They'll gain in other ways too but many of the benefits of electricity are indirect. For example, irrigation could double or treble the yield of their dry fields. With electricity they could install small pumps to lift the water from the river to their fields. It's no good installing electricity and leaving it at that. You've got to educate people how to use it best and develop other things such as agriculture at the same time.'

We reached the top of the cliff and turned on to the canal which ran through the terraced fields. Large sections of the trench had been dug and men were reinforcing parts of it with cement lining. One of the main problems was the large number of small side streams that trickled down the hillside. For each of these a culvert had to be dug and lined to protect the canal from erosion.

The Kathe Khola valley was about ten miles long from the rising of its headwaters to the point where it joined the Kali Gandaki. It was steeply V-shaped, widening at its head and narrowing to a bottle-neck gorge where it entered the Kali. On the southern side where Titeng lay it was flanked by cliffs but, on this northern slope, terraced fields came right down to its edge except for the small cliff where the penstock was going. Above the cliffs lay the fields and multitude of villages that gradually petered out into rocky pasture land and forest as the altitude increased. The main walking path along the valley lay on the northern side about a hundred feet above the canal. The river itself was fast-flowing and filled with boulders. In the dry season its waters were a languid translucent blue in the deep pools and it was easy to jump across from boulder to boulder. But the rains transformed it to a turbulent muddy-brown with the debris brought down from the unstable slopes.

'Look, do you see that village?' said Duane, pointing to the top of a side tributary near the head of the Kathe Khola. 'That's Khannegaon. They used to mine copper there. The smelting was done by wood fires and in time the forests were destroyed. So the government imposed restrictions on the felling of trees and the industry was forced to close down. With electricity it would be possible to restart this. Another local cottage industry that could benefit is the paper-making. At the moment they have to rely on the sun to dry the sheets so they can only make it in the dry season.'

'What about cooking? If they could use electricity instead of firewood that would prevent the trees being cut down.'

'The problem is that it may not help in time. First of all you have to develop a suitable small fuel-efficient cooker and then you've got to persuade people to use it. It calls for a big change in their customs. But in the long-term, yes, it is the answer.'

After three miles on the canal which wound in and out of the bulges and dips of the hills we reached the point where it diverged from the Kathe Khola.

'We won't need to make a dam,' said Duane. 'Just a rough barrage of stones and mud to divert the water into the canal. There's no point wasting money and building something fancy – it'll only be swept away in the monsoon floods. Better to make something simple that can be repaired cheaply and easily with local resources.'

'Will you be taking all the water from the river?'

'Only at the driest time of year. But even then there'll still be water flowing below the 'intake' because of the side streams that come in.

'The barrage and intake will be here, and over there we'll have the settling tank,' he said, pointing to a flattish piece of land close to the river. 'The main problem for hydro-electric schemes in Nepal is the amount of sediment the rivers carry. It can damage the turbines and if you build a dam, the lake behind it silts up very quickly. With the settling tank the sediment can sink to the bottom and by opening a gate it can be flushed out. As an extra precaution there'll be a grating just before the water flows down the penstock – that's to stop any sticks or bigger stones going down.'

We surveyed the jumble of greenish-white boulders that almost hid the river at this point and stretched up the opposing slope like scattered waste paper. The terraced fields had been split by two ugly jagged scars that ran the length of the hillside.

'Came down two years ago in the middle of the night,' said a villager who saw us looking across the valley. 'They say there was a huge landslide way up in the forest on the mountain top. I remember there was a loud roar and suddenly trees and boulders and earth came crashing down the valley. All the bridges were destroyed. See where the side river makes a sharp turn about halfway up the mountain? The trees and boulders jammed there and the waters piled up behind. Suddenly the water burst out of the valley and flowed straight down the hillside. Tore out these two gullies . . . swept the fields away . . . the whole hillside fell down! All that's left of our fields are these boulders. But we're lucky only four people died that night – they were sleeping in their stable in the fields. If there had been a village in the way many people would have died.'

We stood silently for a while. Words were not adequate to express the way we felt. Who were *we* to try to tame the rivers of this land? We crossed the boulders and returned by a roundabout route to Titeng. The village appeared to cling more precariously than ever to its shallow ledge on the mountainside.

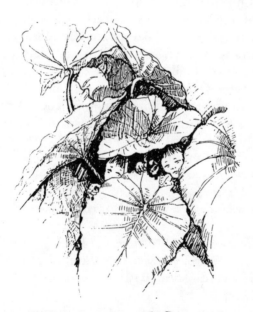

Children hiding in the Tiralu leaves

8

The eyes of the stomach

Sitting in the cowshed beside Grandmother I surveyed the now familiar ridges and dips of the Kathe Khola valley. Streaks of green, the first tinges of spring, touched the slopes where a few stalks of wheat struggled through the stony ground. The month of March was drawing to a close.

'Look – the Queen Birds are here,' said Grandmother, pointing to where a pair of scarlet minivets flashed their crimson and chrome colours on the guava trees. 'That means the wheat should be good. After the Chaitra festival we'll harvest it and plant the maize. Then when the rains come we'll cut the maize and plant the rice. Ah! – that's the best time of year! *Everyone* turns out to help. The women talk and sing as they plant and the men joke, and when it's over we'll kill a pig and have a big feast. Do they do that in your country at rice-planting time?'

'We don't grow rice in England. It's too cold.'

'Don't grow rice? What does your family grow on their land then? Maize? Millet?'

'No – it's too cold. We can only grow wheat, barley, oats and potatoes.'

'Eh?' Grandmother was bewildered. Even on the highest slopes around Baglung they still grew maize and millet, and I could see her mentally classifying England with the wastes of the high Tibetan plateau.

'What we can't grow ourselves we buy from other countries and bring by ship,' I explained. 'My parents don't own any land – we buy the food we need in the shops. Only a few people are farmers.' Grandmother looked at me puzzled so I hastened to reassure her that in America where Duane came from they grew plenty of rice and maize.

'America?' queried Grandmother, thinking it sounded slightly familiar. 'Which district of Nepal is that in?'

Every conversation with the villagers sooner or later got on to the topic of food. It was not surprising, for food with its associated agriculture was the pivot of their lives.

'If you were very rich and had as much money as you wanted, what would you spend it on?' I asked Bhakhu one day as I handed him a rupee coin for running a message to Duane.

'I haven't got any money,' he objected.

'Well, just imagine somebody's given you thousands of rupees – what would you spend it on?'

He furrowed his brows and pondered this problem at some length. Finally he looked up and said, 'Sister, I would buy *meat* and . . . *milk* and . . . *yoghourt* . . . *tea* . . . *sel-roti* . . . and . . . *and bananas,*' he finished emphatically, listing all his favourite foods.

Nepalis regarded the stomach as the most important organ of their bodies. Whereas we talked of seeing with 'our mind's eye', they talked of seeing with 'the eyes of the stomach'. When getting a job they spoke of 'raising the stomach', using the same word as in 'raising chickens' or 'raising children', and Gurkha soldiers described their years in the army as 'cooking our pension', and their years of retirement as 'eating our pension'.

All foods were classified as either 'hot' or 'cold', this classification having, to our minds, little apparent system to it, and bearing no relationship to the actual temperature of the foods concerned. For example green, black and red lentils were 'hot' but yellow lentils were 'cold'. Maize, millet and wheat were 'hot' when baked as *roti*, but 'cold' when boiled as porridge. Roast potatoes were 'hot', but boiled potatoes were 'cold'; small bananas 'hot', large ones 'cold'; brown sugar 'hot', white sugar 'cold'. Goat and chicken meat were 'hot', but pork and buffalo meat were 'cold'. About the only logical items I could find were the spices such as chilli, garlic, and ginger which were understandably defined as 'hot'.

The significance of this food classification system became clear when a person was sick, for diseases were also defined as either 'hot' or 'cold', the definition once again bearing no relationship to the temperature of the person's body. If he was suffering from a 'cold' disease such as a fever he should eat only 'hot' foods if he wanted to get better, whereas a 'hot' disease such as diarrhoea was treated by only eating 'cold' foods. Certain diseases were treated by specific remedies such as hot water with spices, mashed green lentils, or mint chutney.

Whilst Duane and I did not follow their food classification system, we did find that food took on a new significance. Motivated by the desire to broaden our diet I devoted many hours to tending our small garden. Rows of cauliflowers, lettuces, peas and beans surprised me by coming up; I knew nothing about gardening and had haphazardly thrown the seeds in. But the credit really had to go to the family's goats:

'Goat's manure is better than cow's or buffalo's,' Wife One had declared when she saw me preparing the plot, and before I had finished digging she had carried down two *doko*-loads of goat's droppings fresh from their stable.

The villagers watched my gardening work with interest. It was harder than I had anticipated since we had to carry water from the spring to irrigate. They themselves kept small kitchen gardens at the end of the rainy season when the soil still held some moisture, but this time of year grew nothing.

'Cauliflowers?' they inquired. 'They'll be tasty in the *tun*. Will you give us some?' I distributed seedlings to everyone who asked, but most died from lack of water.

Grandmother offered advice and criticism freely. 'Why do you put in all those sticks and branches with the peas and beans? Just let them lie on the ground. Potatoes? You can't grow potatoes here – the red ants'll eat them.' She was right, of course.

As we watched the peas and beans shoot up, the carrot tops grow curlier and the lettuces fatter and crisper, our mouths began to water. It was the height of the dry season – the worst months of the year for food. I scoured the bazaar for green vegetables but there was not a single spinach leaf to be found – only some dried kidney beans and red hot chillies. At least it simplified the decision of what to cook. But for Naina Singh's family the situation was more serious: their supplies of rice and millet had run out and it would be two months before the wheat was ready to harvest. Devi's Mother and Maila were despatched to search for grain. They travelled several hours from village to village until they found a family with a surplus of millet they were willing to sell. Buying in the bazaar was not considered because of the high prices. Naina's family was luckier than some – thanks to his winter months of labouring they had enough cash to buy the grain. Other families bought food on credit, and several consecutive years of poor crops started an upward spiral of debts that ended with the forfeiture of their land.

Water was also in short supply. Titeng was fortunate to have two springs that flowed throughout the dry season, but many springs dried up and people had to travel long distances to fetch water or rely on a small polluted water hole. As the heat built up, flies and parasites began to breed in the water causing outbreaks of disease; dysentery was widespread, and with the lack of water children went unwashed for days and large infected sores developed on their arms and legs.

We now realised the advantages of the dark and smoky Magar houses which discouraged the flies. I suffered from continual itches and although we swatted hundreds of them fresh reinforcements arrived each day from the nearby stables. Reluctantly (we had wanted to keep our house as simple as possible), we decided to put mosquito-screening on the downstairs room where we kept the food and did our cooking; the flies were a pest and we had already had one bout of dysentery.

We ordered a roll of mosquito-screening from Kathmandu and when it arrived tacked a patch on to our downstairs window. The villagers, inquisitive as ever, gathered round to watch.

'Ah! So you've taken my advice at last,' said Naina happily. 'Now nobody can break in.'

'Yes, that will keep the thieves out,' said the headman.

They were always worried about thieves and continually warning us to keep our things locked up. In fact we never did – and never lost a thing. They themselves were scrupulously honest, but strangers did wander through the village from time to time. Perhaps we were just lucky, but we suspected it would take a very sly thief to slip past Grandmother's sharp eyes.

'No!' said Duane. 'This is to keep the flies out, not the thieves.'

The headman pushed back his cloth *topi* and scratched his head, and Naina screwed his face into a series of grimaces – a sign that he was thinking hard.

'All that money and work just to keep the flies out?' the headman asked, incredulously.

'Pah!' said Naina, less restrained. 'You're crazy! They'll still come in through the door!'

'No, they won't,' we replied, and showed him the screen door that Duane had made. He had fastened a spring so that it closed automatically. This was a novelty, and for weeks our fly problem continued while the children played with the screen door, opening it and watching it slam a hundred times a day, oblivious of the squadrons of flies that zoomed in. I took the opportunity to give a short health talk to the women. In graphic terms I explained about the unseen little 'bugs' that were carried by the flies from the pigsties and dirt to our food, and made us sick when we ate them. They nodded their heads gravely, but I could see they were unconvinced. 'We have our superstitions and these foreigners have theirs!' they seemed to be saying. 'Unseen bugs – what a joke!' I repeated this talk from time to time and although by the end of the year they agreed with me, they never followed our example or built themselves a latrine.

Fire was the number three problem of the dry season. All around us the landscape was brown and parched, the trees naked – stripped of their foliage to feed the buffalo and goats. One day as I was out walking in the nearby village of Salbot, a chance spark from a courtyard fire landed on the thatched roof of a house. In a matter of minutes the fire had engulfed three homes and was threatening others. I looked on, wishing I could help, but help seemed futile. The inhabitants formed a human chain to the nearest spring, but their meagre pots of water could not dampen the fire. Some seized branches and tried to beat out the flames, and others whose houses were threatened but not yet on fire leapt on their roofs and ripped off the bundles of thatch. If these were removed in time there was a chance the fire could be stopped.

A spark flew high in the air and another roof was set ablaze. Women began to wail in the background but the children, excited and oblivious to danger, chased each other with burning embers in their hands.

In the end the village was saved not by human power but by a wind that rose and blew the flames away from the other homes.

The damage was slight by Nepali standards. No one had died, but the fire had claimed two cows, with three houses completely destroyed and two more badly damaged. As I returned home I thought about the things I had always taken for granted – good food, piped water supply, fire engines and firemen – and wondered what could have been done to save those homes.

Back in Titeng the wind was blowing whirls of dust and straw across the courtyard into our room. Grandmother pulled her shawl over her face and huddled close to the wall with her back to the wind. A tailor from Damaigaon was visiting and Bhakhu, Laute, Kali, Gophle and Devi were lining up for new shirts and dresses. With speed and precision the tailor wrapped a piece of material round each child, snipped with a gigantic pair of black scissors, gave the flywheel of his battered sewing-machine a deft flick, and zipped up the seams. They were hardly well-fashioned clothes, but the children didn't care. They pulled them over their old clothes and strutted round the village to show their friends.

Inside our house I hastily pulled our mattresses away from the windows and put as many things away as possible. The wind rose to a scream and the sky exploded in a crack of thunder. I closed my eyes at the violent blast of wind that followed. It lifted the straw mats off the floor and they flapped up and down like over-fed vultures trying to take off. Straw missiles bombarded the room, books and candles dropped from their places on the walls and sheaves of paper fluttered round like frightened doves. Any moment I expected to see our entire furnishings blown through the doorway.

I tied down what I could and wedged the mats in the window spaces as a flimsy protection. I was amazed to see the tailor still sewing merrily in the courtyard even as the wind whipped the material into knots around his sewing-machine. Suddenly, like spurts of machine-gun fire, heavy drops of rain spattered inside our room. Wife One hurriedly put the grain away and carried Grandmother inside, and the tailor reluctantly retired to the verandah. The rain fell faster and faster, in heavier and heavier drops. Then the hail started. Round white balls shot off the roof and spun round the yard. Bhakhu and Laute chased after the biggest ones, and in the thick of the hail Devi's Mother and Saili plodded in from the fields with drenched clothes and heavy loads of firewood on their backs.

The storm continued to build up. Thunder and lightning followed in quick succession and Baglung was obscured by a thick wedge of driving rain. I dragged our possessions further inside our room, wrapped myself in a sleeping-bag, and with Beethoven's 4th piano concerto on the tape-recorder prepared to sit out the storm.

When it finally blew over several hours later, I was surprised to see that once more snow had fallen on the surrounding hilltops. The air was fresh and clear and Annapurna glistened in the distance. This was the first of the sporadic violent thunderstorms that heralded the end of the dry season and the approach of the monsoon. It was a signal that the maize could now be planted even though the monsoon was still three months away.

It was about this time that I started feeling the need to have a job. It was no longer sufficient to say that I was Duane's wife. Everyone else in Titeng worked, even Grandmother, but I had neither fields to farm nor children to look after, and the housework for just two people could hardly be called heavy in their terms. Reading and writing did not count as work to the villagers and for some reason I felt it important to be seen to be productive in their terms.

At first I had planned to spend my time doing whatever the village women were doing, but having experienced all their tasks at least a couple of times my determination began to weaken. Their work was both monotonous and physically demanding, and on top of that I often didn't have the necessary skills – I couldn't climb trees to cut the fodder, I was slow at cutting grass, and the cows and goats didn't respond to my herding. Besides, my main interest in working alongside the women was the chance to talk and get to know them, but enjoyable though this chatter was, they had work to get through and I was holding them up. So I started looking round for something more suited to my skills.

In Kasauli I had taught our housegirl to read and write, and I wanted to do the same thing in Titeng. None of the women could read or write, and a small literacy class would provide an opportunity to also talk about their health problems. I started with Naina Singh's two wives:

'Would you like to learn to read and write?'

'Who? Us? We're far too old – we'll be dead before we've learned!'

'What about you?' I said, turning to Saili and Devi's Mother.

'We couldn't learn! We don't know how. We've never been to school to learn how to study.'

'It doesn't matter. It wouldn't be like school – I know you can do it.'

But still they shook their heads. I must have looked disappointed for Devi's Mother came up to me and said, 'It's all right for you Sister, but what use is it to us? We don't *need* to read and write to do our work.'

I went through the village asking in every home and their answers were all the same: 'What's the point? There aren't any books in our village, and the grass still has to be cut and the water carried.'

Sadly I was forced to see their point of view and agree with them. If they were to live the fields had to be tended and the women were the labourers. Even if I did teach them to read and write there was no way they were going to escape the cycle – not yet.

Instead I approached the Campus in Baglung. The name was rather misleading. It consisted of just two classrooms, an office, a library, and a garden with flower beds neatly demarcated with upended bricks but no flowers. Although affiliated to the University in Kathmandu, it essentially provided a high school training. I spoke to Mr Adhikari the English teacher – a small rotund Brahmin who owned a rice shop and half of Baglung – offering to help the students with English conversation. 'Why do you want to help the students?' he asked. 'They don't want to learn anything. You must come and teach *us*!' The other six teachers agreed and insisted on starting right away. So we sat down in the garden on the wind-blown cliff top – the hazy mass of Dhaulagiri at our heads, the sacred Kali River at our feet – and talked about England and its way of life. It seemed a strangely remote and unfamiliar land.

After a while I progressed to teaching the students. Not being a trained teacher a conversation class seemed the best policy. But the students had an English examination in two weeks' time and had not covered the syllabus. 'You must teach them Phonetics and The Dictionary,' ordered Mr Adhikari. I began to regret my rash offer of help. I knew nothing about phonetics or the dictionary. How could I possibly teach them in two weeks?

'You'll find a book on phonetics in the library,' said Mr Adhikari with a smile as he left.

Nervously I prepared material for my classes and on the first day waited tense and dry-mouthed for the students to arrive. Nobody turned up. Mr Adhikari had forgotten to inform them. Even after that misunderstanding was sorted out it was hard to establish a schedule. My class was the last in the afternoon, and if their previous class was cancelled – a common occurrence – the students did not wait around for mine. Then there were frequent holidays that they forgot to tell me about. I would walk in from Titeng only to meet my students lounging in a tea-shop. 'Good afternoon, Sir. Where you go?' they would ask innocently in their best English.

'To the Campus for your class,' I would reply, not bothering to correct the Sir.

'Oh Sir! No school today. Hol-i-day!' And they smiled their most disarming smiles and offered me a glass of tea so it was impossible to be annoyed for long.

I discovered my main qualification for the job on the first day we had an actual class. 'Do you speak Arpi?' asked the students, and they went on and on about Arpi until I was thoroughly mystified. Finally they produced their English grammar book and pointed to a passage. 'R.P.', said the text, 'stands for Received Pronunciation as spoken by the BBC and people in south-east England'. I wasn't sure whether I spoke R.P. but I reassured the students that I came from Kent and you couldn't be more south-eastern than that. Having sorted out this problem we began the class, which was when I discovered that whatever accent I used the students couldn't understand me. Their standard of reading and writing was quite good but they were not used to speaking or hearing it spoken, so the first lessons were

notable for the lack of communication between the students and
myself.

My biggest frustration however was the group of five female
students. Though liberated enough to attend school, they could not
bring themselves to sit within ten feet of a boy. The rooms of the
Campus were large and lofty, and the girls sat in the farthest corner
where I knew they could not hear my quiet voice. When I begged
them to move forward they shuffled their benches a few inches and
stopped. So there they sat, day after day, my most regular attenders,
unable to hear a word I said. Eventually when I had gained more
confidence I persuaded the students to abandon their rigid lines of
benches and tables and sit in a circle on the floor. This worked better
but still the girls were too shy to speak when the boys were present.
Apart from the benches, tables and blackboard, the room was totally
bare, and this taxed my imagination as I tried to make the classes as
interesting as possible.

The boys were a typical mixture – a row of long-haired rebels at the
back who paid little attention to the lesson in progress, and a row of
obedient scholars at the front who answered all the questions. In
between sat the rest, the more affluent ones dressed in the latest fashion
of 'cowboy' jackets, jeans, and high-heeled shoes, and those from the
villages in rubber flip-flops, cloth *topis* and untailored shirts and
shorts. Several appeared to be only twelve or thirteen years old.
Officially they had to be at least fifteen for admission, but in practice it
was easy to cheat. The standard of high school graduation was
relatively low, so that a bright boy who started school at five (earlier
than most) could easily finish by thirteen.

The students and teachers presented me with a contrasting segment
of society to the Magars of Titeng. There were the educated élite of
Nepal, almost exclusively from well-to-do Brahmin, Chhettri or
Newar homes in the vicinity of Baglung. There were only two
Magars in the class, and no low-caste students. Although there was no
discrimination on the basis of caste, very few low-caste families could
afford to send their children through the full ten years of school so that
they could graduate, even though the fees were less than 50 pence a
month. In remote areas where there were no secondary schools only
the wealthy could pay for their sons to stay in lodgings in Baglung in
order to attend the high school there.

Besides giving me more sympathy for the teachers in the local
schools, my job introduced me to Jamuna who became a close friend.
She was the only female teacher on the Campus. Clever and attractive,

Jamuna stood out from the rest not only because she was more articulate and her English far better than the English teacher's, but she was the only one not married. In Nepal to be female, over thirty, and not married was highly irregular, and Jamuna shared with me how she had resisted her parents' attempts to marry her off. Coming from a wealthy élite Kathmandu family, Jamuna didn't lack for suitors, but she was interested in more than just marriage. When Jamuna moved to Baglung her mother finally resigned herself to this situation and began to marry off Jamuna's younger sisters instead – a break with Nepali etiquette that must have raised a few eyebrows in their social circle.

Jamuna taught political science and economics and was interested in the status of Nepali women. When she heard I lived in a Magar village she immediately wanted to come and talk to the women to gather some more information for her research. So one afternoon she arrived in the village in her elegant sari and high-heeled shoes. The first women to catch her eye were Wife One, Wife Two, and Grandmother who were sitting in the courtyard spinning and weaving. Jamuna had prepared a questionnaire to evaluate their 'awareness', and I wondered how they would respond to someone of the same sex and nationality. I introduced Jamuna and she began by asking them their names.

'Names?' said Wife Two with a laugh. 'Whose names?'

'Your name.'

'*My* name? But I don't know that! I'd have to ask my mother.'

'Well – never mind your names – how old are you?'

'Age! We don't know our age.'

'I used to know my age,' said Wife One, counting up the number of children she had borne and working backwards from there.

Many of Jamuna's questions were hypothetical and, as I had found, these were the hardest to elicit answers.

'Do you wish you had gone to school?'

'We had to work in the fields. We couldn't go to school.'

'But if you had had the chance, would you have gone?'

'I don't know!'

'What about your children – do they go to school?'

'We send them, but they don't obey. They play truant,' said Wife One helplessly.

Jamuna sighed. She had almost as hard a time understanding their village vocabulary and accent as I did, and in some ways had less understanding of the villagers' way of thinking. I realised then that an educated Kathmandu Nepali was just as much a foreigner to the Magars of Titeng as Duane and myself.

Jamuna tried her final question: 'What do you wish for most of all?'
There was a moment's pause.

'Wishes?' said Grandmother scornfully, speaking for the first time.
'Who has time for wishes?'

Discouraged, Jamuna and I retired to the upper room to discuss
Freud and Indira Gandhi's politics over glasses of tea. I suspected that
the women were neither as ignorant nor as lacking in ideas as they
chose to make out; on rare occasions I caught a glimpse of something
deeper. But they did not analyse or articulate their feelings, and I
mused over the advantages of seeing life through 'the eyes of the
stomach' – free from the torment of 'If only I had done such and
such . . . .'

After Jamuna had left I asked the women what they thought of her.
'Very nice person,' they said. 'She spoke very sweetly but *we* couldn't
understand what she was trying to say. We're *so* dumb!' Bhakhu,
watching her stumble down the rough path in her high-heeled shoes,
summed her up more succinctly: '*Hinna nasakne manche*,' he said,
'She's a not-able-to-walk person.'

There were so many things that Jamuna and I took for granted that
were outside the village women's experience. Photos, for example.
We had recently got back our first batch taken in the village and I
passed them round. Wife One took the top photo and turned it over in
her hands, leaving dirty thumbprints. 'Very nice,' she said without
much expression, and I noticed she was holding it upside down.

'It goes this way up,' I pointed out. 'And it's somebody you know.'

'It's Grandmother,' yelled Bhakhu and Laute who were looking
over her shoulders.

'Grandmother?' repeated Wife One. She turned the photo on to its
side and recognition dawned.

'How amazing!' said Wife Two, also leaning over her shoulders so
that the light was obscured. 'Look every detail is there. There's her
wool, and spindle, even the old basket she keeps the wool in.'

'Let me see, let me see,' said Grandmother in a querulous voice. She
took the photo and studied it in silence. Then she burst into a loud
cackling laugh, 'Why did you take a photo of *me*? I'm just an old
woman. Look – you can see my wrinkles and white hair! Did you
draw this?'

'I took it with a camera – that black box we have.'

'Aah!' said Grandmother.

'*Khich*! *Khich*!' shouted Laute, imitating the sound of a camera being
clicked. 'Show us some more!'

I passed round the photos in turn and the children yelled out the names of people they recognised. 'Look there's Seti . . . Kali . . . Moti with her hand over her mouth . . . and Phupu! There's our old water pot!' Recognition was followed by chuckles of laughter from the subject and sharp criticism if I had caught them smiling or laughing.

'How terrible! Look at me showing my teeth – aren't I ugly,' complained Devi's Mother. 'Sister! How could you take me looking like this? Look at my old *cholo*, all patched and darned.'

'How dark my skin looks,' commented Keshu Ram's daughter. 'And look at you Tulasi, your hair is sticking out all over the place. And little Devi's naked!'

Wife One still insisted on holding the photos sideways but as it seemed to help her recognise them I gave up correcting her. It was noticeable that the children were much quicker at recognising the photos than the older women. But then photos were a recent arrival in Nepali villages and the older women had grown up without ever seeing a two-dimensional picture. They had been brought up to work in the fields, get married, bear children, and so repeat the cycle of their mothers and grandmothers. There was no time for education.

But slowly changes were coming. Primary schooling was now free, and eight years ago Titeng and the nearby villages joined together and under the headman's leadership built a primary school. Most of the boys in Titeng attended the three years of school taught there. After that they had to go to Baglung and pay 7 rupees a month, so many gave up, not just because it cost money, but because their help was needed in the fields. So long as their sons could read and write their names, the parents were content for they could do neither.

After visiting the little primary school I was impressed that the children learnt anything. It was a simple stone building, a mile or two beyond the lower spring, and served Salbot, a Brahmin village, as well as Titeng and Aatmuri. Approaching through the fields I was first struck by the apparent lack of discipline – children were scrambling in and out of the windows and running wild outside. Inside, the three classrooms were more like prison cells than gateways to enlightenment. There was no furniture or decorations apart from some rough wooden benches and two blackboards, and with only one small window they were almost devoid of light. Class One had no benches at all but sat cross-legged on the earth floor chanting the alphabet after their teacher: 'Ka, kha, ga, gha . . . .' In Classes Two and Three a maths lesson was in progress and this too was chanted in unison.

Rote-learning was the rule, and the drop-out rate must have been high
for whilst there were twenty pupils in Class One, only six remained in
Class Three.

Out of the forty or so children in Titeng, only five boys and one girl
attended school. I almost overlooked Seti, the eight-year-old niece of
the headman who was sitting quietly on the floor of Classroom One.
She was unaware that she was making history – the first girl ever to
attend school from Titeng. Would her life hold anything different, I
wondered.

As for the photos I put some into a scrapbook and it became a
popular rainy day pastime to come and leaf through them. The
remainder I gave away, and they carried them off in their *patukas* to
put in the place of honour in the small glass frames that hung over their
doorways containing musty photos of fathers or long-lost uncles
posing solemnly in Gurkha uniform.

Magar boy

9

Off with their heads

'At Chaitra Dasain you'll be able to buy everything you could ever wish for! They even bring things up from India!'

For some months now this had been the promise we received when we asked the shop-keepers for items that were unobtainable in the local shops. Baglung was famous for its celebration of Chaitra Dasain, a religious festival that fell in April at the end of the Nepali year. At this time a huge *mela* (fair-cum-market) was held at Mayathan, the wooded peninsula on the cliff top between the Kali Gandaki and the Kathe Khola, and people travelled for seven or eight days from such far-off places as Dolpo, Mustang and Rukumkot in order to attend.

Like most of Nepal's rich and numerous festivals, Chaitra Desain was Hindu in origin, but both Buddhists and Hindus celebrated it. The statistics divided Nepal into a Hindu majority and a sizeable Buddhist minority, but there was no clear dividing line between these groups and Hindus worshipped images of Buddha, Buddhists celebrated Hindu festivals, and both had incorporated animistic practices. We found that religious devotion varied greatly – from the educated high-caste Uppaddhya Brahmins who studied the Sanskrit scriptures and conscientiously followed every ritual and regulation, to the illiterate low-caste villagers who knew little of orthodox Hinduism beyond the festivals that occurred each year.

The Magars of Titeng fell into the latter group and were labelled Hindu in so far as they participated in the Hindu festivals and holy days, consulted a Brahmin priest to name their children, and were cremated into ashes on the banks of the sacred Kali which they called the 'Ganga', since it flowed into the River Ganges in India. But they couldn't name any of the Hindu pantheon, and the more we studied them the more it seemed that their religious practices derived from a pre-Hindu, pre-Buddhist animism.

When questioned closely they usually admitted to believing in the existence of one God with a capital 'G', but he was too remote and abstract to be of any real influence in their lives, and the day-to-day effective power lay with the gods or spirits which were numerous and inhabited tangible physical objects such as a tree, a rock, a spring, or a river. Scattered around the village were various small altars – a collection of stones tucked behind the spring, a large boulder in the middle of a field, a small hole in the wall of the cowshed – identified by strips of red rags, a daub of cow dung or a sprinkle of red powder. From time to time fresh flowers appeared on them or the ashes of a burnt offering. Naina Singh had an altar to the 'house spirits' in a corner of the room where we ate supper, and later when we knew him better he told us he had consulted these spirits to see if it was acceptable for us to live in his barn. Each morning Wife One searched the courtyard and fields for a few flower petals to place in a copper pot in front of this altar.

'Why do you do that?' I asked.

'An offering to the spirits, Little Child.'

'Which spirits, and why?'

'I don't know. The spirits of the house I suppose. We've always done it.'

Beside the buffalo sheds down by the river was another small altar with crudely carved wooden characters. 'These are the spirits who guard our village,' was the most we could discover when we asked for an explanation. We learned in time that questioning got us nowhere; it was best to observe in silence. Theirs was not a religion of dogma and doctrine, but a loosely connected body of traditions and superstitions handed down through the centuries, whose meaning had long since been lost. Nowadays the festivals served the no less important purpose of providing a break from the daily grind of work, a chance to relax and have fun.

Chaitra festival was no exception. The village rose early as usual but only the women did a few household chores. Chattering myna birds on the banana trees aped the men who gathered in the courtyard dressed in their best clothes, or at least in clean clothes. Gesi Ram and Saili passed by carrying a bamboo coop with a chicken and two pigeons. Saili grinned from ear to ear, obviously delighted to have the day off work and be allowed to accompany her husband on the important task of sacrificing at the temple. 'Older Sister, are you going to the *mela*?' yelled Bhakhu, seeing me watching from our window. 'Later on,' I promised.

The main festivities were taking place at the Mayathan temple beyond Baglung, but Titeng was holding its own private ceremonies for those unable to attend, or unable to afford the gifts for the priests. Three terraces below our house a small field had been cleared and a tall mast of bamboo erected. We joined the crowd of villagers walking down with malnourished chickens in their hands.

Naina Singh was officiating at the site. 'My family are the priests for the village,' he explained. 'If any *puja* has to be performed, I do it.' *Puja* was a Sanskrit word meaning 'worship' in the Hindu tradition, which usually included an offering or sacrifice of some kind. Naina was wearing a clean white loincloth with his head completely shaved except for a tassle of hair at the back. He squatted on the ground muttering to himself and drew from his belt a gleaming *khukuri* – the curved Gurkha knife.

We crowded closer. The early morning mist was still rising and a small wood fire wafted blue smoke into our faces. The villagers threw their chickens on to the ground. Legs tied, earth-bound, they flapped pathetically. Naina lifted a handful of red powder from a leaf plate and sprinkled it around himself and the fire. Then holding the *khukuri* between his toes he seized the first chicken, solemnly pulled its neck through the blade, and threw its flapping headless body to the ground. The crowd cheered and the boys at the back beat their drums and fired an old rifle as the owner ran forward to retrieve the body before it splattered blood on everyone.

Apart from Naina Singh the villagers were in light-hearted and buoyant spirits for this was their holiday and they were out to make the most of it. They laughed and talked and argued throughout the ceremony, identifying the chickens as Naina consigned them one by one to their predestined fate. 'Yes, that one's Grandmother's . . . there goes Phupu's with the ragged wing . . . that one with no feathers is the headman's. . . .' Without exception the chickens were scrawny underfed specimens, the villagers taking the pragmatic view that festivals and sacrifices though necessary were not to be taken too seriously; there was no need to slaughter their best roosters. After each sacrifice Naina allowed the blood from the head to drip on the fire which spat and crackled as it received the offering. Then the ceremony over, the villagers gathered up their dead chickens and returned to their homes to prepare a curry stew.

Towards midday we made our way with Devi and her mother to *Devithan*, the place of the goddess Devi, in the wood on the cliff-top peninsula. Down every mountainside brightly-coloured ribbons of

people curled towards this spot, like streamers pulled by an invisible
hand, perhaps by the goddess herself. Many of the villagers travelled
in large groups bearing in front their communal sacrifice – a young
buffalo strung on bamboo poles, or two or three goats on a lead, their
heads decorated with flowers and red powder. Some had hired bands
to lead their procession.

Close to the wood on a large open space where the buffalo usually
grazed, vendors had set up their stalls. We remembered the shop-
keepers' promise that at Chaitra Dasain we would be able to buy
everything, but in the event we were disappointed. There were no
fruits or vegetables, and apart from some people selling bamboo
baskets and beautifully turned wooden pots, there was only the usual
bazaar collection of flip-flops and hair ribbons. Clearly their view of
plenty was different from ours. But we had not really come to buy; it
was the people we wanted to see.

Magars from the high ridgetops dominated the scene, easy to spot
in their wine-red velvet blouses, rolls of lemon-yellow *patukas*, and
shawls embroidered with tiny flowers. The Brahmin women
favoured shocking reds and pinks, while the latest fashion with the
young men were shirts of violent purple polyester. There were
Tibetans with blankets to sell, holy *sadhus* from the south in orange
robes, Indians with tea-stalls selling hot sticky *jalebis*, and a group of
Kham Magars dressed in sombre black, with broad heavy faces and
wads of rolled tinfoil from cigarette packs stuck through their ear
lobes. In front of them hand-woven wool sacks contained their wares
– walnuts. 'Jungly people!' said Devi's Mother, suddenly feeling
sophisticated and dismissing them with a shrug of her shoulders. For
these Kham Magars, Baglung was the big metropolis. We bought
some walnuts which were delicious though spiced with hairs from the
wool sacks and the dust of eight days' travel.

Passing under an archway we entered the sanctuary of the forest.
Here too vendors had set up stalls along either side of the broad
pathway and the bright colours of the crowds contrasted with the
gentle spring-greenness of the trees. But the collection of tin pans,
aluminium spoons and home-made paraffin burners offered for sale
did not tempt us to purchase anything. Further on in a clearing in the
centre of the forest, was the temple itself, and here the crowds were
thickest, requiring the patrol of Baglung policemen to keep them in
order. Around the temple Brahmin priests – shaved heads, white
loincloths – sat in the shadow of the trees ready to chant portions of the
Hindu scriptures for those who paid them.

Devi's Mother circumambulated the temple clockwise and offered a plate of rice to the priest at the door. We sat outside and waited. The forecourt of the temple was stained a dark and ominous red and a young buffalo calf tied to an elaborately carved stake shivered in the pool of its predecessor's blood. It seemed to know its fate and its large black eyes pleaded mournfully with me. The executioner grasped his long *khukuri* with both hands and held it high above his head, and a Brahmin priest rushed forward to sprinkle holy water on the calf's head; tradition demanded that no animal could be sacrificed until it had nodded its assent. But the buffalo calf stood rigid with fear and only when the priest emptied the whole of his water pot did it give a pathetic toss of its head and the executioner's knife fell. Two young boys ran to dip their feet in the blood that spurted from the severed neck, and the priest stepped forward to claim his payment – the head and one foreleg.

The day seemed to have grown hotter and more humid and I was glad to leave the temple area and slip back into the cool shade of the forest. I took a glass of tea and some doughnut-shaped *sel roti* from a tea stand, and one of my English students greeted me and started talking. He was anxious to dissociate himself from the celebrations. 'These festivals are all right for the ignorant village folk, but we educated people don't believe in them any more,' he told me. 'Religion is just a money-making business set up by the priests.' He was a communist but when I questioned him tactfully he didn't see any conflict between this and the money-lending business that his family ran. I knew they were one of the biggest landowners and several of the Magars in Titeng were in debt to his family.

Besides the temple rites there were other attractions that drew the crowds. One man was selling drums and bamboo flutes and the trees around him were filled with Magar boys playing love-songs and making passes at the girls who walked beneath. There was also a stone-throwing contest, the Nepali version of shot-putting. Hopeful men bulging with muscles and tendons lined up at the top of the fairground with a heavy stone balanced on their shoulders. The contest was simple. They ran downhill to a certain mark and with a loud grunt threw the stones as far as they could.

Further along a magician from India provided cheap thrills for those able to afford the one rupee entrance fee to his enclosure. We paid our fee and pushed our way in through the door, unlike some who preferred to burrow under the canvas walls. The show was slow moving but entertaining. The magician and his partner spent much of their time working the crowd into a frenzy of excitement and anticipation, and only then did they begin their act. They started with simple tricks, making pictures in books disappear and reappear, producing coins from the hats of the audience, and causing sticks to vanish. To us the mechanism of the tricks seemed very transparent, but the audience loved it. We noticed one strange thing – they applauded *before* the trick was performed, and obviously believed it was their clapping that caused the magic to happen.

The magician, his teeth and lips stained a gruesome red from chewing betel-nut, worked the crowd up for his grand finale – a levitation act. A large sheet of material with a small hole was laid on the ground and his partner crawled underneath and lay down with his head through the hole. Then to the beat of drums and a long monologue by the magician, the body was raised inch by inch until it was about a man's height off the ground. We were not fooled, but the crowd cheered with delight. Without a doubt they had got their money's worth.

Back in Titeng we were treated to a second performance by Bhakhu and Laute who tried to imitate the magician and produce coins from their sleeves. Naina Singh, no doubt wishing they could really master that trick, seemed in good spirits nonetheless when he came over to our kitchen for coffee and walnuts. We sensed a softening in his attitude towards us, perhaps helped by a bottle or two of *rakshi*, and we took advantage of this to discuss our roof which had been leaking badly in the recent heavy storms.

'Don't worry,' said Naina. 'This is *my* house. My grandfather built the round house, my father built the square house, but this one I built myself. I am the best house builder in the village – I am the best house builder in Baglung – I am the best in the whole district! I'll mend your roof so that not a single drop of rain can get through. Not one single drop!'

To seal this promise we offered him a second glass of coffee, but he shook his head and said, 'It's time to come to my house. I have some special food I've prepared for you.'

Half-asleep, wondering what this could be, we stumbled our way into their dark house. As usual a cauldron was bubbling on the fire. Naina made us sit down and with great ceremony handed us a bowl of millet beer. Then he dipped a ladle into the cauldron.

'Such a treat! Such a delicacy!' he intoned as he handed us the plates. I took mine and stared at the gruesome morsels in front of me. They were still whole and revoltingly lifelike. How could I leave them without offending him? I could hear Naina's voice ringing in my ears, 'Only the heads – the juiciest, tastiest chicken heads, reserved for the priest for doing the *puja*.' Without asking he poured another ladleful of heads on to our plates.

There was no alternative, so shutting my eyes and fixing my mind on a tasty piece of chicken breast, I forced myself to pick up one of the heads and move it up to my mouth. 'Only the *heads*, all the *heads* . . .' droned Naina in the background. I took a bite. My mouth closed on a piece of rubbery fried comb, and the beak wedged itself between my teeth. . . .

'Grandmother'

10

Water from the
twelve-month-flower

May was here and suddenly it was hot. Forgetting the chill shivers of winter, we delighted in our house-with-no-doors that enticed the breeze to blow through the gaps and cool us off. Titeng caught the light winds that drifted up the Kathe Khola gorge and stayed several degrees cooler than Baglung where the heavy air was spiced with all-pervading toilet odours, and swarms of mosquitoes waited for dusk to whine their high-pitched warning.

The bazaar folk could not understand why we chose to live in Titeng. 'Why don't you come and live in our house?' the shop-keepers would say. 'We have fine rooms for rent. You would be near the shops, and here we have water taps in the street. Why hide yourselves up there? Those Magars are ignorant and simple. No doubt they feed you millet instead of rice – you'll get sick! Now, if you live in our house you can improve it just how you like – lay down a cement floor, install a paraffin oven, or even a refrigerator! You'd be much happier here.'

I would shake my head and diplomatically say that Titeng was more convenient for Duane's work – an unconvincing reply – but the truth was we didn't like the bazaar folk. They were too painful a reminder of the society we had left behind where time seemed spent in chasing money, and greed, not need, dictated how to live. Endless jealous feuds festered in the muggy air of Baglung's narrow streets, splitting the community into hostile factions. Titeng, with its air of gentle passivity, its easy-going inhabitants, its springs and streams and terraced fields, was a world apart from the noise and social intrigues of the bazaar. And it was a world we loved.

We had been in our house-with-no-doors for six months and we could run up and down the ladder without hands and negotiate the toilet path in the dark without stumbling. Our knee joints and leg muscles had strengthened and even squatting presented little difficulty. I had adjusted to wearing a *lungi* – the length of material that wrapped around to form a skirt – and neither of us wore anything except rubber flip-flops on our feet. When we entered a house we automatically removed these and were careful never to touch or point at anyone with our feet, for that was to put ourselves above them. We had learnt to say *namaste* properly, not in the casual manner of a 'Hi' or 'Hello' as we had done at first, but slowly and reverently, pressing our palms together and bowing our heads. *Namaste, I greet the god in you*, was the meaning of the gesture. We had also learnt not to rush things, but to wait until the moment was right to state our case or request some help. In return, the villagers no longer dropped what they were doing when we appeared, but treated us as one of them, sometimes acknowledging our presence with a brief nod or a *namaste*, and sometimes launching into a longer conversation if they had the time.

But the skill of drinking from a *karuwa* still eluded me. The *karuwa* was an elegantly shaped bronze vessel with a spout, commonly offered to travellers who requested a drink of water. The Magars simply tipped their heads back as if they had boneless necks, stuck out their lower jaws and poured the water straight down their throats in a continuous stream, swallowing without closing their mouths or stopping the flow of water. Their lips never touched the vessel which thus remained unpolluted and could be passed from traveller to traveller. But when I tried to copy them, the water invariably found its way to my lungs and I would end up ignominiously spluttering and choking. To save this embarrassment the Titeng villagers usually offered me water in a bronze beaker.

As we became more proficient in the language and their village accent we spent more time just talking to them. It was not always easy to find new topics for conversation with our visitors; theirs were often banal – the state of their crops, their health, their children – and they would question us about facts but rarely about feelings. It was fascinating to see how their language reflected their culture. Un-pleasant things were softened by putting into the passive tense: *the bottle was dropped*, rather than *I dropped the bottle*; a reflection perhaps of their fatalistic attitude to life. There were few words to express feelings. Where we could say nice, good, lovely, wonderful, pretty, beautiful, or excellent, they could only say 'good'. But for rice there were six different words: *dhan* for the whole grain or seed and when the crop was still in the field; *chamal* for the dehusked grain; *bhaat* for cooked rice; *buja* for puffed rice; *chiura* for parboiled beaten rice; and *kanika* for the rice grains broken in husking, as well as individual names for each strain of rice.

As the romance of living in the village wore off, life became more of a chore. Nothing was straightforward, and preparing even a simple meal was time-consuming. The first step was to make sure the water was carried and the stoves filled with paraffin. If the basis of the meal was rice, it had to be sorted – stones, twigs, dirt and broken grains removed – and washed two or three times in full pans of water to remove the dust and starch flour that collected round the grains. The same steps had to be followed for the lentils, and while they were both cooking the salt and spices had to be ground by hand on a stone tablet, the vegetables washed and chopped (we rarely peeled) and the mustard oil we used for cooking strained through a clean cloth, otherwise impurities caused it to splutter and smoke too much. If we were having *roti* (flatbreads) instead of rice, then the wheat had to be ground. Once a month I took a supply to the mill in the bazaar, but however carefully I stored it, weevils appeared and these had to be removed by sieving. Then I would add water and knead the dough to a spongy consistency. It was at this point, when my hands were covered with floury dough and the vegetables about to burn, that the lamp would run out of paraffin leaving me in chaotic darkness.

We had discovered that Bhakhu was always ready to earn an extra rupee or two when we needed help. If Duane or I had forgotten to carry water, Bhakhu was always willing, and sometimes I paid him to wash our clothes as well. Bhakhu was a quick though not very thorough washerman. On Saturdays he would persuade Laute to shepherd the goats and would trot off to the spring with our dirty clothes in a *doko*. An hour later he would return with the clothes full of scrubbed holes and an unplanned 'tie-dye' of colours. He would hang these rags on the guava tree or spread them on a mat in the courtyard where they promptly became dirty again.

'Watch out they don't blow into the pig pen. The pigs will eat them!' Grandmother would cackle.

'Don't leave them in the dust!' I would add.

With the Chaitra festival over, field work began in earnest. Wife Two, Devi's Mother and Saili cut the wheat laboriously stalk by stalk with small curved sickles which they carried in decoratively carved wooden holders tied to their waists. The heads of grain were carried to the courtyard where Wife One pounded them with a wooden stick to separate the grains from the stalk and chaff. The courtyard was stifling in the noon day sun and her only shield was a shawl carelessly wrapped

Above: Wife Two spreads a fresh layer of mud and dung over the courtyard
prior to threshing the grain
Below: Threshing the grain in the courtyard. Taken from our upper room

Above: Rice planting Naina Singh's fields
Below: Looking towards Annapurna – taken from above Titeng

over her head. Thud, thud, thud, went her stick and the dust and chaff lifted into the air and settled in a grimy layer on her face, damp with sweat. In every courtyard the scene was repeated. Even Keshu Ram's daughter-in-law who was eight months pregnant worked hard with the rest, her only concession being to sit instead of stand. As she swung her stick down, her massive belly escaped the confines of her *patuka* and quivered in rhythm to her strokes; her face, impassive, chiselled in stone, registered neither discomfort nor boredom. We nicknamed her Stone-Face.

After threshing, the grain had to be winnowed. It was scooped into circular bamboo trays, tossed into the air and the dust and chaff allowed to blow away. Then the clean grain was spread to dry in the sun and finally stored in the attic. And when every grain of wheat had been cut, threshed, winnowed and dried, they began to plant the maize.

Now at last the men took a turn. Naina Singh and Gesi Ram yoked their large black bull and small brown bull together and guided the plough along the narrow terraces below our house. The plough-head was of wood, carefully formed by Naina Singh from a tree fork with axe and chisel. When he had shaped it, he smoothed down the rough edges and carried it to the Village of the Blacksmiths where they added an iron tip. It was primitive in design, merely scarring a shallow furrow through the sun-baked shell of the field. But this conserved the scant moisture that was in the ground. Behind the plough came Bhakhu with a shoulder bag of maize kernels which he flicked one by one into the furrow, and behind Bhakhu came Wife Two with a long-handled mallet. As the plough returned in the opposite direction it heaved clods of compacted earth on to the previous furrow, covering the maize kernels, and Wife Two lifted her mallet and beat the clods into dusty fragments. Saili and Devi's Mother ferried *doko*-loads of manure from the buffalo shed and spread it on the fields waiting to be ploughed, while Maila worked the terraces with a short-handled hoe, digging the small corners the plough couldn't reach.

I took a turn with the shoulder bag of maize seed. It seemed fairly straightforward. I thrust my hand into the bag, grabbed a fistful of maize and started to sow. But it was not so easy as it looked – the maize stuck in my hand, or fell in heaps on the same spot, and soon I was lagging behind the plough. Bhakhu gave me a lesson and with practice I mastered the technique, flicking out the maize kernel on the forward swing of my arm, and on the backward swing allowing another maize

kernel to roll forward ready to be flicked by the thumb on the next
upswing. The rhythm of the arm-swinging was important for this
allowed the maize to be planted at equal intervals. Every task had its
rhythm in Nepal making it seem less of a chore and more a sacred
ritual.

Bhakhu meanwhile was taking his turn at ploughing under the
watchful eyes of Gesi Ram and Naina Singh. 'Hutt! Hutt! Aaaah
wheee! Ho! Ho!' he shouted, goading the oxen into a brisk gallop.

'Whoa!' yelled Naina. 'They're going to jump into the field below
and the plough will break. You dolt, what did I tell you . . . .'

All the villagers worked long hours, rising at dawn and continuing
till dusk with only a break for their mid-morning meal. We were
impressed by the degree of cooperation they showed. The married
daughters, after planting their husband's terraces, returned to their
parents' home to assist with the planting there. Old Mati Lal, who
didn't own a plough team and only had a few terraces, helped to
plough Keshu Ram's terraces, and in return borrowed his oxen for a
day to plough his own. Lal Bahadur, who had many fields to work
but only his wife to help him, joined hands with Dal Bahadur and
worked their fields together. There seemed to be no tight accounting
for the time spent on another's fields, merely a tacit agreement that at
some point the help would be reciprocated.

On a Saturday soon after the maize had been planted, we
wandered along the crooked paths of the village to the 'terrace row'
and stopped outside Prithvi Lal's house where a group of men were
chatting. They shuffled along the verandah to make room and we sat
down, somewhat diffidently on my part, being the only woman
present. A land survey was currently taking place and they were
discussing whether they would have to pay more taxes once their
fields had been surveyed and registered. As we talked Prithvi Lal's
wife returned from the spring, her head and shoulders hunched
forward to balance the weight of the water pot on her back. She
greeted us without raising her head and plodded past into the dark
interior of the house.

Soft-spoken, shy Prithvi Lal suddenly turned to Duane: 'Can't you
help us put in a drinking water supply like they have in Baglung?
Look at my wife – she has to do all the carrying herself, and this
season there's not much water in the spring.'

'For my family,' interrupted Sher Bahadur, whose wives and
children rivalled Naina Singh's in number, 'we have to make at least
six trips a day to the spring. Nothing is easy for us here.'

'We know how to do the work,' continued Prithvi Lal. 'I was a foreman on the Baglung water project – the one that comes down from the Empty River at the top of this valley. It's brought down by pipe, across the river, and up the other side to a tank. Then it's distributed by smaller pipes all over the bazaar. Each street has its own standpipe where the people can get water.'

'You could do the same here,' said Duane. 'In a smaller way.'

'We'd like to,' said Sher Bahadur. 'We could do the work ourselves, but the pipe costs money and we need cement for building the tank.'

'It depends whether you have a big enough source of water *above* the village,' said Duane. 'Otherwise you'd need a pump and that would be expensive.'

'There's the spring above the village.'

'Does it flow all year or does it dry up some months?'

'It flows all year.'

The land survey men and taxes were forgotten in their enthusiasm for the new idea, and suddenly we found ourselves processing in single file, down the zig-zag path, past Dal Bahadur's house, past the empty patch of ground where a house had been pulled down, and over the stone ledges set in the wall to the courtyard of the headman's house.

The headman's house, like its owner, was humble and rather run-down. Its mud faces were peeling, its balding thatch had developed sooty dandruff, and its verandah was crumbling into dust. The headman greeted us with stooping back and slightly bent knees whose skin hung in sagging wrinkles.

'For seventeen years I've been headman,' he told us. 'They keep on electing me.' He wheezed a laugh. 'Nobody else wants the job – it's too much work and they don't pay me for it!'

The headman had a piercing voice and was a very vocal participant in any discussion. He was headman of Titeng and the neighbouring villages of Aatmuri and Kumaldara. Together these three villages formed a *ward*, and nine *wards* a *panchayat*. The *panchayats* were grouped into districts, and the districts into zones of which there were thirteen in Nepal. The system of government was known as the partyless *panchayat* system, and at its head was King Birendra, descendant of a dynasty of kings dating from the seventeenth century when King Prithvi Narayan Shah from Gorkha first united Nepal into one kingdom. So the headman was the elected representative for the *ward* – the lowest level of the *panchayat* system. He had never been to school and could neither read nor write, but carried out his job conscientiously. His main task was acting as a go-between in village quarrels.

'If a man runs off with another's wife, the husband comes to me and I make sure the man pays back the bride price,' he told us. 'If somebody is accused of stealing I have to settle the dispute. I must see that everything's kept in good condition. You know the bridge across the river on the way to Baglung? That's my responsibility. I make sure it's kept in good repair, and maintain the paths if landslides destroy them. I don't do it all myself – everyone in the *ward* shares the work. Then there's this so-called 'development' work. Eight years ago we all gave our labour and what money we could spare to build the primary school for our *ward*.'

'We came to see you about improving the drinking water,' said Duane. 'We're willing to help buy the pipe and cement if you can organise the labour.'

'We've wanted to do that for some time,' replied the headman. 'The money's been the problem though.'

Briefly Duane outlined the scheme. There were many reasons why it made sense. To the villagers the economic aspect was the most important: the time they spent carrying water could be better spent tending their fields. The Magars believed it was inauspicious to live below their fields, so their villages were located on the ridge-tops, some distance from the nearest rivers. Most villages therefore took their water from a muddy seepage hole perhaps two feet across which had to supply the whole village with drinking water for themselves and their animals as well as water for cooking and washing. Since rain fell in only five months of the year, many of these springs and seepage holes dried up and villagers were forced to travel longer distances to get their water. On top of that the open seepage holes were breeding grounds for mosquitoes and other organisms that carried diseases such as typhoid, malaria, cholera and dysentery. But health was of little concern to them. They didn't realise that the scabies and infected sores on their children would disappear if they had more water or that the many intestinal diseases from which they suffered, and even died, were carried by contaminated water.

The villagers decided to walk to the upper spring to investigate the scheme's feasibility. We took the path that led up and around from Titeng, skirting the wooded cliff with its dizzy views down to the bubbling Kathe Khola. Half a mile outside the village we left the path and scrambled over a dry stone wall into the terraced fields. The path followed the contour on a narrow embankment between the terraces.

Most of the wheat had been cut, but scattered stalks remained tall and straight like soldiers on guard. Half a mile further on we reached the spring.

Like its companion below the village the upper spring was overshadowed by a bush with flaming red flowers. Below, spears of pepper-green mint, beds of cress, and cushions of moist spongy moss marked the course of its waters as they seeped down the hillside. Prithvi Lal picked a flower from the bush and gave it to me. 'Take a twelve-month-flower,' he said. 'It blooms the whole year through.'

Duane cleared away the overgrown foliage and looked at where the waters seeped from the underlying rock.

'There's not much water,' said Prithvi Lal.

'There's enough,' said Duane. 'But we'll need to build a small tank – that will store the water during the night and keep it clean and free from disease. Then we'll lay a pipe from the tank down to the village and install a couple of tap stands.' They surveyed the course the pipe would take and together we returned to the village. The headman promised to organise the villagers to share in the work.

Duane designed a simple reservoir tank and gravity pipeline, and ordered cement and pipe from Kathmandu. Friends from Libby, Montana who had previously worked in Nepal kindly donated the money towards these things. For our part we stood to gain as much as the villagers. For over four months now we had been carrying our water from the lower spring and we had first-hand knowledge of how much time and effort it took. We would appreciate a closer supply for the remaining months.

Meanwhile amongst the villagers much discussion took place on where the two tap stands should be placed. Finally Prithvi Lal and the headman announced that they wished to place one of the taps under the *pipal* tree at the edge of the village by the main footpath so that travellers could use it too. 'It's a hot climb in the summer months, and travellers often stop to rest on the *chautara* under the shade of the *pipal* tree. It will be good if they can get a drink of cold fresh water,' they said. The other tap initially, in deference to us, they wanted to place outside our house, but we persuaded them to locate it beyond Mati Lal's house on the terrace above. The waste water from both taps could then drain into nearby gullies.

Without further delay the villagers, being anxious to lay the pipe through the fields before the rice-planting season, began to dig the trench where the pipe would be buried. Everyone was to benefit, especially the women, and everyone shared in the work, both rich and poor, including the headman. Saturdays were set aside for the work, and in no time the site for the tank was cleared and the walls began to grow. The men undertook the skilled masonry work while the team of women supplied them with boulders and gravel, carried on their backs from the river bed 500 feet below. One of the biggest tasks was transporting the pipe and cement over the 30 rugged miles from the roadhead at Naudara. The cement came in 50 kg sacks and the black plastic pipe was divided into man-size coils twisted round a bamboo framework. Both had to be carried by the traditional *namlo* rope over the forehead. Thankfully the headman organised the delegation of jobs and ensured that each family contributed in a fair way according to their means.

Prithvi Lal directed the scheme in his unassuming competent way, working from the design Duane had prepared though he had never seen a technical drawing before. He was a modest man with remarkable skills who deserved his reputation as the foremost builder in Baglung District. His family were poor with little land and thus depended almost entirely on his earnings as a builder.

'I learnt through experience,' he said as he gently tapped another stone into place on the masonry for the tank. 'I asked a lot of questions and I remembered the answers. I wish I'd been to school but I never had the chance. My uncle Sher Bahadur taught me and my brother to read and write. Every evening we'd crouch over a small oil lamp scratching our letters and numbers with bamboo pens on banana leaves. It was a struggle at the time, but worth it.'

We left for a holiday while the work was still in progress. When we returned after three weeks trekking in the Annapurna Sanctuary amongst some of the most beautiful mountain scenery in the world, I was still excited to turn the corner in the bazaar and see Titeng, a verdant swathe, clinging tenaciously to the mountainside. Yes, it was all real. There was Maila carrying manure to the fields, and Bhakhu and Laute playing near the river with the goats. Our garden had grown and the maize was like a forest, but otherwise it was unchanged.

Grandmother poked her head round the corner of the cowshed and broke into a wide smile. 'You naughty children! You've been away twenty-two days. Have you killed your love for us?'

'No,' we reassured her, amused to think she had counted each day. We sat down and had to report on where we had been, what had happened, and how much we had had to pay for our rice.

'Climbing in the *Himal*? Whatever made you do that! You were both getting nice and fat here, and then you go off wandering and come back thin again,' complained Grandmother.

'You've been everywhere,' said Wife One. 'Here we live and die in the same place.'

'What's happened here whilst we've been away?' we asked, expecting the usual answer of 'nothing, just water and fodder, that's our life'.

'Go and get some water,' interrupted Wife Two with a sly smile on her face. 'No, not that way! Go to the *chautara* by the main path!'

We rushed to the *pipal* tree, and there was the new tap stand gushing water into the women's pots. The tap was on full and the water spurted out with such force that the spray drenched the women's skirts. A stone ledge had been made on either side for loading and unloading the water pots from the *dokos*, and underneath the tap was a rectangular scrubbing area of cement where the women could wash their clothes. A group of travellers had stopped beneath the *pipal* tree and were passing round a bronze *karuwa* of water, holding it above their heads so that its spout directed a stream of water into their mouths.

We stepped forward to try out the new tap and wash the journey's dirt from our faces and feet. Then we filled up our own copper pot. The water splashed and gurgled into it twice as fast as the old spring. With a smile of satisfaction we carried it back to our house.

The sky is weeping

The monsoon was approaching. We listened to reports each day on the All India radio station: 'The front has reached Calcutta . . . in two days it will hit eastern Nepal . . . expected to arrive in Kathmandu on June 20th . . . .'

We made our preparations for its onslaught. I bought a large black 'Made in India' umbrella in the bazaar and Naina Singh spent a morning repairing our roof. The thatch had blown away in several places and his concern was lest the rain should dribble on to his walls, washing away the binding mud plaster. It was not uncommon for quite substantial buildings to collapse during the monsoon because of their soluble mud mortar. Naina Singh patched the gaps with a stiff dried grass, wrapping the strands across the peak of the roof and weaving the ends under the old thatch.

The pre-monsoon storms grew in intensity. The walk to the bazaar became unbearably hot and sticky and Duane and I took frequent showers at the new tap stand or went for a swim in the refreshingly cool, blue-green pools of the Kathe Khola. Just upstream from the buffalo sheds and *swami* trees, the waters flowed swiftly round a bend, washing against the rocky walls of the cliff. It was fun to jump in upstream and float down, carried by the surging rippling current, past the dark wall of the cliff where the waters were deepest and then steer ourselves on to a gravel bank before the waters cascaded in a white froth down the cataracts. Enclosed between the walls of the canyon we felt secluded and alone, but this was an illusion.

'Sa-la-la-la! I saw you floating down the river,' Wife Two would say on our return. 'I was on the cliff cutting grass for the buffalo. Aren't you afraid the waters will carry you away?' It seemed that we could never be truly alone and this was hard to cope with at times. But the advantages of our village life more than compensated for its problems, and we never regretted our choice.

Late one afternoon the monsoon began. To the east, above Karkineta ridge and the Modi Khola river, dark purplish-blue thunderclouds piled up, tower upon tower. The wind increased and white clouds chased each other across the sky. The last hot breaths of stale air were swirled away and in their place, borne on the wind, was the refreshing fragrance of damp earth. I remember thinking how strange it was that we could smell the rain long before any fell. The skies darkened as the thunderclouds expanded and moved westwards obliterating the sun and swallowing up the last patches of blue. There was a flash of lightning followed by a roar of thunder that seemed to shake the rocky foundations of Titeng. The wind strengthened and whipped round the houses lifting the thatch on the overhanging roofs and bending the supple bamboos until they were almost horizontal, then slackening so that they arched back up to the sky creaking and rattling. In the fields the maize leaned backwards with the wind, its leaves streaming behind like pennants.

The lightning and thunder increased until each successive explosion merged into the one before. Heavy drops of rain started to splatter the dust of the courtyard with a plopping sound. Gaining strength and speed they hammered on to our roof, seeking a way through the shield, but the straws channelled the rivulets downwards and outwards to the eaves where they fell in a continuous sheet of water on to the courtyard. Naina Singh had made a good job of the roof and not a drop came through. We lay down warm and snug on our pads for the night, listening to the howl of the storm outside.

When we woke in the morning we knew it was the monsoon. The wind had dropped and the rain cascaded relentlessly from the skies in undeviating vertical lines. Above Galkot and the upper reaches of the Kathe Khola valley fluid clouds poured over the pass in swirls and eddies, like waves breaking on a beach. Northwards, across the Baglung plateau and the interlocking ridges of the Kali Gandaki gorge, soft currents of white mist flowed and ebbed against the dark banks of the mountains.

It rained continuously for three days and three nights. On the fourth day I ventured out feeling like Noah after the flood. It was still raining lightly but there were patches of blue sky as I slithered and skidded my way to the bazaar. It was useless to wear my rubber flip-flops for they gave no hold on the slippery chute of the path. I discarded them and went barefoot, delighting in the sensation of mud between the toes. Moisture glistened and dripped from every leaf, blade and stem. The terraced fields, now under six inches of water, had become terraced

lakes, rising in steep tiers from both sides of the river and reflecting the
changing sky. As the clouds and mist cleared away the gaps of sky
burned an intense volatile blue, and waves of steamy heat issued from
the watery terraces.

Down below, the Kathe Khola had been transformed into a raging
muddy torrent, swollen to a hundred times its dry season flow. There
was no question of wading, for the stepping stones were lost beneath
fresh deposits of gravel or swept away downstream. I worked my way
down to the toy-like suspension bridge. Half the path lay submerged
beneath a newly-created channel and in one place the river had eroded
the supporting bank and the three lowest terraces had collapsed, so I
was forced to wade knee-deep into the water. Smiling ploughmen
passed by, spattered from head to foot with freckles of mud, and in the
flooded terraces teams of women were already at work transplanting
the rice seedlings. As I crossed the bridge the swallows glided and
plummeted above my head.

The bazaar was a ferment of mud, smells and filth. The large
flagstones were so slippery that several times my feet shot from under
me and I sat down in the mire to the amusement of any onlookers. The
Nepalis had an uncanny sense of balance and never seemed to falter.
Plump Newari ladies tripped their way through the squalor in
moulded plastic heels, lifting the hems of their *saris* just enough to
clear the mud without exposing their legs. The village folk, less
concerned with fashion, hitched their skirts up to their knees and
bundled the extra length inside their *patukas*.

There was an air of excitement around. Shouts of laughter rang out
in the clear air as people joked and sympathised with each other in their
muddy predicament. In the fields the women sang as they planted the
rice seedlings.

Despite the promise of fertility the bazaar was devoid of fresh food.
I passed by dusty boxes of shrivelled potatoes and bags of waxy red-
hot chillies nicknamed 'death', but the only hint of green in the shops
were garlic tops. We were down to low levels of cuisine in the village
and for several evenings we had eaten only a porridge of coarsely
ground wheat accompanied by a *tun* of finely ground wheat spiced
with a single chilli. I bought the inevitable garlic and a tin of tuna fish
that I found by chance in the back-shelf gloom of a small store, tucked
between the paraffin and soap. On the way home I was caught in
another cloud-burst. The rain spilled down with a force only possible
in the monsoon and in a matter of seconds my fine new umbrella
yielded to its onslaught and I was drenched. Barely able to keep my

eyes open against the cascade that showered down my face, I abandoned myself to the rain.

Halfway up the hill to the village I met the headman, holding a large banana leaf over his head. He gave me a whimsical smile of empathy and raised his eyes and hands upwards. 'The sky is weeping!' he said. It was indeed, but they were tears of joy, not sorrow.

Reaching the village I found Wife One wandering through her kitchen garden on the terrace just below their house. It contained a few chilli bushes and a couple of guava trees whose fruits were still hard and green. The cucumber and pumpkin vines, traditional vegetables of the monsoon season, were just beginning to climb the trees and were not ready yet.

'What can I cook for *tun*?' she asked me. 'The soya beans are finished.'

I handed her some lettuces and carrots from our garden which were starting to go to seed with the excess moisture of the monsoon.

'What is this? Spinach?' she inquired, turning them over in her hands.

'No. We call it lettuce. We eat it raw. And these are carrots.'

'What caste of vegetable are they?'

'They're like an orange radish.'

'Are they hot like radishes?'

'Try one and see.' I borrowed her sickle and cut the carrots up. Grandmother took a cautious bite and wrinkled her face into a smile. 'They're sweet and good, not bitter at all!' she said, and passed it to Gophle for a taste.

The lettuce was boiled that night for *tun*. When I offered them the remainder of our peas and beans they pulled up the whole plants and chopped them, leaves, stems and pods, into the cauldron for *tun*. They made a change from the nettle heads and fern shoots.

The men spent the rainy days when they weren't ploughing, curled on their verandahs with blankets, but when it rained extra hard they dropped what they were doing, grabbed their fishing nets, and raced down to the river. The flash floods swept the fish from their hideouts beneath the rocks. Flood fishing was fruitful but dangerous; few of the villagers were strong swimmers and further floods could sweep down the gorge at any time.

These floods occurred with little or no warning; sometimes it would not even be raining in Titeng, but the water came from higher up the valley where a landslide might have temporarily dammed the river until the pressure of the waters forced a way through. The noise

first alerted us – a rushing, roaring sound that filled the air – and
looking down from the village we would see the river visibly rising,
swallowing up the grass verges on either bank, engulfing the islands of
boulders in midstream, and tossing spray across the narrow suspension bridge. During one of these floods, Mati Lal's buffalo was
marooned on an island in the middle. The flood waters rose until there
was only a small patch of dry ground beneath its feet. Its mournful
bellows filled the air as it charged this way and that, seeking an escape.
Luckily the waters subsided and an anxious Mati Lal was able to coax
the buffalo to safety.

Fishing was a favourite pastime in which the whole village
participated, even the old grandmothers. When the river was not in
flood the usual method was to dam one of the channels that flowed
round the island. The men would build a temporary dam of boulders
and teams of boys carried baskets of mud to seal it. When this was
completed the waters were channelled down one side of the island and
the women and children spread along the dried-up channel and fished
in the remaining pools, turning over boulders to flush out the fish
beneath. Most could easily be caught by hand though home-made
nets of hemp were also used. The women stuffed the fish they caught
into their *patukas* – none was more than six inches in length, and few
more than three. They seemed a small return for the investment of
time and energy but the villagers were well pleased; they loved fish,
and half the enjoyment was in catching them. Often the children
couldn't wait until they got home, but built a fire right there on the
river bank to cook them.

With the monsoon, supplies for the hydro-electric project were held
up and when Duane decided to go to Kathmandu to sort things out I
walked partway with him. Travel in the monsoon was an uncertain
and even risky business. Landslides were frequent both on the motor
roads and on the footpaths, and fording rivers was no longer possible
so long detours had to be made to use the existing bridges. Because of
this we decided to take an alternative route that led directly to
Pokhara, a larger town and roadhead further north. Walking was
quite different in the monsoon for every path doubled as an irrigation
channel. If they were not already natural gullies for the rain, the
Nepalis made them so by digging trenches and diversionary earth
banks. Harmless rat-snakes slithered out of our way and once we
caught sight of a small but lethal green snake. Fishermen were much in
evidence. Some had gone a step further than the Magars of Titeng and
obtained sticks of stolen gelignite which they lit and threw into the

water. As the fish rose to the surface downstream of the explosion, they dived in and caught them with their bare hands. An alternative method was to carry a large sledge-hammer. This would be rammed on to the boulders and a net spread to catch any fish that might rise to the surface, momentarily stunned by the shock.

Beyond the Modi Khola we diverged from the usual track to Naudara. The route to Pokhara was part of the old walking path to Kathmandu used for centuries before the motor road was built. Now it had fallen into decay. We passed through once-prosperous villages with rows of shops and tea-houses boarded up. Few people travelled this way for it was longer and involved climbing the 9,000-foot pass of Pakkha Pani. But we liked the emptiness. As we climbed higher we left behind all human habitation and the jungle closed in around us, peaceful and still, yet very much alive with the hums, ticks, trills, and shrieks of insects and birds.

Water dripped steadily from the trees and so did the leeches, clamping on to our feet or any unprotected area of warm blood-filled skin. Once their suckers were into our flesh they were hard to remove until they had sucked their fill and were bloated five times their regular size. A lighted match worked best (if they were not too damp to strike) or failing that, a prolonged squeeze removed all but the most persistent. Wearing flip-flops we could immediately spot a thirsty leech and remove it before too much damage was done. Shoes and socks were fatal because you couldn't see inside and the leeches could squeeze themselves through the minutest of cracks. At the end of the day I discovered one had even crawled into my armpit and made a thorough mess. Thankfully they were quite painless but left an itchy sore after removal.

But our sufferings were amply rewarded when, near the top of the pass, where the rainy mist had dissolved and patches of sunlight bathed the forest floor, a pair of Himalayan pandas burst from the undergrowth and bounded up a tree. In the sudden sunshine their fur burned a fiery russet-red. They were about four feet long with long flamboyant tails ringed with bands of black and red. Their small pointed faces, smudged with white and capped by two rounded ears, turned back briefly to see who had disturbed the peace of the forest pass. But before we were fully aware of what we had seen they were lost to sight in the foliage. Hardly able to believe our good fortune, for Himalayan pandas are quite rare, Duane checked our identification in Kathmandu to make sure we were correct.

In Pokhara I said goodbye to Duane and returned alone on the more frequented route, exciting many comments from people I passed.

'You're a woman? You don't mind walking on your own? Our women can't walk like that – they're too weak. Strong in the legs, but weak in the mind. They can't walk alone.'

In Titeng the villagers were also concerned. 'Where's your old man?' they asked.

'Gone to Kathmandu.'

'You walked back alone? And the *bihaauni-siyaauni* didn't get you?'

'The what?'

'*Bihaauni-siyaauni*. You know – stones turn over, branches fall in front of you, you trip over, you hear noises. You never see them but you know they're there.'

'No, I saw nothing like that.'

'Ah, she doesn't understand the word,' said the headman's wife, who spoke in a particularly slow unhurried Magar accent, adding a vowel sound to the end of every word and pronouncing each syllable evenly. 'That's why she isn't afraid. If she knew what it meant she'd be frightened to walk alone.'

Not quite sure of this logic, but unable to argue with it, I left the matter alone and the *bihaauni-siyaauni* continued to let me tread the mountain paths in solitary peace.

But while Duane was away the villagers were convinced I must be lonely and visited me ever more frequently. Each morning Wife One brought a plate of freshly popped wheat or maize and in the evenings Devi's Mother and other friends kept me company. It was hard to keep a moment to myself. 'Aren't you lonely without him?' they asked, jerking their heads in the direction of Kathmandu. I tried to explain that I was not lonely (how could I be with Naina Singh's large family at arm's reach?) but I *did* miss Duane. I was touched by the depth of their concern and perception. Duane had been away for three weeks by now and I was really missing him. So I went down to the *swami* trees by the river hoping to capture a moment's peace and reflection for myself. On my return Grandmother stopped me, 'What have you been doing down by the river?'

'Just sitting and thinking.'

'Thinking about what?'

'Nothing in particular.'

'You've been thinking about your Old One, haven't you?' she said, staring deep into my eyes. 'I can tell. I could see your mind weeping as you walked up the hill.'

12

Rice-planting

With the arrival of the monsoon, the rice-planting season began.

Naina Singh came up to our room one morning. Following Nepali custom he did not refer immediately to the subject on his mind.

'The roof isn't leaking any more?' he asked, squatting by the window and pulling out his pipe.

'No, not at all. You fixed it very well. Thank you.'

'Of course. I know how to fix roofs. I did a good job. Other people wouldn't have done such a good job. But I knew you must have only the best.'

He tidied away some loose ends of thatch and asked when Duane would be coming back.

'Another week maybe. The supplies aren't getting through in this rainy weather and he has to sort it out.'

'Next week we'll plant the rice fields by the upper spring. We'd like you to come and help. It's a special time of year for us. Please say you'll come,' he implored, pressing his palms together in the traditional manner of supplication. He needn't have worried. I was flattered to be invited in this way by Naina Singh himself, and promised to be there. I was rewarded by a rare smile of pleasure. Grandmother too was delighted. 'So you're going to plant rice?' she called out. 'It's fun! All the women work in teams, singing as they plant, and we make special foods to eat in the fields because we work all day. Then when it's finished we kill a pig and have a big feast.'

The planting of rice was an event of religious significance, surrounded by more rituals and traditions than any other event of the agricultural year. It was a sacred occasion, for rice represented life and wealth. To eat was to eat rice, and Nepalis who had just consumed a large meal of flatbreads and lentils would say they had *not* eaten because they had not eaten rice. A reliable index of wealth was the amount of rice land a person owned, and the dream of many hill people was to save sufficient money to buy some rice land on the plains of the *terai* where the fields were flat, the soil rich, and water plentiful.

Despite the high rainfall, rice required additional irrigation from a spring or river. Where no such constant source of water existed the fields were designated dry fields and used for growing maize or millet. The irrigation system for the wet fields was unsophisticated yet quite complex. Water was diverted from springs or streams with small hand-made dams of sticks and mud. Long sinuous ditches following the contours of the mountainside led the water down to the fields, sometimes several miles away. These ditches often had to be carved out of the solid rock by hand, and there was one irrigation channel near Baglung that passed straight through a rocky spur in a tunnel that was barely large enough to have allowed the man who excavated it to squirm along on his stomach.

Each field was carefully graded to make sure it was horizontal, and secured by a low mud embankment about six inches high with a small opening in one corner. When water was released from the irrigation ditch it flooded the top terrace, overflowed through the opening to the next and continued down in this way, each successive field being slightly lower than its neighbour. Often many groups of terraces would be irrigated from the same channel and the water was divided by means of a proportional weir. This was a log with notches which when laid across the ditch caused the water to back up and overflow through the notches. Each notch divided and channelled the water into separate sub-canals, which might be further subdivided by another notched weir. The size of the notch determined the volume of water – a wide notch was used for a large area of terraces and a narrow notch for a smaller area.

When there wasn't enough water for all the channels of the system to work at the same time, the water was shared on a rota basis. A common system was the 18-hour rota where the fields were divided into three groups. The first group received water from 6 am to 12 noon, the second from noon to 6 pm and the third from 6 pm to 12 midnight, when the first group would start their shift again. Each group was responsible for keeping track of the time and 'turning on' the water when it was their shift. In the days before watches and clocks, and still today in some parts of Nepal, time was kept by means of a water-clock. This was a clay pot with a small hole in the bottom which allowed the water to drip through at a steady rate and thus enabled them to keep track of time. The 18-hour rota was more favoured than a 24-hour rota because it meant the night shifts alternated between the groups. Nobody enjoyed the midnight trek to the rice fields, especially if they were far away and the paths clogged with evil spirits. In places where water was very short, a member of the family would be assigned fulltime to watch the rice fields and make sure that nobody stole down under cover of darkness and rediverted the water to *their* fields.

On the appointed day Naina Singh called and invited me to eat the morning meal with them first. Most of the family were already out in the fields and had been since dawn. I ate the wheat porridge and feeling rather solid and weighed down climbed the hill to the rice fields.

Like a still-life painting come to life, yesterday's empty arena of terraced fields was filled with the joyful drama of rice planting. Everyone was there: Keshu Ram in his army-issue khaki shirt, threadbare but still proud, Lal Bahadur with his broad bare back leading a team of oxen, Sher Bahadur with all thirteen of his offspring, and of course the headman, who tottered towards me on legs whose wrinkled folds of skin were caked with mud.

'So you've come to learn how to plant rice?' he wheezed, adjusting the *topi* that never left his head. 'That's good. This is the happiest time of year for us.'

Bhakhu, Maila and Naina Singh were already at work with their hoes, digging blocks of mud and earth from the fields to form the embankments. Gesi Ram, covered from head to toe in mud, was balancing on the rear foot of the plough as the family's two oxen careered across a narrow terrace spraying arcs of mud behind them. Wife Two, Saili, Devi's Mother and Jethi (the married daughter) were pulling up handfuls of rice seedlings from the nursery beds – a couple of terraces that had been specially prepared and irrigated two months ago.

The irrigation system had been 'turned on' and the water was flooding over the abandoned stalks of the previous maize crop and flowing in a hundred small waterfalls from terrace to terrace. Once a field was thoroughly soaked the plough was taken over it two or three times, churning the soil and water to a thick creamy mud. As the plough teams finished the field, the women gathered up the bundles of rice seedlings, and threw them down with a splash into the mud of the finished field.

'Come on, Sister! What are you waiting for? Here's your bundle!'

I picked up the bunch of rice seedlings roughly knotted together by their own leaves. Gently untying them, I eased their tangled roots apart and ran my finger down their smooth translucent gold-green leaves.

They were bruised and slightly torn at the point where they had been tied. I was holding in their terms a handful of gold dust, yet the women around me treated them so casually. They were already at work, without a second's glance, thrusting the gold deep into the mud so that only their tips were exposed. I stepped into place beside Devi's Mother and Jethi.

We worked calf-deep in liquid mud, not the clean fresh water I had always imagined as a child studying the illustrations in my Children's Picture Atlas. The Atlas had not mentioned the other sensations: the way the sticky mud sucked my feet down, the hard knobs of the previous season's maize stalks that cut my feet, the shower of mud that fell on my hair and back as the plough went by on the terrace above, and the morning's meal of wheat porridge that sat heavily in my stomach. I was slow and clumsy and wasted much time at first trying to disentangle the roots of the individual seedlings. 'Don't worry – plant them two or three together,' Naina called out, seeing my problem: 'That way they'll grow up strong and not too tall.' It was important to space the seedlings evenly and make sure their roots had been pushed down deep enough into the liquid mud so that they didn't float to the surface again. As I worked, my mind concentrated on the immediate problems. Was I planting in straight lines? Should I have been planting in straight lines? I looked around – it seemed haphazard but there had to be a system to it somewhere. I was working in the middle of the team in the space they left for me, but somehow my lines never seemed to correspond with theirs. I tried to realign myself but still I would be out of step. I straightened my back and watched them work and pinpointed the problem: *my* mind worked in straight geometric lines, but theirs were loose and flexible, expanding and contracting to fit the contours of the fields which were anything but straight.

As we reached the end of the terrace, bunching closer and closer together with the narrowing of the field, Devi's Mother said, 'Go and sit down Sister. Take a rest. We're used to this but you're not.' I was hot, sweaty, tired and covered in mud. Obediently I sat down on a still unploughed field under a *syo* – an umbrella of bamboo and leaves perched atop the maize stalks. 'Has it eaten your back?' asked Wife Two, smiling as always so that her eyes closed to two cat-like black slits. She tucked the ends of her *lungi* behind her knees and squatted down on her sturdy brown legs on the embankment edge and I noticed her toes splayed wide apart so that her feet though shorter were almost twice as wide as mine.

'What about you? Is your back aching too?' I asked. Wife Two had plenty of wrinkles on her face but always seemed younger and more vigorous than Wife One. 'Oh yes, my back aches plenty,' she said, shaking with laughter as if it was a great joke. 'But it's not so bad as weeding the maize and millet. At least we keep our feet cool in the water.' She pulled out her tobacco pouch, stuffed some dried leaves into the clay pipe and offered me a puff. I shook my head and she agreed. 'No, you don't need it. You can eat when you like! As for me, I can't work without this – it takes away my hunger pangs.' Again she shook with laughter.

Nobody knows when the mountains were first carved into terraces nor whether the idea started in Nepal or infiltrated from other parts of Asia, but without them even more top-soil and nutrients would be washed away in the monsoon. Prolonged heavy rainfall could put tremendous pressure on the terraces and to discourage landslides the farmers were careful to build up the embankments and shape the terrace walls to just the right angle. To maintain the soil's fertility they trampled in the old maize stalks as well as the branches of a certain tree, but otherwise no fertiliser was used. After each field had been ploughed two or three times with the regular ploughhead, a wide shallow plough with four prongs like a rake was taken over the field to make sure the mud was mixed to the same consistency throughout. This plough being lighter and shallower went much faster, and the children climbed on to its wooden frame for a sleigh run through the mud until they overbalanced and tumbled into its soft oozing depths. Even the women had time for play as well as work. Devi's Mother and Jethi challenged each other to a race. Jethi, like her mother Wife Two, had a great sense of fun, and tried to disrupt the rhythm of Devi's Mother by planting seedlings out of line on her side of the field. Devi's Mother replied with a flick of mud that sprayed us all and soon there was a free-for-all mud fight as we tried to topple each other into the mud. Little Devi, naked except for tatoos of mud and annoyed that she was being ignored, pushed up her mother's blouse and tried to suck milk as she bent over planting. 'Not now, you naughty one, can't you leave me alone?' laughed her mother, and Jethi, smiling mischievously, scooped up a handful of liquid mud and smeared it over her breasts. Defeated, Devi broke into a howl of protest.

In the afternoon I took a break from planting to do some sketching. The light was intense, and the reflections shone in the still water of the planted terraces, azure-blue and turquoise, like the patterned wings of the roller birds that swooped in the sky overhead. If I closed my eyes then the sound of rushing water engulfed me and the smell of mud, pungent and fresh, cleared my sinuses and stirred memories of childhood mud-pies. Bhakhu and Maila stopped work to look over my shoulder until Naina Singh noticed they were missing and scolded them to return. Maila pretended not to hear, while Bhakhu crawled inside a *doko* covered with a *syo*, curled himself up like a cat, and fell asleep.

Towards 4 o'clock Wife One arrived with a *doko* of food and millet beer and we gathered round on an unploughed terrace. She handed us hot wheat *roti* which we dipped into a spicy chutney made from the lumpy bitter-gourd. Wife Two fetched a potful of water from the irrigation ditch to add to the fermented millet mash. She squeezed the swollen mash of grain between her none-too-clean hands and drained the liquid into our bowls. Dehydrated by the hot sun and hard work, I gulped the beer down and lived to regret it – there must have been swarms of bacteria in the ditch.

'Is the chutney too spicy for you? We like it this way, hot and bitter,' said Wife One.

'Look at my feet,' complained Jethi, pointing to the pits in her soles. 'They've been "eaten" by the mud. Last year my feet were so swollen I could hardly walk at the end of rice planting.'

After the break Bhakhu and Laute ran off along the ditches to hunt for crabs but I took the younger children back to the village. Devi clasped my hand tightly all the way. She was barefoot and I marvelled at the way she didn't once stumble or stub her toes on the rocky path. Exhausted by the work and sun, I was just drifting off to sleep that evening when Bhakhu turned up. He had stepped on a newly sharpened hoe in the rice fields and given himself a deep gash along the sole of his foot.

I made him soak off the layer of mud and grime in a basin of hot salty water, cleaned the cut and daubed it liberally with iodine. I had no plasters so I used a torn strip of material from my old *kitenge* blouse for a bandage. I was a little annoyed and not optimistic about the prognosis when the next day I saw Grandmother proudly wearing a new patch of *kitenge* material on her old black blouse, and Bhakhu shovelling manure in his bare feet, the bandage missing and the wound exposed. Cuts and sores so easily became infected in Nepal. But I repeated the soakings and iodine treatment and to my surprise and satisfaction Bhakhu's foot healed nicely. After that incident my medical reputation received a boost and the children came to me whenever they had a cut. They particularly liked the iodine; the fact that it stung when I put it on only assured them that it was strong medicine.

It took three days to finish Naina Singh's fields so I had plenty of practice at rice-planting.

'How useful it is to have an extra daughter-in-law!' joked Wife Two.

'How fast you've learned, Sister,' said Devi's Mother. 'Look at how neat your rows are.'

'But I'm too slow. You plant twice as many as I do in the same time.'

'Don't worry. By next year you'll be planting as fast as us.'

As we finished each field we stood back to admire our handiwork – the graceful pattern of whorls and rosettes made by the seedlings which leaned some forwards, some backwards, depending on which direction the planter had faced. We planted steep fields and shallow fields, wide fields and narrow fields, slowly working our way down the slope. Even the smallest scraps of land within reach of the irrigation water were carved into terraces, some barely large enough to stand on, and we reverently planted three or four rice seedlings in each. These smaller fields had to be dug by hand for they were too small to hold the plough teams. Even the embankments, too precious to remain as mere mounds of earth, were planted with sprouted soya beans or black gram lentils carefully thumb-pressed into the soil about six inches apart. Once these were planted it became almost impossible to balance along the narrow ledges between the fields without sliding into the mud. When the last field was completed Devi's Mother ceremoniously grouped the remaining seedlings together, planted them in the centre of the final field and bowed to them. With this small ritual she committed the fate of the seedlings to the gods.

But the Magars did not leave everything to the whim of uncertain deities. Many kinds of animals liked to eat the succulent seedlings so constant vigilance was essential or whole fields could be cropped to their roots. Some farmers built temporary shelters in their more distant fields and lived in these for the duration of the rice season. In Titeng it was the beautiful *langur* monkeys with their coal-black faces and ruff of white fur who were the biggest pests. They descended on the young rice fields in squabbling hordes, leaping gracefully from bank to bank with their long expressive tails flaring behind them. To my dismay Naina Singh produced an old gun and fired a volley of shots into the air, but the monkeys bounded effortlessly away, unfrightened and unharmed, swinging their babies from their bellies.

When all the families had completed their rice planting I was woken one morning by ear-splitting squeals, and looking out saw Lal Bahadur hanging on to the tail of one of Naina's black pot-bellied pigs. It was half in and half out of the pig pen and refusing to move. Prithvi Lal arrived to help and together they caught hold of its hind legs, tied a rope round its belly and dragged it out. Then sticking large *khukuris* in their belts they set off for the *swami* trees by the river, dragging the pig behind them on its belly leash, still squealing its protests.

'Each year we must sacrifice a pig by the river,' Prithvi Lal told me on the way down. 'This keeps our ancestors happy and placates the river. One year we didn't sacrifice and the river flooded its banks – several people died – so now we sacrifice each year. If we don't, our ancestors will make trouble for us – spoil our crops, make us sick, or cast a spell on our buffalo.'

They laid the pig on a massive flat-topped boulder that was split into two halves by a deep fissure. 'The first time a pig was sacrificed here the stone split in two,' said Lal Bahadur. 'It was long ago, but that's what they say. So that proves that the goddess lives here in these *swami* trees.'

He grasped the *khukuri* with both hands and with a swift sawing motion pulled the knife through the pig's throat. Convulsions racked through its body and the men strained to hold it down. While it was still alive the blood from its throat was sprinkled across the cracked boulder to placate the goddess. I turned away; I had been expecting the quick chop of the buffalo sacrifices. This seemed a painful, ugly way to die. Instead of skinning the pig the men lit a fire and roasted it, and the flames spat and crackled as the fat from its body slowly melted. It was a slow smelly process and the children who had been rapt observers during the actual slaughter, grew bored and jumped into the river to play football with the blown-up stomach. When the hair had been roasted off the pig, the men weighed and divided out the meat, taking care that each family received an appropriate share according to their size.

That evening we dined on wheat *roti* and pork. Wife One piled six or seven *roti* on to my plate and Naina gave me a generous helping of brains and other titbits from his special pot. 'Only me and the other elders eat this,' he said, as he busied himself preparing leaf bowls of rice and meat and red powder to offer to his ancestors. I ate till I could eat no more, but when I got up to leave, Wife One called me back.

'Where are you going? You haven't eaten rice yet.'

'I'm full. I can't eat any more.'

'*Roti* and meat – that's just a snack! Come and eat rice.'

Ignoring my negative answer she plumped a pile of pink-bran rice on my plate so then I had to eat for fear it would be wasted.

The next day they performed a *puja*-ritual in their fields to ensure a good crop. Early in the morning each family went out to their newly planted terraces carrying leaf plates and wooden *tekus* of *ghiu* (clarified butter). Placing a sage shrub on the edge of a field, they laid down beside it the leaf plates of rice, red powder and incense, placed some maize stalks and *ghiu* on top and set them alight.

All that could be done to safeguard the crop was now complete. In the weeks that followed we watched the rice grow until the thousand terraced lakes became a thousand stairs of velvet-green.

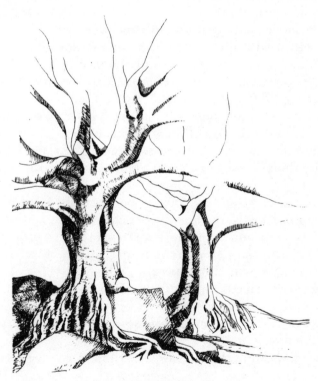

Swami trees by the Katue Khola

13

Season of festivals and fertility

The monsoon continued to favour us with its pervasive wetness. The rice fields below Titeng changed from a light sulphurous green to a deep viridian, and at dusk released clouds of metallic-blue dragonflies into the air. At night time too the frogs came out and filled the air with their guttural croaks. In the village the canary-yellow flowers of the cucumbers and pumpkins trailed around the roof-tops and trees, and in the woods and shady hollows ferns uncoiled and fragile begonias bloomed. The mud walls of our house were saturated; mould started to grow on our books, our towels, and even our camera, and my long hair stayed permanently damp. Food rotted in a day if we forgot to eat it, but it was perfect yoghourt-making weather. Every evening we boiled our left-over milk, added a teaspoonful of old yoghourt and by the next morning had a jarful of fresh creamy yoghourt. With the monsoon our diet improved and we feasted on maize and a whole new family of knobbly, lumpy and often bitter vegetables that I had never tasted before.

The guava tree below our courtyard developed egg-sized dark green fruit and attracted the interest of both children and adults. One morning I woke up and found myself staring straight into the eyes of Bhakhu. He was balanced in the topmost branch of the guava tree, exactly on eye level with our upper room.

Looking closer I spied Gophle, Laute, Kali and two of the teenagers – all perched like vultures in the flimsy branches, munching on green guavas. The tree was not very big and seemed likely to collapse under their combined weight.

'Why are you eating the guavas? They're not ripe yet,' I yelled to them.

'If we don't eat them now, others will,' Bhakhu called back, and threw us some guavas through the window.

I selected the softest and tried to sink my teeth into it, but only managed to puncture the skin. It was bitter and astringent; how hard it was to understand their tastes! Duane and I had been looking forward for some months to the ripening of the guavas, and now it seemed they were to be consumed unripe.

The guava tree was the only one in the village and drew people like a magnet. Wife One tied a bundle of prickly branches round the base of the tree to forestall some of the younger thieves, but this did not deter the older ones. The tree, though growing on Naina Singh's land, was regarded as belonging to the whole village, and everyone was free to help themselves. Fruit was so scarce and so much enjoyed we were surprised they didn't bother to plant more fruit trees. But the villagers said, 'If God wants us to have more fruit trees, he will give them to us.'

It was the season of growth and fertility. In respect of this the religious calendar marked a succession of festivals culminating with Dasain, a ten-day festival and the most important of the year. The first of the season was Sak Rati, memorable for us as the time Bhakhu nearly set the whole village ablaze. It was the fire-throwing festival and each person doused a stick of their choice with oil, set light to it and threw it as far as they could into the fields below. Bhakhu, over-zealous with the oil, was determined to throw his the furthest. He swung himself round like a tiny gyroscope, opened his fist, and sent the fiery missile humming a straight course towards the nearest building which happened to be Naina Singh's round house. It landed with an explosion of sparks on the thatched roof.

'You crazy one!' screamed Naina. 'What are you trying to do? Kill us all?'

The women dived for their water pots and Gesi Ram and Naina scrambled on to the roof to try and beat the flames out. Titeng, with its houses cramped so closely together, was particularly vulnerable to fire; it only needed a blaze in one house for the sparks to spread and catch the rest of the village. Luckily the fire was quickly put out, thanks to the prompt reaction of the villagers and the monsoon which had left the roof still damp from the day's rain.

After that the festivals followed each other in quick succession. We watched the famous masked dance of Lakhe, the monkey dance of Hanuman, we paid out rupees to the cows and evil spirits of Gai Jatra and Indra Jatra, and finally we followed the Brahmin women down to the Kali Gandaki river to celebrate Tij, the women's festival. Tij was the one day of the year when the women were relieved of their field work, their household chores, their husbands, their children, and

were free to dress up in their finest clothes and jewellery for a festival
of singing and dancing. The day began with a ritual bathe in the river,
when the women cleansed themselves from the 'stain' of menstru-
ation. The devout washed themselves once for every time they had
menstruated during the past year and then offered sacrifices at the
temple. After that they retired to the sacred wood on the cliff top to
celebrate their regained purity with songs and dances. Their songs
were long ballads describing the year's main events including the latest
scandals and gossip. As few of the women could read or write, the
words had to be retained by memory and extra verses or even whole
songs would be extemporised, one woman singing the lead line, and
the crowd picking up the refrain.

But these festivals were mostly celebrated by the Newar or
Brahmin castes who lived in Baglung, and the villagers of Titeng
happily ignored them with no apparent retribution from the gods.
They were busy with their field work. Although the pressure of work
had eased now that the rice and millet were planted, they still had to be
tended. Wife Two, Maila, Saili, Bhakhu and Devi's Mother worked
the millet fields in a long row, pulling out the weeds that sprang up
overnight, and resting in the shade to suck on chilli-spiced lemons
when they became tired.

It was a familiar routine followed for centuries by their forefathers
who had worked the same fields in the same seasons. Change was on
its way and slowly seeping into even the remotest areas, but the
villagers remained suspicious and would take a lot more time and a lot
more persuasion before they adopted new practices of farming. That
year Keshu Ram, the ex-Gurkha soldier who supplied our milk,
decided to experiment with some insecticide. According to Naina
Singh, whose word was not always to be trusted, Keshu Ram was the
wealthiest man in the village. He owned about the same amount of
land as Naina Singh, but he had a smaller family and with two sons in
the Indian Gurkhas a regular cash income to supplement his grain
harvest. Because his greater wealth made him less vulnerable to the
consequences of taking risks, and his Gurkha service had given him
more contact with the outside world, Keshu was somewhat open to
new ideas. That year he had planted his millet earlier than most, and
now it was being devastated by a marauding breed of black flies. On
advice from Kanchha, his youngest son who was still home on leave,
he visited the Agriculture Development Office in Baglung and
returned with an insecticide and spray apparatus, and soon we saw
him walking back and forth spraying his millet fields.

When we questioned him however he shrugged his shoulders, doubtful of its efficacy: 'This is what they told me to do. I don't know why, but I'm doing it.'

'Ha!' scoffed Naina from his own territory. 'That won't work. You're wasting your time and money.'

We reserved our judgement for later, but time proved Naina to be right, and despite the insecticide Keshu still lost a good percentage of his millet crop. We weren't sure why it had failed to work, but it meant the trickle of change in Titeng was temporarily halted.

Once the rice and millet were firmly established the men worked hard one Saturday and brought the water pipe through the centre of the village and installed a second tap stand beside Mati Lal's house, two terraces above ours. Prithvi Lal was solely responsible for the design and the supervision of the work, and we were pleased that he had acquired this new and much-needed skill. Now we listened day and night to the sound of water splashing on the cement washing area, for the villagers, unfamiliar with the purpose of taps, never remembered to turn it off. Luckily there was sufficient water in the spring so we didn't bother to remind them, and we were happy because this tap stand was even closer than the one under the *pipal* tree and made our life easier.

With both tap stands completed I discovered that the old spring in the lower rice fields made a perfect bathroom, quiet and secluded, for the women no longer went there. Here I could forget about wearing a petticoat and wash naked, hidden beneath the weeping foliage of the poinsettia and the tall dense rice plants. I would hang my clothes on a convenient bough of the poinsettia and squat down beneath the wooden water spout on the wide flat stones slippery with neglect and green monsoon moss and mould. Through the blades of rice I could see the opposite mountainside, stippled with terraces and houses, and above the poinsettia leaves, the shimmering blue sky. Fishes and tadpoles came to tickle my toes and once a crab crawled out of his hideaway and nipped my ankle, but a lather of soap usually sent them scooting for shelter beneath the rocks and rice plants. After washing I would wrap my towel around me and move into the sun to drip dry in its warm rays. Once or twice I caught sight of faces in the distance, peering through the millet stalks to see what I was up to. But they never bothered me and I was left to enjoy my solitary bathroom in peace.

14

Too many people; too little land

On the long summer evenings Duane and I liked to wander through the village and sit and talk to the villagers. This was the time when their work was over for the day and they were relaxed and ready to chat. As the evenings were hot and very still, Duane often went bare-chested.

'Where's your shirt?' yelled the Screechy Woman to Duane one evening. Her voice had a squawk like a myna bird. 'If you walk round naked like that the wind will blow through your stomach and make you sick.'

We laughed. We tried to follow their customs but sometimes Duane took a perverse delight in doing things that were strange to them just to enjoy their reaction.

'Oooh! Your hair has turned quite bla-a-ack since you came here,' said the Screechy Woman, turning her attention to me. 'It's just like ours now.' This was a private joke that she never failed to make, for my hair was fair and bleached a lighter shade each week with the sun.

The Screechy Woman would never pass by without exchanging a comment, a joke, or a word of encouragement. Her own hair was particularly black and thick and had not had a comb pulled through it for months. A few straggling ends were caught together with a torn strip of red cloth, but the bulk of it had escaped and flared away from her scalp in stiff spikes. She always wore a black threadbare skirt and a mostly black blouse whose patches seemed held together by the layer of grime that stretched from her neck to her fingertips and toes. She wore no jewellery save for two very worn twisted brass earrings. The Screechy Woman was a constant reminder to me that their way of life was not always as happy as it appeared.

She had married a nephew of Sher Bahadur and come to live in Titeng twenty-five years ago. After five years of childless marriage her husband deserted her for another woman and never came back. Her parents were both dead and her brothers unwilling or unable to support her, so the Screechy Woman remained in Titeng and her husband's relatives donated a small plot of land and a room for her adjoining the 'terrace row' in which Sher Bahadur lived. In some countries her situation would not arouse comment, but Nepal was a society of families, and singleness and childlessness were both believed to be the result of sin, so the Screechy Woman was doubly cursed.

But she was not alone in her misfortune and it was quite common for women to be abandoned by their husbands. Next door to the Screechy Woman Sher Bahadur's own daughter Kali had been left in a similar predicament. Sher Bahadur had arranged her marriage and Kali had gone to live with her husband in his village. The family was large however and their landholdings small, so after a year of marriage her husband announced he must go to India to find work in order to support them. Years passed and no news filtered back from India. Finally Kali decided he was never going to return, and she and her young son left her husband's home where she was unhappy, and returned to Sher Bahadur's already overcrowded house.

In the highest house at the western end of the village lived a family of women – Nanakala, her daughter Dil Maya, and her granddaughter Lal Devi. Nanakala was about fifty years old. She too had once been married, but after the birth of her first and only child Dil Maya, she became sick and was unable to work as hard in the fields as formerly. She suffered severe pains down her back and legs. Her husband, through lack of sympathy or force of poverty, took another wife to work in the fields and turned Nanakala and her child out of the house. They returned to Titeng where her parents gave her two fields which her brothers helped to farm. That was twenty-seven years ago. In due course her daughter Dil Maya married, moved to her husband's home, and was in turn abandoned by him. So she and her seven-year-old daughter Lal Devi returned home to keep Nanakala company. The land left to Nanakala was not enough to support the three of them, so Dil Maya had to work for the bazaar landowners, earning six rupees for a ten-hour day carrying manure, hoeing, digging, and planting. To supplement this Nanakala distilled millet beer at home, selling the *rakshi* in the bazaar for five rupees a bottle.

The increasing pressure of population was of concern to them all for it was the cause of most of their problems. At one time when land was plentiful the Magars had been slash-and-burn cultivators and hunted wild pig and deer in the dense forests that covered the lower mountains. As their population increased they had settled down to farm permanent fields and established their villages, gradually cutting down the forest as they brought more land under cultivation. As the forests and grazing lands disappeared, they were forced to cut down on the animals they raised and this meant less manure for the fields which suffered increasingly from erosion and loss of fertility.

'When I was young,' said Keshu Ram, 'there was more land and fewer people. There were only six or seven houses in Titeng. Now there are sixteen.'

'How do you manage?'

'Well, when a man dies we divide his land into parts. Each son gets an equal portion. If one son doesn't want to farm, his brothers will farm his share.'

'And if there's not enough land to feed them all?'

'They take extra work in the bazaar if they can find it, or go to India and get a job, perhaps as a night watchman. The Indians like us because we're so honest. Some try to join the army – that's the best money.' Keshu paused and trimmed his toenails thoughtfully with his long curved *khukuri*. 'It's not right,' he continued, 'to join the Gurkhas and fight other men's wars and kill people . . . but, if there isn't enough food at home, then it's all right. What else can we do? Some families move away. You know the derelict house in the middle of the village near Dal Bahadur's? That belonged to a family who moved away six years ago. Didn't have enough land here so they sold all they had and bought some land up the Myagdi Khola, north of here. It's high up on the mountainside where it's very cold, but good land, and cheap too. Another family bought land down on the *terai*. They're both rich men now, so they say. Perhaps if we had moved we'd be rich too, but what to do? Here at least we have our brothers and sisters and we manage to get along.'

'Yes, it's not so bad here,' agreed the headman. 'If only we could get rid of our debts. They're our biggest problem. If they were gone all would be well.'

To gain a better understanding of their economic situation I decided to conduct my own unofficial survey and talk with each of the families in Titeng. I tried to do this without letting them know they were being interviewed, but my memory was not always good enough to retain the facts and from time to time I had to resort to taking notes. This made them a little uneasy. 'What are you writing these things down for, Sister? Are you going to hand it to the Tax man?' I laughed. Taxes on the meagre amounts of land they owned were only a few rupees a year and were surely the least of their problems.

Getting figures on their landholdings was not easy. At that time their land had not been surveyed so they had no way of knowing its areal extent. Instead they measured their land in 'ploughs'. Four ploughs of land meant the holding was such it took a pair of oxen four days to plough. This was a very rough measure; it took no account of the sharpness of the plough, the strength of the oxen, or the number of rest stops. Some measured their land by the volume of grain it produced – so many baskets of maize cobs or *pathi* containers of rice. The problem here was the harvests varied so much from year to year – did they measure in a good year, a bad year, or an average year? Still, somewhat hesitantly, I assigned a rough areal measurement to their landholdings which at least enabled me to compare within the village.

There were a total of sixteen households in Titeng, varying in size from sixteen members (Naina Singh's) to one (the Screechy Woman's), but averaging eight members per household. The average household owned less than one acre of land – not very much on which to support a family of eight, but the villagers invested much effort in their fields, intensively farming every corner of them and, as the climate was favourable, managed to get two crops a year. Still it was not usually sufficient and at least one member would find some outside building work during the winter months which brought in a supplementary income of £150 per family per year. The bulk of this would go on clothing and extra grain to feed the family.

It was interesting to compare my figures with the way they perceived themselves. Keshu Ram and Lal Bahadur owned the most land, about two acres each, and both had good cash incomes, but Keshu Ram's family was double the size of Lal Bahadur's, so clearly Lal was better off. Yet the villagers saw Keshu Ram as being the wealthiest. Everyone agreed that old Mati Lal's family were the poorest. They owned virtually no land. But that year both Mati Lal and his son worked fulltime as labourers on the hydro-electric project and by my calculations, even allowing for them buying all their food, ended up with the largest surplus of income over expenditure. According to my figures, Nanakala's family of single women was by far the poorest. The three of them managed to subsist on a tenth of an acre of land and £37 cash income a year, far less than Mati Lal. But probably they didn't count in the villagers' reckoning because they were all women.

It was clear from my survey that the villagers viewed wealth in terms of land ownership, and this was not a false view. Those families with a high cash income but little land had no security; they were dependent on intermittent seasonal jobs and had to buy all their food at current prices with no buffer against inflation. In addition, having the disposable income in their pockets, they were tempted to spend it on non-essential things – drink, cigarettes, more stylish clothes – to the detriment of their family's well-being. But the change-over from a grain to a cash economy had already begun, and we wondered how Titeng would fare as the pressure of population forced more and more people to give up farming and seek other employment.

Already nearly every family was in debt to the Newar and Brahmin money-lenders in the bazaar, owing anything from 200 to 5,000 rupees. In a year when the weather cooperated and their harvests were good, they could keep their accounts balanced, but extra expenses such as a wedding or funeral forced them into debt. Although Lal Bahadur had plenty of land he was still paying off medical expenses and funeral debts incurred thirteen years ago when his father died after a long sickness. With interest rates ranging from 20% to 40% it was hard to keep up the interest payments and they had little hope of paying back the principal. Death was no escape for the debts passed on to their sons and grandsons until they were paid off. The payments might be made in cash or grain and until they were completed the debtor was obliged to work for the money-lender whenever called upon. If he defaulted on the interest payments, the money-lender would take his land.

'One time all the land across the valley was owned by Titeng,' said the headman. 'But we lost it when we fell into debt. The Brahmins are too clever for us. We Magars will never be advanced; we spend too much money drinking and feasting.'

The headman's youngest son was home on leave from his police post in Kasauli. He was the most educated man in the village having studied for the full ten years of school.

'Nothing's nice here,' he whispered confidentially to us, thinking we would agree. 'The songs aren't nice, the houses aren't nice, the people aren't nice. You must excuse these people – they are ignorant and poor.'

I felt hurt. Titeng had become my own to such an extent I didn't like anyone to criticise it. I also felt angry that the headman's son should so despise his own background and society.

His comment arose more from embarrassment than anything else. But I was upset because I felt that Duane and I were partly responsible for his attitude. It was an attitude conveyed by the very presence of

Above: Devi and friends help to mix the white clay for the Dasain 'lipnu'
of the houses
Below: Naina Singh receiving the Dasain 'tika' from Grandmother

Favourite walk through the woods above the cliffs near Titeng

foreign aid workers in the country – 'we know better; we have something you need and don't have'. How could we offer them more education, better methods of farming, new technology and other things that could improve their standard of living, without making them feel their present tools and methods were useless and they themselves inferior? The fact was that although improved technology had brought widespread benefits to some developing countries, it was quite frequently being shown that the local people knew best and that their methods of production were well suited to their environment. Improved strains of maize introduced to Nepal, for example, gave much higher yields, but these improved strains were not so resistant to disease and drought, so that for villagers like those of Titeng who could not afford to take risks, it was perhaps better to stick to their low-yielding but reliable strains.

Education was another problem. It was badly needed and could bring about tremendous changes, but if those who continued to higher education or secondary school learnt to be ashamed of their backgrounds and despise farming, education was perhaps doing more harm than good. We were aware of how easily our own prejudices were conveyed to them. If we saw a 'Made in Nepal' label on a product we said to ourselves it was inferior in quality and would soon break or malfunction. When we contracted a Nepali to do a particular task we thought how *we* could have done it more efficiently. Thus it was not surprising the villagers felt that everything in England or America was bigger and better than in Nepal.

'You can do everything. You have machines to do the work in your country. How happy you must all be!' was their frequent comment, with the insinuation: 'You're clever, and we're dumb.'

To counteract this we were at pains to point out all the instances where we thought their way of doing things and their society was better than ours. We tried to explain the problems our urbanised, industrialised society had that theirs didn't. They found this hard to believe for to live in a city, where the land was flat, the shops had everything you might need and you didn't have to walk, sounded the ultimate in happiness. But they *did* need to be reassured that we liked their country.

'Why have you come here? Do you like it here?' they would ask wistfully from time to time. We only had to see their smiles when we affirmed how much we liked Nepal and its people, to know that we had said the right thing.

By mid-September the monsoon was dying. The children of Baglung stood on the ridges and cliff tops to fly their rice-paper kites, a signal for the winds to come and blow the monsoon away. In its brief four months of life it had left nothing untouched. The terraced fields bore stands of ripening millet and rice, springs had been replenished, and forests regenerated, but millions of tons of fertile soil had been removed from the mountain slopes of Nepal and washed down by the rivers to the Ganges Plain and the Bay of Bengal. But still the monsoon lingered on and in a final storm – its death throes – the rain opened up the holes in our roof again and poured though.

On my way back from the bazaar one day I made a detour to the hydro-electric office to see if the mail runner who went once a week to Kasauli had brought any letters for us. It was a clear sunny day and the waters of the Kathe Khola had diminished considerably and regained their sparkling turquoise colour. Already Duane was able to wade across on his way to the site, saving himself a thirty-minute walk to the bridge and back. I stood on the cliff beside the office and looked down at the river, debating whether to risk crossing it myself in order to return to Titeng.

In the end laziness won over caution and I scrambled down the cliff and walked upstream to our swimming spot where the river was free of boulders and flowed more slowly. Hitching up my long skirt in my hands I stepped out. Even at this relatively gentle crossing spot the river was flowing more deeply and strongly than I had realised, and it lifted me off my feet before I was even into the mainstream current. I retreated to the shore and thought again. I didn't like to be defeated so I decided to swim. I had done it before when the water was lower, but as the current was still strong I removed my long skirt so that I could swim faster and reach the other side before the river carried me on to the boulders. I bundled my skirt into my bag, and, standing on the boulder that jutted out furthest into the river, threw the bag as hard as I could across the river. It easily reached the other side, but my rolled-up skirt had turned the bag into a ball and it rebounded from the rocks and bounced into the river.

I stared as it disappeared down the chute of a small waterfall, surrounded by bubbles and spray. It took a while for my predicament to sink in, but when it did, I was dismayed. I was in my T-shirt and underwear in a culture that didn't approve of women even showing their calves. Hoping that my bag would be washed ashore or stuck in a pool of water behind a boulder, I swam across and searched downstream, but without success. There was no option but to return to the village in the state I was in.

A voiding the regular path, I chose the cow-path that led up from the river to the village. It was hidden most of the way by trees and was only used when the villagers took their cows down to graze, so the chances of meeting someone were slight. I scrambled up the path as far as it went, but for a short section I was forced to join the regular path. People were coming and going on it. I peered through the bamboos waiting for a break in the traffic and trying to calculate the best moment to emerge. Finally two men passed by and then the way was clear. I stepped out stealthily hoping to follow unseen, but they must have sensed my presence for they stopped and turned round to stare in the unabashed way Nepalis do. Too late to stop and too embarrassed to speak, I marched up the path as if I roamed in this attire every day. I could only hope they took me for a long-haired man. They stepped to one side to let me pass and silently fell in behind me, too astonished to talk, until I turned off the path and took a shortcut up the zig-zag path through the terraces to our house. Thankfully I did not know them, and even in my embarrassment I was able to laugh as I imagined the story they would tell to their friends of the evil white spirit that stalked them out of the woods.

For once I was grateful for the steep incline that obscured the village until I had practically entered it. Reaching our garden terrace I made a quick reconnaissance. The courtyard was clear. I leapt up the steps and dived for our room, congratulating myself that I had made it unseen.

'What happened to you today?' asked Wife One when we went to eat supper.

'Nothing,' I said nonchalantly.

She exchanged a knowing look with Wife Two and smiled, and I realised my story was out.

'Well,' I said, 'You know the river. . . .'

'I warned you about swimming in the river,' said Wife Two at the end of my story, laughing so much there were tears in her eyes. 'Sa-la-la-la-lah, it flows!'

As the monsoon waned and the river became truly fordable, it was a delight to wake up in the mornings and look out at the new day dawning. Annapurna graced us once more with her frosty presence, and in Baglung Dhaulagiri's fluted ice face glinted above the slate roof of the bazaar, seeming so close in the freshly cleaned air that one could reach out and touch her.

15

When the flies stopped biting

The months passed by. Each day the sun rose, chased away the night shadows, and illuminated the Kathe Khola valley walls that marked the outer boundaries of the world of Titeng. Each day the villagers ate their morning meal, tied their small-bladed sickles round their waists, loaded their hoes into empty *dokos* carelessly swung on their backs, and set out for the fields in single file. Each day they carried water, fed the buffalo, tended the fields, prepared their food, and worked until darkness fell and then returned to their homes, pulled their shawls over their heads, and the world of the strange night spirits took over. When the sun rose the next morning, the previous day's work had been obliterated; the weeds had sprung up again and the same chores waited to be done. Like the kernels of maize caught in Wife One's grinding stone, they went round and round, trapped between the rocky walls of the valley, until the rough cycle of life wore them down and they died. No wonder Hinduism and Buddhism talked of ways to escape this wheel of life.

To me, a product of western culture, used to the constant stimulation of new ideas, new people and new places, their daily existence seemed monotonous and restricted. Their life as I perceived it could be simplified to a code of 'Grow food – Prepare food – Eat food – Sleep'. Did they ever ask if there were other choices; did they ever question why this was their fate in life; what, if any, were their hopes and unfulfilled ambitions, and what sustained the onward momentum of their lives? These were questions I wanted to ask, but it was hard to find answers.

For the women, their world was particularly confining. Its limits were a triangle formed by their home, their parents' home, and the bazaar. Even the latter, less than an hour's walk distant, they only visited occasionally. During the year of our stay, Wife One to my knowledge went to the bazaar twice – once at the Chaitra festival, and once when Gophle was sick and after a lot of persuasion from me she took him to the clinic. Why didn't they go more often? Lack of time was part of the answer, and perhaps lack of money, for what fun were the shops if you could not buy anything? But it seemed there was more to it than that.

These restrictions did not apply to the men, who went to the bazaar frequently, if not daily, to indulge their craving for *rakshi* and to make the occasional business transaction such as selling their buffalo. But even the men, with the exception of the two ex-Gurkha soldiers, were not well-informed about what lay beyond the valley walls. Baglung bazaar was often the extent of their worldly experience and their contact with the products of modern civilisation was limited. In the whole village there was not a single plastic utensil except for ours. There were no books, and no factory-manufactured articles; only the copper and brass cooking pots and the heavy iron farming tools that were hand-forged by the blacksmiths up the mountain.

We had brought with us a few photos from home, and these provided them with their first rather inaccurate impressions of a life beyond their own. During the rainy days of the monsoon it became a favourite pastime to climb the ladder to our upper room and leaf through the pages of the photo album. They commented mainly on things they could relate to – the flatness of the land, the beautiful flowers, the size of the houses – pushing aside such things as motor vehicles that were totally outside their experience. But when I explained what a car was, and how a network of roads covered our country and everybody travelled by bus or car, they were fascinated. The closest most of the villagers had come to a wheeled vehicle were the small aeroplanes that flew overhead, or the helicopters that landed infrequently at Baglung bearing some government dignitary or foreign aid consultant. Dhan Bahadur for example was typical. He was a married man of about forty years who worked with Duane on the hydro-electric project. One day he came round to beg us a favour: could he take our mail to Kasauli just once so that he could ride on a bus? He had seen the buses at Naudara but never ridden on one and his biggest desire was to do so once before he died. Perhaps twice, he added as an afterthought. So Duane arranged for Dhan Bahadur to relieve our regular mail runner for one week. He came back vowing never to go on a bus again, having suffered from severe motion-sickness! If that was the extent of Dhan Bahadur's articulated ambitions, he typified the older men of the village who were content to maintain the *status quo*, not seeking a way out of their humdrum life.

The concept of recreation as a separate and special activity chosen for its enjoyment value was quite foreign to them. Even when they stopped for a smoke or a chat it was always in the middle of working, and if work was slack then they turned the grinding stone at a slower pace than usual and weeded the fields in a more leisurely manner. Whereas I would hurry through my work in order to have more time for recreation. Two of my favourite spare-time activities were walking and bird-watching. Beyond the upper rice fields there was a path that rambled round the forested sides of the gorge on the cliff tops, where I might see the crested green magpie, a fantail fly-catcher or the rich cobalt and tangerine of a beautiful-niltava, as well as flocks of the common jungle-babblers and bulbuls. The Magars only went there occasionally to gather wood or cut leaves for the buffalo, so it was peaceful and still. These walks of mine puzzled them in several ways, first because it was incomprehensible that anyone should want to walk unless they had to, and secondly because the path led to nowhere but the forest – the habitat of ghosts and evil spirits.

'Where've you been?' they would ask on my return. 'To the forest! Why? Looking at birds? Aren't you afraid of the spirits? Eeyeh! If we have nothing to do we lie on our verandahs and go to sleep!'

'But *if* you had the chance, where would you go?' I asked.

'Where? Nowhere. Because I can't,' replied Bhakhu, shrugging his bony shoulders, unable to cope with the hypothetical question.

'What about you, Jethi?' I persisted, turning to Bhakhu's older married sister who was visiting.

'I will go where my husband takes me,' she said. 'We can't choose where we go. It's written on our foreheads by God at our birth.'

Strangely even the ex-Gurkha soldiers with their experience of foreign travel seemed to accept this view and were little inclined to alter their way of life or even desire anything different. It was only when I met Gore, the thirteen-year-old son of Dhan Bahadur (of bus-trip fame) that I discovered someone with a vision of possibilities beyond Titeng.

'I've come because I hate just sitting on a mat in my house with the flies biting my legs,' Gore announced the first time he came to call on me. I was astounded. It was the first and only unsolicited remark I ever heard that expressed dissatisfaction with the limitations of life in Titeng. Gore immediately grasped the questions I was asking and the speed with which his words came tumbling out indicated that he had given some thought to these issues.

'I want to be a soldier and travel to foreign countries,' he told me. 'I want to go to Dolpo and Kathmandu and England and America and . . . lots of places!'

So Dolpo and Kathmandu were 'foreign countries' and even the bazaar was foreign territory to be visited only in the safety of numbers. After all the villagers identified themselves as *Magars*, not Nepalis, and as such kept themselves to their mountainside, away from the towns where they didn't belong.

Gore was bursting with curiosity and had opinions on many subjects. More than anyone else in the village, Gore's mind was actively searching, and while Bhakhu and his friends were content to leave school and mind the goats, earning a few rupees now and then so that they could go to the bazaar and buy a glass of *rakshi* or a packet of cigarettes, Gore wanted more.

It was Gore's dislike of sitting in his house with the flies biting, that led to their first experience of recreation for its own sake, without the sanction of a religious festival, a wedding or a funeral. Duane was away in Kathmandu and the children were in our upper room keeping me company when Gore suddenly asked, 'Sister, do you have a machine that takes a photo of our voices?'

I picked up our radio/tape-recorder from the 'rat's freeway' shelf under the eaves. Although the villagers were familiar with the radio part of it they had never until now queried the other half. I showed Gore and his friends how it worked and they immediately wanted to record a poem of their own.

'How do we do it, Sister?'

'Just speak – like you do to me.' They nudged each other and giggled.

'You first . . . no, go on . . . after you . . . .'

Finally Gore plucked up courage. 'Kukurika!' he announced, as though it was the evening news. 'By Gore Thapa Magar and Ram Bahadur Thapa Magar.'

He and Ram paused for a moment and then burst into a loud unmelodic chant:

> Kukurika! Kukurika!
> The red-crested cock is crowing,
> For the mother has just delivered.

> We must sacrifice a chicken
> So that she can eat meat.
> When she has eaten her share,
> I shall eat the head.

When I played it back they howled with delight to hear their own voices, especially where they had made mistakes or stuttered. We quickly filled the tape with more songs and poems and several versions of the national anthem. Word soon spread around the village about the amazing black box that 'catches your voice', and in twos and threes they came up to listen to the tape. I encouraged them because I wanted to record some of their songs. But the adults didn't have the natural facility of the children, and self-consciousness left many of them tongue-tied when their turn came. They liked to sing when they were working in the fields or minding the goats, and when they walked home late in the evening they sang a coarse, lilting, almost yodelling song to frighten the ghosts away. But sitting in our upper room surrounded by an audience, shyness overcame them.

'What shall I say? I don't know what to say,' was Wife One's first recorded sentence on tape.

'Go on, just say anything like "I must go and cut grass for the buffalo",' urged Bhakhu, saying the first and most obvious thing that came to mind.

'I must go and cut grass for the buffalo,' repeated Wife One in a wooden voice. 'Ah! I feel so silly,' she cried, pulling her shawl in front of her face in embarrassment.

Although they enjoyed hearing their speeches and poems, they liked it best when I recorded them unknowingly in their pre-performance warm-ups or off-stage comments. They never grew bored of listening to the tape played over and over again.

'Come on. Let's hear it again,' they would plead.

'But I've already played it five times.'

'Just once more. Look, Tulasi has come. She must hear it. And here's Kali – she hasn't heard it yet either.'

'I'll play it once more if you'll sing a song for me.'

'Kali! You have the best voice,' they said, turning to Sher Bahadur's oldest daughter. 'Sing us a song!'

Kali looked away in embarrassment. 'I've just come to listen,' she said shyly. 'My head is aching, so I haven't gone to work in the fields.'

'You've got to sing.'

'No. I can't. I'm too shy. People will hear me.'

After a lot of persuasion she sat suspiciously in front of the tape-recorder, shawl pulled over her lowered head, and hand in front of her mouth so that her face was almost obscured. After a few false starts she uttered a tremulous note, low and sustained, that grew in volume until it filled the room and echoed off the four bare walls, ending in a dissonant trill. Slowly a sad haunting melody unfolded, each note nasalised and drawn out, almost to a wail – a poetic melodious wail, sung with intense emotion. I listened mesmerised as her unaccompanied voice rose and fell, catching the subtle quarter tones that gave Eastern music its distinctive sound.

I could not grasp the meaning of all the words, but the intensity of the music lifted me out of my surroundings. I forgot I was sitting on the hard mud floor. I forgot that my legs were stiff and aching. I forgot about the villagers pressing around me.

At the end Kali paused, staring almost in a trance through the floor. Then she lifted her head and smiled shyly. 'My headache has gone away with the singing. Was that all right?'

'Very good!' I said.

'Delicious!' cried the Magar women, using more idiomatic Nepali.

'Now please tell me what it means,' I begged. 'I could only understand a few of the words.'

'Oh Sister! The beauty is all in the words. It's no fun if you don't understand the words. I'll sing it again – this time you'll understand.'

> My husband has gone to Malaya,★
> What shall I do?
> I grind my corn alone;
> Life is short and seldom do we meet.
> I have no one for a friend,
> I am lonely and pass my life weeping.
> Why did he bother to marry me?

The song was strangely appropriate, for Kali's husband had indeed abandoned her – not for the army but for another woman. Here in the songs seemed to be the feelings and thoughts that I had been searching for in their lives.

'Sing us another song,' begged the women.

'All right,' said Kali, smiling now.

★i.e. He is a Gurkha soldier.

Wherever I go the landslides fall;
If I go here,
If I go there,
They fall.
What is my fate?

'Do you have songs like this in your country?' asked Kali.

'We sing songs, but they're not like yours.' I picked up my guitar and sang them 'As I walked out over London Bridge'.

'That's nice,' they said politely at the end, but it was obvious they preferred their own. We had brought tapes of various kinds of music with us – rock, folk, and classical – but only two of them ever evoked any comment. The first was a portion of Mike Oldfield's Tubular Bells which includes a lively hornpipe jig. They loved this: 'Oh! Music we can dance to! Do you have any more like this?' The second piece was the last movement of Beethoven's Appassionata Sonata. At the end of this dramatic movement Wife Two breathed a deep sigh and smiled. 'It goes sa-la-la-la-la,' she said, making the sound they used to describe the rippling of the river, and I wondered if music was after all a universal language.

From that day on I was besieged with callers who wanted to hear the tape played again and again. It didn't matter if I was busy; they would squat patiently in my room until I finished what I was doing. One particularly rainy day my room was packed with women and children. They liked to stand or squat at the end of the room or on the ladder as if to say 'We've only just come to look and we don't mean to stay'. Some of them were actually standing on the sloping roof of the chicken house, peering in so that only their eyes and the tops of their heads were visible. Wife One had brought her spinning and most of the younger women were nursing their babies. In the front rows, packed closely against the magical black box were the children – Gophle, Laute, Bhakhu, Gore, Kali, Seti and Ram – and inevitably, *laato* Maila. There had been teases and jibes from the women when Maila pushed his way in.

'Hey, this is no place for a man – only women here. If you come and gossip with the women, you'll turn into one yourself!'

'What sort of a man is he? Not able to plough, not able to carry, not able to marry!'

Maila didn't care. He wrinkled up his face and laughed and I noticed that he was wearing Gesi Ram's cast-off shirt.

Jit Bahadur's wife wanted to sing. She was a wild-looking woman who lived at the far end of the village with her husband and only surviving child – a twelve-year-old boy who was mentally handicapped. I switched the recorder on.

'Ah-dheri! I'm too shy! No, no, I can't!' she burst out. But after much coughing and spitting she began to sing, off-key and croaky and with *ad lib* comments spliced between the lines. 'I can't sing . . . what a terrible voice I have . . . I can't remember the words . . . when I'm on my own in the house it comes all right, but now I can't sing anything at all!'

At this point Maila, who was leaning right over the microphone, gave a loud explosive belch, obliterating her song. It was the finish of Jit's wife. She collapsed into gales of laughter and retreated to the back rows with her eyes streaming.

'Maila! You coarse oaf! Now look what you've done,' scolded Mati Lal's wife. Maila grunted an excuse and spread his hands. All of this was recorded on the tape and when I played it back they howled with laughter, especially Maila.

After this episode the men wanted to have a turn, and Ratna and his teenage friends, Damar and Jagat Bahadur, asked if they could come in the evening after work. 'It's not fair, the women have all the fun, while we have to work,' they said, not used to seeing their womenfolk enjoy themselves.

I consented, little knowing what was in store for me, and when I returned from supper at Naina Singh's house, I found my room packed to capacity. All the men had come, and the women and children, not wanting to be usurped from their privileged position as guardians of the black box, had also turned up in force.

The party was in full swing. Jagat Bahadur had brought along his bamboo flute, and Damar and Ratna a *madal* drum each – long oval-shaped drums beaten with a hand at either end. These three were the leaders of the gang of teenagers – young, unmarried, and carefree. With money in their pockets from their jobs on the hydro-electric project, they could afford such extra luxuries as long trousers, shoes, and vivid floral shirts, in which they strutted round the village or bazaar on their days off, vying for the attention of the unmarried girls. A cloud of blue smoke drifted towards the rafters from the cigarettes and pipes which all were smoking. Nepali manufactured cigarettes were cheap enough to tempt even the poorest, and children became regular smokers at eleven or twelve, often trying their first puff while still being nursed.

Jagat Bahadur played a lilting melody on his flute which the drums and singers picked up. When I played the tape back, the drums sounded like an artillery of guns firing. I explained that to make a good recording they must play the drums much more softly. This was not popular at all. We started again with the drums *sotto voce*, but as the drummers warmed up, they became louder and louder. It was extemporaneous with a remarkably skilled syncopation that on first hearing seemed to bear no relationship to the leisurely free-spirited rhythm of the song – quite an accomplishment for someone like Damar who was both playing and singing. Further colour was added by the discordance between the pitch of the drums and the pitch of their singing.

The hours passed by and the singing intensified in fervour and volume. Light-hearted banter passed back and forth between the young men and girls. Damar and Jagat had persuaded two of them, Hira and Kali, to sing a duet. As bodies swayed from side to side with the music, the smoke pall thickened. More women crowded in the doorway, their chores over for the day, with their babies bundled tightly on their backs or sucking sleepily at a nipple. I stifled a yawn. It was late. I usually went to sleep at 9 in order to cope with the 5 o'clock start to the day, but tonight, in spite of feeling tired, I was enjoying myself. The community bond was strong – the bond of being indeed one family. Everybody was accepted within this embrace, even myself and Maila, and the handicapped son of Jit Bahadur.

The song was in solo-refrain style, slow at first, with the girls picking up the men's words and repeating them. For once their voices were well-blended and in tune. As the song progressed, the tension increased and the singing became faster and more impassioned. In their excitement the men thumped their sticks on the floor and yelled catcalls to spur on the singers, and the mud walls resounded with the hollow timbre of the drums.

Hira and Kali alone seemed unmoved by the tension building in the room. They faced each other like modern-day images of Buddha – bodies immobile and faces expressionless. Only the cigarettes glowing in their hands and the slight sheen of sweat on their smooth olive-brown faces indicated some feelings beneath the calm surface as the poignant words echoed back and forth:

> My mind weeps. Who can explain it?
> Our love is like the pipal and banyan trees.
> Salala relai!
> We met by chance near the stream,
> Like two charged arrows is our love.
> Take my love – fill your life with my love.
> Salala relai!

I cannot accept your spring of love.
You will forget me.
You must love me all your life or not at all.
Salala relai!

Accept my love.
If not, my life is spent.
Salala relai!

Your love I accept, but if it fades,
I'll shed tears till my own life is dead.
Salala relai!

Never! Though spring comes and the forest is green,
My mind shall weep with the memory of your love.
If you love me, come with me;
The way is far, but you've won my love.
Salala relai!

The room was hot and the singing lulled me into a half-sleep. Here in their songs were the feelings that they suppressed at other times. Here was evidence of a struggle with their *karma* (destiny) and a concept of romantic love strangely inconsistent with their tradition of arranged marriages. The batteries of my tape-recorder finally ground to a halt long past midnight and I said goodnight to them. They were bitterly disappointed. 'But we've only just come!' commented old Mati Lal's wife as she descended the ladder.

From then on my life was not my own. Throughout the day, women and children came up, and at nights the men joined them. They talked of nothing else. The families from the far end of the village who had missed out on the early days of recording came to demand a turn, and Gore declared that the day he recorded his Kukurika poem was the best day of his life. But it was becoming too much for me. I did not even have an hour to myself. I started turning them away, but it was hard to resist their pleas. 'We have only an hour free, and then we have to go and weed the millet. Please let us hear it through once. We weren't able to come the night you recorded,' begged Nanakala and her daughter from the top end of the village.

I took to leaving the house in the early morning and not coming back until late afternoon, but they waited patiently in the courtyard until I returned. Even when I was sleeping I was not left alone. I would wake up in the middle of the night to find my room filled with people waiting for me to get up. They would never forcibly waken me, but once I had taken the fatal step of talking, that was the end of sleep.

'What's going on?' I would ask through half-closed eyes.

'We've come to record songs.'

'Go away. I'm sleeping.'

'But Sister!' they would laugh, 'You're not sleeping – you're talking to us!' In my sleepy state I couldn't summon up the vocabulary to refute this logic.

I began to feel like the sorcerer's apprentice, unable to control the magic I had let loose. I longed for Duane to return and help me deal with the situation. Nepalis showed more respect to a man, and when we were together they gave us more privacy. Now that Duane was gone they were convinced I must be lonely and stepped up their visits. In the end help came from an unexpected quarter.

It was the time of another festival and everyone, including the women, had a holiday from work. As it was wet the men spent most of the day sitting on their verandahs drinking home-brewed *rakshi* and playing cards. In the late afternoon Lal Bahadur and Ratna asked if they could come round and record some more songs that evening. I was feeling tired and my reluctance showed.

'Please,' they begged. 'Our sisters have returned from their married homes and we want to show them the tape-recorder.'

So I relented. They didn't come until about 9.30 or 10 pm, and I was already half-asleep. The room was soon packed with people and the singing more boisterous than last time, due no doubt to the *rakshi* they had been knocking back. I leaned against the wall and fell asleep.

When I woke up around midnight, the singing was still going and the room was bulging at its mud seams with people. Every family seemed to have come. There was Keshu Ram and his bevy of daughters-in-law, Jit Bahadur's family, Sher Bahadur and his brood, and even Gesi Ram, normally so anti-social. All the women and children were present including several from neighbouring villages. Only the headman and Naina Singh seemed to be missing.

I had forgotten to boil our milk, a chore that we had to do morning and evening to prevent it souring, so I squeezed my way through the network of arms and legs and babies, and went downstairs to the kitchen. While I was inside the kitchen I heard

Naina Singh's voice bellow out from the verandah of his house, '*Sahib*! I don't like it! It's not good. This commotion and singing must stop.'

I was paralysed with tiredness myself and in full agreement with him. Still, I did not know quite how to handle his complaint. Almost the entire population of Titeng was upstairs in my room, and it would be rude to ask them to leave. Why did Naina Singh direct his complaints at me, I thought. I decided to stay hidden on the ground floor, keeping the rest of Naina Singh's chickens company, and await further developments.

Naina continued to yell. 'I don't like it. Stop this racket right now!' The singing stuttered to a halt, someone beat out a last tattoo on the drum, and an embarrassing hush fell on the upper room. I culd feel the tension through the floor.

Then one by one they left – Lal Bahadur, Ratna, Damar, Jagat, Gore, Bhakhu, Laute. Even the older men of Naina's age – Keshu Ram, Jit, Mati Lal, Dal Bahadur – shamefacedly picked up their things and departed. Naina stood at the bottom of the ladder ticking them off like an angry school teacher. Then the women left, hiding anonymously behind their shawls, trying to pretend they had never been part of such a rowdy gathering. I watched them pass by in single file from the kitchen. Nobody said a word.

When all had left I came out of my retreat. Naina caught me at the bottom of the ladder. 'Sahib! It's not good – this *noise*. These young people will go on all night. It *must* stop.'

'Yes,' I said, feeling like a guilty child.

Upstairs I found Devi's Mother and Saili still hiding in the shadows, too scared to come out and face their angry father-in-law. They were holding an inquest on what had happened and muttering about Naina Singh. Turning to me, they delivered their conclusion: 'Sister! It's all *your* fault! You should never have let the men join in. From now on we must keep it just for the women!'

It seemed I was not popular with either side. After that episode they still continued to come during the day to record more songs, but the novelty had worn off and their enthusiasm waned; Duane came back and their interest turned to other things. Once or twice on festival days we risked a big recording session, but in Dal Bahadur's *goth* at the western end of the village – well away from Naina Singh.

16

Babies, witches and broomsticks

Layers of *patuka* could no longer disguise the fact that Saili's tummy
was visibly swelling. When she carried the heavy loads of firewood
her movements were slower and beads of perspiration gathered on her
smooth forehead. No allowances were made for her condition; birth,
like death, was part of the familiar cycle of the seasons and was
accepted as casually as the sunrise each day and the monsoon each
year.

Like every aspect of their lives pregnancy was governed by a system
of rules and superstitions. We knew that these beliefs existed, but
coaxing more precise information from the villagers was like prising
the leeches from our feet in the monsoon season.

'Yemi's mother died with a baby in her stomach because she ate
chillies and bitter spice while pregnant,' Grandmother shouted in a
hoarse whisper one day as we were watching four-year-old Yemi
playing with Devi in the courtyard. 'They cut her up and took the
baby out.'

These rules were not consciously taught or learnt, but were
acquired over the years as naturally as walking and talking. No one
questioned their validity and the villagers would often assume these
rules to be universal and so didn't bother to explain them to us. We
preferred to collect this information informally, and if it was not freely
offered we didn't push hard; we were not anthropologists and we
didn't want to destroy our friendship with the villagers for the sake of
knowledge. But our curiosity was hard to control and sometimes led
us to commit a *faux pas*.

'When is your baby due?' I asked Saili, when her stomach resembled a soft overgrown pumpkin and I was finally certain of my
diagnosis.

There was a shocked silence. Saili blushed and giggled and hid her
face under her shawl.

'We don't talk about it,' whispered Devi's Mother. 'We pretend nothing is happening until the baby is born. Then we can talk.'

'Why can't you talk beforehand? It happens to everyone.'

'Don't say that!' gasped Devi's Mother, rocking on her heels with laughter. 'We mustn't talk about it because of the shame!'

That was the most I could get out of them and I hoped I had not blundered too much. I could sympathise with the problems facing health workers. How could you encourage mothers to come for ante-natal check-ups when they would not admit to being pregnant?

This code of conduct governing pregnancy and birth began the day a girl first menstruated. From time to time we had arrived in the evening to find Wife One absent and Wife Two supervising supper. They wouldn't tell us why; they just said that Wife One was in the stable with Grandmother, but when this occurred with monthly regularity we discovered the reason. Wife One remained in the stable and had her food brought there by Bhakhu, for when a woman menstruated she was unclean for five days. She could not enter her own house, she could not touch other people, and she was not allowed to prepare food.

Sex was never discussed in the village in our presence, and even family planning could be an embarrassing subject. Only one man told us quite openly that his wife had 'done family planning', but this was unusual and pregnancy and birth continued to be a recurrent additional burden for the women.

We went away for a few days and when we got back I realised that Saili was missing.

'Where's Saili?' I asked, half suspecting what the answer might be.

'She's in the round house,' Naina's wives replied. In their strange modest way they made no mention of a new baby. I decided to play their own game and pretend that I wasn't interested.

'Can I go and see her?' I asked casually.

We entered the small round house together. Its circular walls made it even more cave-like than the other house. It was very dark and still except for the flies that buzzed in the doorway light and the remains of a fire that glowed dimly in the central grate. As the room began to take shape and Saili's form materialised on the far side of the fire, my first impression was that I had guessed wrong; there was no sign of a baby. But then Saili shifted her weight and what had looked like a bundle of rags quivered in response. I started over to have a look, but Wife One pulled me back.

'Touch this,' she ordered, pulling out a glowing coal from the fire. I hesitated. My hands were not protected by layers of calloused skin like hers, but when I quickly tapped the red-hot coal I was surprised to find that it didn't hurt.

'We must do this until the baby is named. Then it has its own protection from the evil spirits,' said Wife Two.

'We all have to do it, even the father and mother,' added Wife One in her sensitive way, afraid that I might have been offended. 'We never know when an evil spirit has jumped on our backs, and we might carry it inside without knowing.'

Freed from my evil spirits, I bent down and gently pulled at the thin layers of cotton rags. The bundle puckered up its mouth and clenched a tiny fist. It looked pathetically fragile and defenceless. I replaced the covers and brushed away the horde of flies that had settled on the dribble of mucus running from the baby's nostrils. It was a boy. That was good, and Naina Singh would be pleased for this was his first grandson.

'You have a beautiful son,' I said to Saili, trying to find the appropriate words to express my admiration. 'He's fat and white. Very fine.'

'What's so fine about that?' Saili answered, nevertheless blushing with pride.

As Saili was no more talkative than usual, Wife Two told me about the baby's birth. It had taken place in the round house, in the peace and tranquillity of the night time. Custom dictated that birth must take place in a dark room, often the stable, so that evil spirits could not observe the birth and steal the baby. Naina's two wives had assisted Saili; her husband and the other men had stayed away so as not to be contaminated. After the delivery the placenta was buried in a plot of land behind the house. For ten days Saili remained ritually unclean, forbidden to touch anybody or their utensils, and she ate her meals from separate plates in the solitude of the round house. Some mothers had to stay inside throughout the ten days but in Titeng they were not so strict and on sunny days Saili padded into the courtyard and laid the baby on a soft wad of rice straw in a *doko*.

On the eleventh day Saili washed herself and her clothes at the water tap, laid out a grain offering to the gods, and drank a concoction of cow's urine, barley, sesame seed, and *sun-paani* – water that had had gold placed in it for good fortune. Meanwhile Naina Singh and his son Gesi Ram journeyed to consult the astrologer – a Jaisi Brahmin – over the naming of the new baby. They took with them the exact hour and day of the birth and the Jaisi consulted his astrological calendar to determine which letter the names should begin with. Then blowing up the fire and scattering patterns of rice flour and red powder around it, the Jaisi began the *puja* rites.

When smoke had filled the room in thick swirls and endless leaf bowls of rice and rupee coins covered the floor, the Jaisi suddenly called for quiet:

'His names shall be – Narendra! Netra Lal! Netra Prasad!' he announced, writing the three names on a *pipal* leaf which he handed to Gesi Ram. These were the child's official names but Gesi Ram and Saili called their son Nar Bahadur, thus concealing the child's true identity so that the evil spirits were fooled and could not harm the child.

They were right to be concerned about the child's well-being for an alarming number of children died in the first five years of life from infections such as measles, pneumonia and diarrhoea, which could easily be prevented or treated. Diarrhoea in particular could be treated at almost no cost by a solution of water, sugar, and salt that the mothers could prepare themselves. Unfortunately they believed the child was trying to get rid of excess water and therefore withheld all liquids from a child with diarrhoea.

Malnutrition was another hazard. When we first arrived in the village Gore's two-year-old sister Dhane looked like a famine poster with stick-like arms and legs and an enormous swollen stomach. Her hair was patchy and a dull brownish colour. She cried most of the time, but even for that she could not summon up much energy. The 'Crying Disease' the villagers called it, but they knew of no cure. Gore's family were poor and had no rice, which was more digestible than maize or millet, and Dhane's new baby sister took all the mother's breast milk. I explained how to make a weaning food out of the maize and millet and soya beans that they had, but Gore's mother only shook her head and said, 'There's nothing you can do when they have the "Crying Disease".' I was sad and disappointed that they wouldn't listen to my advice, but thankfully Dhane recovered when their buffalo calved and there was once again a source of milk for her.

Almost four children out of ten died in the village before they reached five years of age. Of the nine children that Wife One had borne for Naina Singh, five had died in infancy, and of the four that remained, one was physically and mentally handicapped. Infant deaths were so common that the villagers did not bother with a ceremonial cremation unless the child was more than nine or ten years old, merely burying the small ones outside the village. They felt grief in the same way that we did, but they had a more fatalistic attitude towards death. It was so familiar they were forced to come to terms with it, and the close family bonds of the village and the hard physical demands of field work, which had to continue if the rest of the family were to survive, helped them to cope.

It was hard to know how to improve their health care when sickness and health were so inextricably tied to their system of belief. Classifying these beliefs was difficult. To call them merely super-stitions was failing to recognise their far-reaching consequences, yet to label them 'religion' raised the problem of which religion. 'We're Hindus,' said Naina Singh as he conducted another festival sacrifice; 'We're Buddhists,' said Prithvi Lal in his gentle manner, neither of them aware of any contradiction. But the majority of Magars were not worried to assign a label or definition to their faith. The truth perhaps lay in their tribal past before they adopted either Hinduism or Buddhism, when the Magars had been animists – spirit worshippers.

Certainly central to their beliefs was the view that their world was pervaded by evil influences, variously called gods, witches, spirits, and ancestors, that would harm them if certain rules were not obeyed. These evil spirits could be encountered anywhere, but particularly in the natural world – the fields, the trees, the mountain tops, the springs, the rivers, and above all, the night-time.

The Magars rarely went out after dark, and never alone, for fear of the evil spirits. If the women were late getting back from the fields they sang a loud yodelling song to keep the evil spirits at bay. Outside the village was a silk-cotton tree that was believed to be haunted and was avoided at all costs after dark, even though it meant a long detour. At least one villager's death had been attributed to passing beneath the silk-cotton tree after dark. In March and April when its brilliant red flowers were in full bloom, flocks of hair-crested drongos were attracted to the tree, and these black birds with their long forked tails and cackling laughter were strangely reminiscent of the demons in medieval manuscripts, so we could almost share their belief that the tree was haunted. Then there was the *tuni* tree that was so infested with evil spirits, the Magars could never use it for building their houses. Fortunately the spirits were destroyed when the wood was burnt as a fuel, and throughout Baglung district the pungent smoke of the *tuni* tree issued from the village homes.

Their fields were a major source of concern as an untamed spirit there could ruin the whole harvest. The spirits however could be appeased in various ways. The most common method was to perform a small *puja* with a grain or animal offering. Each farmer was responsible for doing the *puja* rites in his own fields.

'It's such a bother,' muttered Naina Singh, coming back from doing his. 'Our fields are so spread out we have to do *puja* in each little field. Other families have their fields close together so they only have to do it once. But we have to be careful. One year we didn't bother with the small fields down by the river and one of our bullocks dropped dead while ploughing there.'

Twice a year the whole village joined in *maj puja* which was performed to protect the houses and their inhabitants from sickness and death. Small altars were constructed at the entrances to the village with rounded stones or carvings to represent the gods. *Puja* was also done at the lower spring, otherwise the snake-spirit who lived in the water would cause the villagers to grow one leg longer than the other.

It was thanks to the evil spirits that Phaedrus came to live with us. Phaedrus was a black chick that I found cheeping in great distress in the middle of the village one day. I picked him up and searched for his mother, but there were no hens in sight, so I took him to Gore's house which was the closest.

'Have you lost a black chick?'

'No,' they answered, looking rather embarrassed.

'Are you sure?' I persisted.

'Well actually we threw him out.'

'Why? Because he's black?'

'No, you see only three eggs hatched.' As I looked quite blank they continued, 'You can have one or two chicks, or four or more chicks, but never, never, three. So we had to offer this one to the spirits.'

'Can I keep him?'

'Why not, if you want to? You'll only have one chick and that's all right.'

So Phaedrus came to live with us. He was a very gregarious chick and loved human company, and was happiest when sitting on my shoulder under my long hair, or better still, on my face. To the villagers it merely confirmed that all foreigners were slightly crazy. Who else would keep one black male chick that had no hope of ever laying an egg? Phaedrus lived with us for several happy weeks and then one day we returned home to find one of his legs broken and a wing damaged. Phaedrus refused to eat and grew weaker, and then since he was obviously in pain, Duane reluctantly helped him to an early grave. We suspected the children had been too heavy-handed with him, but perhaps the spirits had only claimed their rightful due.

Some of these beliefs were widespread but others were extremely local, and it was easy to see how new traditions arose from the close juxtaposition of two or more unfavourable events. Thus, when Bhakhu's goat fell down the cliff, it was remembered that a Muslim (not commonly found in Nepal) had once died in the fields nearby. The Magars' conclusion: the goat fell down the cliff *because* the Muslim had died there, and fresh rites must be performed to exorcise his spirit which was still haunting the place.

'Why aren't women allowed to plough?' I asked Devi's Mother during rice planting.

'Once a woman ploughed and the gods became angry and sent an enormous landslide that swept everything away. So now women don't plough any more,' she replied.

'One year we planted white millet,' said Lal Bahadur. 'That year my grandfather died so now *my* family don't grow white millet any more.'

At times we suspected some rules were invented on the spur of the moment to suit their own purposes. When the roof of our latrine needed repairing I went to Gesi Ram to ask him to cut some thatching grass for me.

'Tomorrow,' he promised.

My heart sank. I had heard that reply before. 'Tomorrow' could mean anything from twenty-four hours to twenty-four years, and we had already put up with the leaky roof for several weeks.

'Why not today?' I pleaded.

'Because today is Wednesday and you can't cut thatching grass on a Wednesday.'

I knew there was no answer to one of these statements. I had not heard this particular rule before, but neither had I asked for thatching grass. I would never have questioned its validity had I not met three Brahmin girls later that day. Each one was carrying an enormous load of long luxuriant thatching grass.

'Don't you know you're not allowed to cut thatching grass on a Wednesday?' I said smugly, pleased to show off my knowledge of their customs.

'No, no, you've got it wrong!' they laughed. 'It's all right on a Wednesday. It's *Tuesday* you're not allowed to cut thatching grass!'

The rules were endless – you mustn't eat salt or spice when your child is sick, you mustn't plough after the first hailstorm of the year, you mustn't leave home on a Saturday, you mustn't arrive home on a Tuesday, you mustn't travel south on a Thursday . . . . If all these rules were followed conscientiously, normal everyday life would become impossibly restricted. So there were ways and means to get around them when some forbidden activity was unavoidable. For example when Wife Two had to travel south on a Thursday to visit her mother who was dangerously ill, she deposited a small leaf bowl of grain and flowers at the beginning of the path as a peace offering to the spirits not to trouble her on the journey.

Despite these precautions and propitiations, the spirits still troubled the villagers. Generally the first sign of this was ill health, and the initial treatment was to call in the *Phukne*-man. My introduction to the *Phukne* was through a man who came to our house complaining of tooth-ache. His jaw was swollen so I tentatively suggested he should buy some antibiotics at the compounder's shop in Baglung. A few days later I found him sitting in a courtyard with another man and I was shocked to see that the whole right half of his face was enormously swollen.

'Didn't you get the medicine I suggested?' I asked.

'No, I haven't gone yet,' he muttered through the left half of his mouth. 'What medicine did you say?'

We discussed the matter again and then I realised with a shock of embarrassment that I had actually interrupted the treatment of a traditional healer to recommend some western medicine, for the other man was a *Phukne*. While we were talking he had calmly started to stroke and blow upon the affected cheek, muttering to himself. The *Phukne* seemed unperturbed that his patient should be considering an alternative system of medical care while in the middle of his own treatment! '*Phukne*' according to the dictionary means 'to blow, to go free, to come undone, to cast a spell, to cure a disease' and this sums up the theory and practice of the *Phukne*-healer. They were the lowest level of traditional healers and each village had at least one. They were called in for commonplace sicknesses, particularly in children, and their method of treatment was to blow upon the affected part with a soft rapid 'phoo, phoo, phoo!' either with their bare lips or through a bamboo tube.

I met the tooth-ache man a week later and his face was back to normal size.

'I see you're feeling better. Did the medicines help?'

'I never took the medicines,' he replied. 'The *Phukne* did the job.'

If the *Phukne* failed to work however, the next step was to visit the *Lama* or *Jhankri*. This was a more serious matter for the *Lama* required a gift of grain and money and often a chicken or two as well.

'Evil spirits can attack any part of the body,' explained Naina Singh. 'If it's on the feet, that's very bad, because when you plant your fields the crops will fail, but the worst place is the eyes, because then you go blind. The *Lama* goes into a trance to divine which particular spirit is affecting you and then uses spells and herbs to cast it out. If it's a very powerful spirit the *Lama* will shake all over as it comes out.'

My curiosity was aroused so at the next opportunity I accompanied a woman to visit the *Lama*. The *Lama* lived in a village higher up the mountain and as we were walking there the woman confided that she was having trouble with her menstrual periods – black blood instead of red blood, and too much pain.

We were ushered into the *Lama*'s consulting room – a bare mud floor with a grinding stone in one corner, a few upturned *dokos*, a short-handled broom, and a straw mat on which we sat down. If I had been expecting fetishes and the like, I was disappointed. Everything seemed very normal, almost ominously so, and we waited in silence. A shaft of sunlight threw diamond patterns on to the floor from a small carved window, and lit up a curl of blue smoke that suddenly erupted from the ashes of the morning's fire. After a long wait the *Lama* shuffled in. He was old, with streaked white hair, and sagging wrinkles beneath his eyes and knees. He gave me a long cool look. I fidgeted uneasily.

'I've just come to have a look. Is that all right?' I asked.

He continued to stare.

'I can give you medicine for your spots,' he said suddenly, moving closer to take a good look at my face.

'No, no,' I said, slightly alarmed. 'I've only come to have a look.'

He gave me another long cool stare, and then reluctantly left my evil spirits and turned to the woman.

'Black blood? Did you say *black* blood?' He bent over and looked into her eyes. 'Black blood is the sure sign of a witch.'

The woman filled a bronze plate with rice and rupee coins and pushed it towards him. He said nothing but continued to stare at her until she pulled out a couple more coins and threw these on top of the pile. Apparently satisfied with these gifts he mixed up a bowl of dark red liquid which he signalled her to drink.

'What kind of illnesses do you treat?' I asked in an attempt to relieve the tense atmosphere with some conversation.

'Everything.'

'And what sort of a success rate do you have?'

He gave me another long cool look that made me prickle all over. '*I never fail*,' he said slowly and distinctly, and turning his back on me began to pull out a pouch of dried roots and herbs. Selecting some he crushed them, adding other strange powders and instructed the woman to take a pinch each day. She got up and I thought the treatment was over, but he directed her to the window where she sat down in the diamond shafts of light. Now his half-muttered incantations changed tone and grew in volume. Suddenly he grabbed the broom that was leaning against the wall by the grinding stone and started beating it up and down the woman's back. Clouds of white dust billowed upwards and the three of us began to cough for the broom was clogged with flour from the grinding stone. His shaking and trembling increased and soon he was beating it all over her head and stomach with furious energy. When the poor woman was beaten and white all over, he stopped as abruptly as he had started, and looked suspiciously at me.

'I can give you treatment for your spots,' he repeated.

'I really have to go. I'm in a hurry. I have to see someone.'

'It won't cost you very much. All you have to do is. . . .'

I grabbed the surprised woman by the arm and hurried her out of the house before he could attack me with the witch's broomstick.

Back in Titeng I went to see Old Mati Lal who was always a good source of local information.

'Mati Lal, do you *really* have witches in Titeng?'

He looked at me quizzically and then broke into a loud cackling laugh. 'Didn't you know? Every man's a thief and every woman's a witch! Ha! Ha! Ha!'

17

Death and Dasain

After her brief ten days of rest Saili want straight back to work, for it was harvest time. The women applied a fresh layer of mud and buffalo dung to the courtyard and the sun baked it into a hard cohesive surface on which to pound the grain. Harvest days were the best of the year – sunny, but not hot, with the cut rice lying in stiff brush strokes of golden-brown on the green canvas of the slopes, and the air so clear after its monsoon wash each detail was magnified and the shouts of the harvesters echoed for miles.

Naina Singh and Gesi Ram erected a sturdy pole in the centre of the yard and the newly harvested rice and millet were pounded by the women and then the almost grainless stalks tossed around the pole to be trampled by the oxen, ensuring that every last grain was saved. The children loved it; with screams of excitement they danced round the pole with the oxen, tumbling on the mounds of straw and turning cartwheels and somersaults in its soft depths.

From time to time Saili would lay aside her pounding stick to nurse her baby. Keshu Ram looked down from his courtyard with disapproval.

'Mother's milk – that's no good!' he shouted to me. 'Now in your country you feed them cow's milk from a bottle, don't you? I saw them doing it in India. The Memsahibs feed their babies cow's milk and their babies grow up big and strong. Mother's milk makes babies weak.'

'Cow's milk isn't very good,' I said, hastening to correct him. 'Mother's milk is best really. Some people in our country feed their children on cow's milk but that's because they can't be bothered or they don't have enough milk of their own.'

'Is that so? I always thought mother's milk was no good. Look at how big your babies are and how small ours are.'

Other people joined in the conversation and we discussed the

problem from courtyard to courtyard. It was strange to think that
almost a year ago these people had been unknown faces to us, masks
from which two slanting inscrutable eyes stared out. Now we could see
behind the masks. We could see human beings who despite their
different looks, different customs and culture, shared emotions that
were remarkably similar to our own: Saili trying to act off-hand about
the birth of her son, yet glowing with pride; Naina Singh anxious for us
to be impressed with their ceremonies and traditions; Wife One worry-
ing about the well-being of her family. Yet we did not fool ourselves
that we knew them well; their deeper secrets couldn't be unlocked in
only a year.

'We must go,' said Devi's Mother, shaking me awake on a cold autumn
morning.
  'Where?'
  'To *maita ghar*.'
  'Right now?'
  'Yes.'
Like a true Nepali I abandoned my plans for the day and within ten
minutes was ready to leave. *Maita ghar* was a married woman's childhood home, where her parents and brothers still lived. Both Saili and
Devi's Mother came from the same village, high up on the slopes at the
head of the Kathe Khola valley. They had wanted me to visit their *maita
ghar* for some time, and we had even planned a trip in the monsoon, but
the night before we were due to leave it had rained heavily and the rivers
were too swollen to cross. Now Saili's brother had been sent down
from her parents' house with the message that an uncle had died and
Naina Singh was obliged to send a *mana* of rice and a bottle of *rakshi* to
the funeral. Saili begged to go but the family wouldn't hear of it.
  'How can you go?' scolded Grandmother. 'The way is long and steep
with many rivers to wade across. It wouldn't be safe for you to travel
when your baby's still so small.'
So Devi's Mother was delegated the task of bearing the gifts to the
bereaved family. She was delighted as it meant she could visit her own
family as well.
  'We'll leave Devi behind, then we can walk faster and maybe get there
and back in a day,' she said to me. But little Devi sobbed and stamped
her feet, and as usual won her own way.
  'Come on then! You'll have to walk all the way!' Devi walked the first
mile and then her mother strapped her on her back and carried her for
the rest of the journey. She looked snug and warm on her mother's

back, shrouded in a shawl so that only her tiny bare toes were visible. As we waded the river below Titeng her mother picked up a stone and threw it into the waters to ask the river spirits to bring good luck to Devi and keep us all safe on the journey.

On the other side of the valley the path was broad and level for the first two hours. We stopped at a bamboo tea-shop at Dobhan, the junction of two rivers, and I had some tea while Devi's Mother smoked a pipe of tobacco. A mill had been set up here – one of the first in Nepal to be operated by a water turbine – and women crowded in the tea-shops as they waited to husk their rice or press the oil out of their mustard seeds. Inside the milling shed clouds of white dust filled the air, and the two operators looked like ghosts as they shifted the sacks of flour around. We had to shout to make ourselves heard above the thunder of the water that cascaded down the metal penstock, through the spinning turbine and tumbled out beneath the shed into a canal that led it back to the river. But the women didn't mind the noise and they didn't mind the long wait. It wasn't often they had a day like this to sit in the sun and talk to their friends.

We followed the right fork of the river, shadowed from the sun by steep cliffs, but at last the sun found us and I shivered as its rays warmed through me. We waded back and forth across the river for the bridges were insubstantial – a single log across a ravine, or two or three bamboos tied together. We passed several traditional-style water wheels for grinding, heavy wooden wheels attached by shafts to massive grinding stones and turned by a chute of water – the same principle as the more sophisticated turbine mill we had seen at Dobhan.

The valley became narrower and we passed into the cold shadow again as the mountain walls closed in around us. Once more we crossed the river then started to climb steeply up a ridge. On the opposite side of the valley an unbelievably steep mountainside, carved into a maze of terraces running from ridge top to valley bottom, obscured the more distant views. Another hour's climbing and we stopped to rest at a thoughtfully provided *chautara*. I was hot now, but the wind blew icy blasts up the mountainside. We struggled on again. At each step we covered more distance vertically than horizontally, and Devi's Mother had to rest frequently. She was getting into territory she knew well, and people began to ask who her strange-looking companion was, not realising that I understood Nepali.

Finally the incline lessened and we found ourselves approaching a village scattered across a wide shelf near the top of the mountain. As we left the main path and balanced our way along the terraces to the home of Saili's sister, the cliffs of Baglung were just visible, and so was Titeng, a tiny pimple at the foot of the mountainside near the entrance to the valley. Beyond them lay the peaks of the Annapurna range and the deep blue sky.

A crowd of people had gathered in the courtyard, muffled in shawls, smoking their clay pipes. I hadn't realised till then that I was actually being taken to the funeral itself. Devi's Mother introduced me, 'She's come to enjoy the funeral,' she announced to the crowd. I squirmed inside with embarrassment, but the crowd nodded their heads as if it was commonplace for people to come and enjoy funerals.

Soon my own qualms at intruding on so solemn an occasion were put to rest. In fact everybody *was* enjoying themselves. There was plenty of good food and bowls of *rakshi* were passing freely around. It was hard to believe somebody had just died. Only the old wife and a daughter showed some signs of sorrow. I came across them squatting in a hidden corner, their eyes red and swollen and their faces streaked with stains.

The two sons of the deceased man presided on the verandah, dressed in soiled white with turbans wrapped round their shaven heads in honour of the dead. As each guest arrived they presented their gifts to the sons and received a red *tika* of rice paste in return. Devi's Mother disappeared inside the house, so I sat myself down on a mat next to some women making leaf plates. They fired the usual questions at me: 'Where have you come from? How old are you? Are you married? How many children do you have? Why not? How much money do you earn?'

'Here, make some of these,' said a woman with broken front teeth. She passed me some *sal* leaves but I had forgotten the technique so once again I was shown how to pin them together with slivers of bamboo into the intricate leaf plates. On the terrace below more women stirred giant copper cauldrons of rice and lentils and soon I was called inside the house to eat rice with Devi's Mother.

Moving outside into the sunny courtyard again I was accosted by a very drunken ex-Gurkha soldier, happy for the opportunity to show off his knowledge of the English language.

'In England you say "alraait". In Nepal we say "raamro". You say "vairy goo-ud sirr",' he slurred in the unmistakable accent of a British colonel.

The men around the courtyard listened attentively behind their cocoons of blankets. Such fine entertainment was not usually provided at funerals. The soldier offered me some more *rakshi* and

when I covered my bowl with my hand to show I really meant 'no' he
poured it over my hand. Then a man came round with a bowl of
fermented rice pudding and slapped portions of it into the palms of our
hands as they had run out of plates. The ex-Gurkha was becoming
annoying; he was so drunk now that I couldn't understand what he
was saying, and as he still insisted on speaking English to me it was
becoming embarrassing. I was relieved when Saili's mother and father
came up and introduced themselves. They were bursting with
questions about their new grandson.

'How's Saili? How's the new baby? Why hasn't she come to visit
us?' In her anxiety the mother didn't give me a chance to answer.

'Saili's fine. But the baby's still too young to travel,' I said,
repeating Grandmother's words.

'What does it look like?'

'Well – it's small and wrinkled, and pink and white!' They both
laughed.

'And how old is it now?'

'Twenty-one days.'

'Are they feeding her good food? Does she get chicken and *ghiu*? Is
she feeling well? Do they make her work?'

'Light work. Near the house, not in the fields.' I lied slightly,
thinking of Saili pounding the grain in the courtyard. I had seen no
sign of a chicken being slaughtered – traditional food for a woman
who has just delivered – but I did my best to reassure her mother that
Saili was looking healthy and getting good treatment in Naina Singh's
household. From the look in her mother's eyes I could see she was not
totally convinced and obviously wished she could have had her
daughter under her own care.

After a while the conversation shifted to the subject of funerals.
Most of the men there had just got back from carrying the body down
to the 'Ganga' (Kali Gandaki) to be cremated. 'It's best if a man can die
with his feet in the holy water, but so long as he's cremated on the
banks of the Ganga it's all right. When that's all over we have this
feast,' explained Saili's grandfather, a tiny man with unusually white
hair. The blind grandmother sitting beside him nodded her head in
agreement. 'Do they do it like this in your country?' she asked.

'In England we usually bury people, but some are cremated. What
happens when you die? Do you go to "heaven"?'

'When we die? I don't know. That's the end,' answered the
grandfather.

'Are you afraid of dying then?'

'Afraid? No. What's there to be afraid of?'

'What about your spirit – does that die too?'

'If a man isn't cremated properly, if his relatives don't do the proper rituals and sacrifices, or if he dies a sudden violent death, his spirit may come back to trouble his relatives. When I die, my relatives will carry my body down to the Ganga. It'll be the duty of my daughter's husband to perform the rituals of my cremation. No, there's nothing to be afraid of so long as they do the rituals properly.'

'You're not reincarnated after death?'

'No. After death, there's nothing. It's the end.'

He seemed so dignified, this old man, looking forward to the quiet finality of death which could not be many years away, and I could sense the feeling of relief that there was, after all, an end to life. Is it only in countries where life is so comfortable and easy that death has become an event to be feared?

It was too late to think of returning to Titeng that same day, so I spent the night at Devi's Mother's home. At this height it was much colder than Titeng and I regretted that in our hurried departure I had forgotten to bring my sleeping-bag. Devi's Mother and her sister-in-law Maiju fussed around and gave me the best of their threadbare blankets.

'Sister must have a pillow,' said Devi's Mother.

'I don't need one,' I protested.

'But you always use one! I've seen them up in your room.'

Despite my protests they bundled some clothes into an old sack for a pillow and gave me a straw mat. I went to bed on the verandah of the house, looking out on to the crescent swathe of terraces and the ghostly shadows of Annapurna. The blankets were infested with fleas and bedbugs that feasted on me all night, but as the cold was intense I had no choice but to keep them tightly pulled around my neck. I returned to Titeng the next morning with a crop of itchy flea bites to remind me of the day I had the gall to 'enjoy' a funeral.

Although they didn't believe in the Hindu doctrine of reincarnation, the Magars did celebrate Dasain – the biggest festival of the Hindu year. When Devi's Mother and Wife Two struggled into the courtyard and laid down their *dokos*, one of red clay and one of white clay, we knew that preparations for the ten-day festival had begun.

It was traditional to give every house a fresh coating of mud at Dasain. After the ravages of the monsoon the houses were shabby, with mud washed away and stones exposed. The new layer of mud acted as a plaster, binding the stones together and filling up the crevices to prevent the wind blowing through. It was also a ceremonial cleansing, for dung from the holy cow was mixed with the mud, thus purifying the houses and their inhabitants in readiness for the festival.

The first day of Dasain dawned with an almost tangible spell in the air. Annapurna awoke and seared the sky with her ice-cold blaze. As the sun rose higher the spiders' webs glistened with dew, and above the gorge two lammergeiers, encased in gold, circled in ever-rising spirals towards the heavens.

There was a shout from outside and Devi's Mother came into our room bearing a shallow tray of soil which she handed ceremoniously to me.

'*Jamara* – these are for you. Give them a little water each day and keep them in a dark place.'

'What are they?'

'You'll see,' she said with a mysterious smile as she left.

According to Hindu tradition the festival of Dasain celebrates the triumph of Good over Evil, when King Rama, an incarnation of Lord Vishnu representing the forces of Good, overcomes and slays Ravana, King of the Demons. King Rama however was only able to vanquish Ravana by invoking the name of Durga, the Mother Goddess, and the source of all power and energy in the universe. So on each day of Dasain a different incarnation of Durga is worshipped, particularly important being her incarnation as Kali, the Destroyer, in which form she demands the blood of animal sacrifices.

But the Magars of Titeng knew nothing of this. When we asked them why they celebrated Dasain, they could only tell us what they did: 'We slaughter a buffalo; we receive *tika*'. When we persisted Prithvi Lal said, 'We don't know why. Our forefathers had a reason, but we've forgotten it. Now it's just a *riti*.'

During the first few days of Dasain teams of villagers set to work with their hoes clearing the footpaths of the area, pulling up the weeds and grass that had encroached during the monsoon and repairing any landslides. And each family *lipnu*-ed their house with a fresh layer of mud. The colour of the mud varied from white, grey and black, to all shades of red, orange, ochre and brown, depending on the type of soil available in the locality. On the *terai* near Kasauli, people used to decorate their houses a light yellow ochre colour, but sometimes made special trips into the hills to bring back a supply of the more favoured red mud. High up on the mountains where the soil was rocky and

poor, the houses were often left undecorated or given only a token
smear of mud around the doors and windows. In Baglung the
traditional colours were dominant – red, varying from a light ochre to
a rich burnt sienna, with contrasting upper or lower storey in white.
Additional decorations were painted around the windows and doors
in a black paste obtained from old torch batteries. As there was no red
mud near Titeng, Devi's Mother and Wife Two had crossed the river
and climbed the hill to Raato Maato – the village of Red Mud. We
could see Raato Maato clearly from Titeng for the hillside at this point
was a rich deep red, badly gullied and almost devoid of vegetation
except for clumps of bamboo. When it rained this area became a
slippery chute lending truth to the saying '*Raato maato, chiplo baato*' –
'red mud, slippery path'. Now with Dasain upon us, the area was
honeycombed with small quarries where the women came to dig their
supply of red clay.

Wife One mixed the white clay in her large copper cauldron, adding
potfuls of water until it became a runny white paste. Then Gesi Ram
borrowed our ladder and balancing himself and the cauldron precariously on the top rung, splashed the white-wash on to the wall of their
house with a brush made of stiff twisted grasses, beginning in the
topmost corner under the eaves of the peaked roof. As the mud dried it
turned from a dark grey colour to a gleaming spotless white.
Meanwhile Devi's Mother prepared the cauldrons of red mud and
cow dung to decorate the lower half of the house. We worked hard all
day until Bhakhu, looking like a ghost with chicken-pox, decided to
pour red mud over Devi, and then it developed into a contest to see
who could get the messiest. It took us two days to finish the inside and
outside of Naina Singh's complex of houses, and throughout the week
the smell of wet clay hung in the air.

'Nothing particular happens during these first few days,' said
Prithvi Lal. 'We *lipnu* the houses and make preparations. Then the
seventh day is *phulpati*. Each village has to send a *teku* of milk, some
fish, and fruit and vegetables to the *koth*. In the bazaar they must take
them to the Anchaladish in the Zonal Office, but the villages around
here, we go to the *koth*. It's three hours' walk up the mountain, *ooota!*'
he said, pointing with his chin across the valley.

'Why do you take it there?'

'A holy man stays there and meditates throughout the ten days of
Dasain. He lives in a cave on the mountain top, and he'll conduct *puja*
with the offerings we bring and give us the *phulpati* blessing.

'Usually we put up the *chamche*,' he went on, referring to a sort of

primitive ferris wheel made of wood or bamboo, 'but last year we had
some trouble. Too many people came from the bazaar to play on it –
gangs of policemen from the barracks, very drunk. They made such a
commotion we couldn't sleep. So this year the headman has said "No
chamche".'

The villagers carried on with their normal schedule of field work
until the eighth day when they sacrificed a buffalo in the middle of the
village. By the ninth day excitement was building up. Families who
had not yet finished *lipnu*-ing their houses made a last-minute rush to
do so, and all through the village, fires smoked as the women distilled
gallons of *rakshi*. On this day we gorged ourselves on chicken, for each
family sacrificed a cock and dripped its blood over their sickles,
ploughs, hoes and other farm implements to bring them good
harvests in the year ahead. The Magars were very pragmatic in their
approach to religion, and the meat of the animal sacrifices was always
kept to eat. Almost every family invited us in for a plate of chicken or
buffalo meat, until by the afternoon, feeling rather sick from the
unaccustomed amounts of meat, we escaped to the river and
recovered our senses with a very cold bathe.

When we returned we found the headman had relented and decided
they could put up the *chamche* after all.

'What to do? The young people insist,' he wheezed to us. The
chamche was only erected at the time of the Dasain festival, some
saying that at Dasain everyone must get their feet off the ground.
Whatever the reason, enjoyment of the *chamche* and the other swings
that proliferated in the villages during Dasain, was not limited to the
children and quite old grandmothers also took their turn. The Titeng
chamche was erected beside the *pipal* and *banyan* trees at the entrance to
the village. It was cleverly made without a single nail in the whole
construction. As it had no self-propelling mechanism, two people had
to stand beneath it and as each wooden seat descended they grabbed
hold of it and yanked it down. When it was the women's turn, Devi's
Mother and I squeezed on to one of the four wooden seats and grasped
the side supports tightly. Three or four men stepped forward and with
a heave started the large wheel turning. We were rudely yanked up
into the air, paused momentarily at the top and then with a sudden
lurch were thrown outwards over the tree tops. I banged my head on
the overhead beam and for a brief moment parted company with the
wooden seat, but Devi's Mother gripped me firmly round the waist
and we went down together leaving our stomachs in the sky, only to
be whisked upwards again. By the third turn I had learnt to duck my

head at the right moment and to lean backwards like a sack of potatoes so that I didn't fly off the seat. It seemed that the men deliberately gave the wheel an extra hard yank when they saw *our* seat arriving near the top!

'Are you enjoying it?' Ratna Bahadur called out. 'Watch out for your hair! Once a woman's hair got caught in the axles and she stepped off the *chamche* bald!'

When we were thoroughly giddy and our stomachs had been pulled and stretched like pieces of dough, the young men showed us how it should be done. Ignoring the seats, each of them clung to the overhead beams with their hands and propelled the wheel round with contortions and jerks of their bodies. As if that wasn't hazardous enough they then used the seats, which were actually individual swings mounted to the wheel, but turned the wheel so violently that each seat turned a somersault over its overhead beam as the wheel went round. It seemed a dangerous and exhausting form of recreation!

Late that night as we went to sleep we heard the shouts and screams coming from the *chamche* and the pounding of the *dhiki* as Wife One and Wife Two frantically prepared enough rice for the next day's feast.

When we woke the next morning on the climactic tenth day, the village was strangely quiet. For once the *dhiki* and the grinding wheels were silent, and only the roosters who had been spared the sacrifices disturbed the peace of the morning. As the sun rose and warmed the air, small groups of men collected in the courtyards, dressed in their cleanest least-darned clothes. Women of the wealthier families brought out their finest shawls and jewels – arc-shaped gold clasps for their hair, earrings, pendants, and turquoise and coral necklaces. Saili climbed down the notched post from her room looking like an Eastern princess, with a wine-red velvet blouse, a new *sari*, and in her ears enormous solid gold earrings shaped like flowers and connected by a thread which passed over the top of her head, in case their weight should be too painful on her ear lobes. Even Wife One, normally dressed in the most threadbare of clothes, had made an effort for the occasion and emerged in a newly made tie-string blouse, though still of sombre black.

As soon as they heard we were up, the men started climbing our ladder to bring us gifts – leaf plates of meat and every make and shape of *roti*, some warm and light, some cold and greasy, and pints and pints of *rakshi* in old discoloured bottles stoppered with corn cobs. All morning I refilled our small kettle with water and dispensed coffee to everyone who called. We tasted the meat and *roti* but, with our spoiled western palates, found they were not so tasty, and so we hit upon the expedient of offering them round with the coffee, and the men were happy enough to consume their own gifts when we pointed out there was too much for us to eat on our own.

'Very good, Sahib, very good!' Naina Singh intoned between mouthfuls of bread and alternate gulps of *rakshi* and coffee. 'Today we receive the *tika*. Everyone will be coming to *my* house because Grandmother is the oldest person in the village, and she must give the *tika* to everyone else. You must come and watch.'

Towards 10 o'clock Devi's Mother called us over for the *tika* ceremony. 'Don't forget to bring your *jamara*!' she yelled. I brought out the tray of dirt they had given us on the first day of Dasain. It had sprouted yellowish-white barley seedlings, three to four inches long.

The ceremony took place in the buffalo shed where Grandmother lived. She too had on a new black tie-string blouse, and her iron-grey hair was neatly plaited into a single braid down the middle of her back. Beside her an ornate copper plate on a pedestal was filled with a mixture of rice, curd, and red dye, and beyond that, the bunches of barley sprouts.

Naina Singh fussed around: 'Come on, come on. Hurry up! Everyone else will be arriving soon and our family won't have finished. Where's Bhakhu? Where's Gesi Ram?' He squeezed us into front-row seats and we sat down on small circular maize-leaf mats on the floor of the shed. The buffalo calf nuzzled me and blew on my neck whilst its mother stared with trepidation from beyond.

'Now, are we all ready at last? I shall go first,' explained Naina Singh. 'Are you watching carefully? No, wait a minute. I must face Annapurna.' He shifted his position and squatted down facing north-eastwards across the Kathe Khola valley in the direction of Annapurna and made a deep obeisance to the mountain. Then Grandmother gave him the *tika* mark, smearing the sticky mixture of rice and curd over his forehead bit by bit. All the while Naina muttered directions to her: 'Spread it all over my forehead. Mind now! Don't leave any gaps!' When it was done to his satisfaction, Grandmother passed him a bunch of barley sprouts which he stuck under his *topi* so that they dangled down like a clown's tassle. Then he bent over and touched his head to Grandmother's bare feet and got up.

'Now move along! Next one. Where's Gesi Ram? Well, you go next, Bhakhu,' he directed. Each member of the family squatted in turn before Grandmother and received the *tika* of rice and curd and the barley sprouts. When it came to the turn of the granddaughters, Kali and Devi, instead of them bowing down, both Grandmother and Naina Singh touched *their* heads to the little girls' feet and handed them shiny rupee coins. I was puzzled at the time but later found out that unmarried virgin daughters are accorded a ritual status almost like that of a goddess in the Magar tribe, and although for most of the year they are treated less favourably than the boys, at times like the Dasain festival they are worshipped accordingly. Kali and Devi squealed with pleasure and rushed past us to the courtyard outside.

When each member of the family had received the *tika*, Naina turned to us, 'Now it's your turn please.'

'It's not our custom to do this,' we said, hesitating a little.

'You are part of our family and we must honour this by giving you the *tika*,' said Naina.

'You *must* have the *tika*,' pleaded the women. 'Why don't you have the custom – does something bad happen to you?'

'No, nothing happens. It's just that we have different beliefs.'

'That doesn't matter,' said Naina. 'We understand. You believe in different things but we don't mind. Please let us give you the *tika* as a sign of our friendship.'

Naina Singh was quite agitated, and Keshu Ram, the headman and other men who had now arrived, solemnly nodded their assent that we must indeed receive the *tika*. Religious differences were suddenly not important; they were overwhelmed by love and friendship.

Slowly Duane got up and sat down in front of Grandmother and the tension in the buffalo shed relaxed. Naina issued his directions even more stringently than before: 'Spread it all over his forehead. Do a good job now. Careful! A little bit more – more – stop!'

Then it was my turn. I held my head as still as possible but the cold clammy rice tickled my forehead as Grandmother applied it. When she was finished I bent down and touched her feet with my head to express my thanks.

'No, no,' said Naina. '*You* don't have to do that!'

We sat back on our mats as the other men of the village and even some from the villages of Aatmuri and Kumaldara stepped forward to receive their *tika*.

'The oldest person in each family gives the *tika* to the rest. Then each of these people must go to the oldest person in the community to receive their own *tika*. That's why they come to Grandmother,' explained Naina Singh.

'Why have people come from Aatmuri and Kumaldara?'

'Because they are relatives of our village.'

'And who gives Grandmother her *tika*?'

'There's nobody older than Grandmother, but somebody will come from Raato Maato to give her her *tika*. That's the village where she was born.'

'Do you have festivals like this in your country?' the men asked, and we told them all about Christmas and Easter and our beliefs and customs.

'It's a strange thing, religion,' commented Keshu Ram. 'You worship different gods to us. You keep different festivals. But we're all the same! I cut my arm and blood comes; you cut your arm and blood comes. We die; you die. We're all one! But our gods – they got divided. They separated and became two. So now you kill cows and eat them, whilst we worship cows and drink their urine. Isn't that strange?'

When everyone had received the *tika*, Wife One called us inside and handed us gigantic servings of rice, *roti* and meat. Then Saili and Devi's Mother got ready to leave for *maita ghar* where they would receive another *tika* from their own parents. Gesi Ram was going with them and Naina Singh called the whole family together to give them a proper send off. Gesi Ram presented his mother with a length of bright red material and all of them bent down and touched her feet as a mark of respect. Then Naina Singh took over and uttered a long rambling prayer to Parameshwor – the Great God – imitating the chanting of the Brahmin priests. Every now and then he paused in his monologue and asked for approval of what he had said from the people listening. 'Let it be! It shall be so!' intoned the other men fervently, and Naina continued his prayer.

Gesi Ram remained impassively staring at the ground but when I caught Saili's eye her broad face broke into an even broader grin and her shoulders heaved as she struggled to suppress her giggles. Failing this, she pulled her shawl over her face. Naina showed no sign of stopping and I hoped that Saili could last out without letting the family down. From time to time Naina seized a handful of rice and threw it over their heads or plastered some more to their foreheads. Unfortunately, although we listened carefully, neither Duane nor I could fully make sense of Naina's mutterings which rambled on with no beginning or end to his sentences. But we gathered that he was asking blessings on his family and their journey to *maita ghar*, and both of us caught his final pragmatic plea:

' . . . and, O Parameshwor, keep them from stubbing their toes on the rocky path!'

18

Farewell

Winter was here again. Cold, crisp mornings when our breath condensed into clouds of white fog in the chilled air. Grandmother was once more carried into the courtyard by Maila, and in the bazaar the government officials set up their offices – their desks and chairs and bulky ledger books – in the sunshine of the streets, the only place where it was possible to stay warm. Abandoned stalks of maize drooped like sad scarecrows on the barren terraces and the fodder trees were shaved to naked stumps. But up at the spring beside the new *cementi* water tank, the twelve-month-flower still bloomed.

Across the valley the small stone power house nestled amongst the boulders. Most of the civil works for the hydro-electric project – the canal and penstock – were completed, and only the machinery which had not yet arrived from India remained to be installed.

'One more month and then we have to go home,' I told Naina Singh's family.

'Why do you have to go? It will be bitter when you leave us.'

'We have family and friends we haven't seen for years. We're homesick for our own countries. But we'll be back.'

They shook their heads sceptically. 'How can we be sure? You'll like it too much in your own country. Everything's nice there. Why would you want to come back here?'

Wife One, sad at the thought of our leaving, served us rice garnished with a glob of *ghiu* every evening, hoping to fatten us before we left. It tasted delicious after the monotonous mounds of porridge, but it disturbed me she should waste her best food on us when her own children needed fattening.

Devi, Kali, and Gophle started coming to our kitchen each morning just as we were boiling the kettle for our breakfast drink of coffee. We didn't like to encourage them to expect something, but it was hard to resist their pleas of 'Sister, tea please!' when we saw their runny noses and bare arms and legs pressed against our screen door.

In a vain attempt to capture some of the 'feel' of Titeng, I wandered through the village taking as many photos as I could, and sketching when my film ran out. Their conflicting attitude towards photos caused me much frustration. I wanted to catch them in informal poses as they went about their daily chores, but they had other ideas. Going through the village I came across Lal Bahadur and his wife squatting in their courtyard with their youngest son. Their manner and pose were so typical, their clothes of the traditional home-spun Magar cloth, that I stopped to take a photo.

'One moment!' cried Lal Bahadur as I was about to press the shutter. He ran inside the house and re-emerged in long trousers, a fancy western-style shirt, and an absurd pork-pie hat imported from Hong Kong in place of his *topi*. Worse still, he refused to pose with his wife but wanted his photo taken with his friend Ratna. The two men stood to attention and stared grimly at the camera like soldiers at arms. 'I wanted to take it as you were before,' I sighed.

'Please! We want a photo like this.'

Everybody wanted their photo 'like this'. The same ridiculous hat, long trousers and fancy shirt were passed to each man in turn so that I ended up with a set of almost identical photos. Nothing I could do or say would persuade them to act normally.

Wherever we went we were invited in for snacks of roasted corn and sorghum, or bowls of millet beer, and we distributed the last drop of the *rakshi* we had accumulated over Dasain to our numerous visitors. We ate rice with the headman, and with Ratna's family in their humble one-roomed hut, lit only by the embers of the fire. Ratna's father, old Mati Lal – the faithful night watchman for the project – sat in a corner wrapped in blankets, pale and listless. He had been sick and unable to work for several weeks with a fever.

'I get up for a day or two,' he croaked, 'and then the fever comes again and I have to lie down. I don't like being unable to work. With only two *muri* of fields, I've always taken whatever job I could find, even if it's only kneading mud for mortar. All my life I've worked, and a man who works has no sin in his stomach. I don't know what will happen when I'm gone – my son's a hard worker but he wastes his money on cigarettes and fancy clothes.'

Despite their poverty and Mati Lal's current loss of income, their generosity was unimpaired, and his wife fed us rice and meat and some milk that she must have bought for they had no buffalo of their own.

Time and again in Nepal we found that generosity increased with poverty.

By now everyone knew we would be leaving soon, and they came round to hear the news from our own lips. 'Are you *really* going? It will seem empty in the village when you've gone. What shall we do in the evenings? No more singing!'

Their sorrow at our impending departure was thankfully lightened by the thought of what we would do with all our things. This thought had occurred to them a whole year ago, within a few days in fact of our arrival. 'Will you be taking all your things with you when you leave?' they had inquired solicitously. Now they asked the same question with renewed enthusiasm and it posed a difficult problem.

'All this stuff!' said Jit Bahadur's wife. 'You'll need too many porters to carry it. How will you take it all with you?'

'Oh, we can manage,' I said airily. 'We can take a lot on the plane with us.'

'What about your pots and pans? You won't take them, will you?'

'How can I cook without my pots and pans?'

'Oh, Sister! *You* can afford to buy some more!'

'But they don't make these fine copper and bronze plates in our country.'

'Look, promise that you'll give me those pots with lids when you leave. You know, the ones with the rice and sugar. Just a small gift. For me to remember you by . . . .'

'Sahib!' said Naina. 'When you leave, will you give us your red water barrel? Just for us, a special gift to my family . . . .'

'Sister,' called Devi's Mother. 'Will you be taking your velvet *cholo* with you? It would make a fine dress for Devi . . . .'

'Brother! Will you give us your radio . . . ?'

'Sister! Will you give us your warm sweater . . . ?'

'What are we to do?' I said to Duane. 'We can't promise something to everybody.'

'It seems to me that if we just give things away we'll be doing more harm than good,' said Duane. 'It's impossible to do it fairly and everyone'll be jealous. Besides, it encourages them to expect handouts. I think the best idea is to sell the things we're not taking. Sell them at a price they can afford – a few rupees – and that way they can choose what they want.'

So we made plans to have a sale. I sorted out the clothes and other belongings that we wanted to keep and threw them into our suitcase and tin trunk. Then we gathered up what was left and spread it out –

pots and pans in the kitchen, clothes and other things upstairs – and I passed word round that the next morning we would be holding a sale.

Promptly at first light they were waiting outside. 'Sister, wake up! We've got to go out to the fields soon and we don't want to miss our chance at the sale!' We opened the door to the kitchen and they rushed inside. In a short time everything was chaos. Bodies obscured the doorway and windows so that it was quite dark inside. Those pushing to get in blocked the way of those trying to get out. I squeezed my way into the fracas.

'Tulasi!' Nanakala was calling in a loud voice. 'You can't take all those bowls. Sister promised them to me.'

'No, they're mine. I got here first.'

Jit's wife and the Screechy Woman were having a tug-of-war over some rat-chewed Tupperware containers. Meanwhile I saw Kali-the-singer slip off with the other items they had claimed and left unguarded in the course of their tussle. Lal Bahadur's wife marched in and with one sweep of her hand knocked everything off the lowest shelf into her uplifted skirts, Keshu Ram's wife had somehow managed to break into the tin trunk where we had stored the things we didn't wish to sell and was trying to escape with her trophies and, in the middle of all this, Mati Lal's wife turned slowly round in circles, 'But all the good stuff has already gone!' she lamented.

It was true. I looked around and the shelves did seem to be bare. Then I discovered Wife One crouched in a corner, immobile. I thought she must be ill, but when I bent down I saw that under the folds of her long skirt she was quietly squatting over an enormous hoard of bottles, cartons, pots and pans. Unable to carry them all herself but refusing to relinquish them, she had sat down to defend her haul against other contenders.

It took us some time to restore order, retrieve the things we were not selling, and persuade Wife One she could not take everything. In order to do things fairly we imposed a quota on the amount each family could buy. When the kitchen was cleaned bare, including the mats off the floor, they went upstairs to examine the remnants of our clothes and a few other things.

'You don't have much!' exclaimed the headman's wife. We couldn't help laughing; we had been trying to tell them this all year and finally they had realised.

'Don't you have any *nylon-sylon* things?' asked Kali-the-singer hopefully.

'What are these?' said Saili, picking up an enormous pair of thermal underpants belonging to Duane, and measuring them against her for size. They came over the top of her head so she reluctantly discarded them and they were seized by the headman. He also carried off an old pair of sandals left behind by a friend, being the only person in the village with feet large enough to fit them.

The most popular items were our towels because of their thickness and warmth, and the women took them to wear round their heads. The young married couples bought our two cotton mattresses, Gesi Ram the one, and Ratna the other. It made us happy to think that their love-making would be done in comfort from now on.

'Are you selling this?' said Saili, fingering the long Tibetan dress I was wearing.

'All right,' I said on the spur of the moment. 'I'll give it to you later.'

At last everything was sold except an orange batik shirt and a pair of denims belonging to Duane. I sold them to Bhakhu for half-price, and a moment later when I looked out he was prancing round the courtyard like a circus clown in these overlarge clothes.

Our sale was over, and we were exhausted. We sat back on our now bare mud floor and recounted the many hilarious moments to each other. We had inadvertently sold several things we were planning to keep, so Duane was left without a change of clothes, and we both had to go shopping as soon as we reached Kathmandu.

On the morning of our last full day, we took a final walk to Deorali, the place of the pass, to pay our respects to the mountains whose temple spires had guarded us throughout the year. Graceful Machapuchare, the holy fishtail mountain, the massive flank of Annapurna I, the pyramid of Annapurna South, the saw-toothed Nilgiris, and beyond the gorge of the Kali Gandaki the frescoed face of Dhaulagiri surrounded by her sibling peaks, the sweeping snow ridge leading up to Churen Himal and Gurja Himal and, shimmering insubstantially in the distance, the lonely shape of Hiunchuli Patan.

To be there was to be exalted; to be close to God.

Our eyes followed each corrugated ridge and valley, stirring memories. We had walked over many of them – the overpopulated Kathe Khola valley and its encircling mountain ridge, the plateau of Baglung balanced atop the cliffs, the forested and now snow-covered summit of Ghorepani, the snaking Kali Gandaki, and the terraced slopes of Karkineta on the way to Naudara and the road. In the rarefied air the shouts of a young Magar goatherd echoed up the mountain. We began our descent.

Part-way down, in a ravine, we met a blind man. His hands were thrust forward into the palms of an old woman who held her hands behind her back and led the way. Both were bare-foot. Haltingly they moved forward, one step at a time, the blind man trusting the woman to guide him.

To me he epitomised the struggle for life in the mountains of Nepal. In faith the villagers planted their crops, married and had children. Blindly they began each new year not knowing what it would bring, whether a landslide would destroy their homes, a hailstorm their crops, or disease take their children. Life was harsh even for the fit and strong; it had no mercy on the weak or crippled.

The blind man and the woman reached the bottom of the ravine. The path ended here and continued on the far side of a rushing stream. To fill the gap a tenuous line of boulders jutted out of the falls and deeply-scoured pools. Not difficult to jump for those with eyes.

The blind man hesitated. He put one foot tentatively on a rock. One step – two – three – and still miraculously he was balanced on the boulders. He was halfway across when he hesitated too long. The old woman impatiently jerked his arms forward and he fell into one of the pools. She pulled him out roughly but his feet were wet now and he fell again, cutting himself badly. He fell twice more as they scrambled up the muddy embankment on the far side. Briefly stopping to wipe the grit from his face and hands, he placed them once more in the woman's and continued down the rocky path.

Our bags and *dokos* were packed. We had handed our red water barrel to Naina Singh – a concession to the special place his family held in our hearts. We had said goodbye to the villagers. Wife One called us into their smoke-laden dark room for the last time. The red plastic barrel stood incongruously at the end of the row of graceful copper pots. She had prepared a special farewell meal which we ate alone, in silence, for the other members of the family had already eaten and gone to the fields. Afterwards she drew us into the light of the doorway, made us sit down, and gave us both a dab of *ghiu* on our heads and a red *tika* mark. Wiping away the tears on her cheeks, she produced two *mala* of brilliant marigold flowers and hung them round our necks.

I wanted to embrace her, but I knew she would not understand the gesture, so instead we solemnly pressed our hands together in the *namaste* position. We had come to give, but how much more they had given us.

We had learnt that complete understanding of one another is not necessary for friendship; that the emotions of pain, sorrow, laughter and love are common to us all, and the sharing of these can overcome any differences in culture, language or education. We had seen the cycle of the seasons: summer and winter, drought, monsoon, seedtime and harvest, lean times and times of abundance. We had shared in their cycle of life, in their times of sorrow and toil, in their times of dancing and celebration. We had seen death; we had seen birth.

We picked up our rucksacks and said goodbye to Grandmother in the courtyard. Our two porters had gone on ahead. In silence we left the huddle of houses and clambered down the steep mountain path, past the barren terraces of red earth that rested, waiting for the cycle of seasons to revolve, for the rains to baptise them afresh.

Glossary of Nepali words

Chamche	A type of primitive ferris wheel erected during the Dasain festival
Chautara	Stone bench surrounding a tree on which to rest loads and sit down
Cholo	Tie-string blouse worn by the women
Chula	Small, wood-fired stove made of stones and mud
Dhiki	Rice-huller
Doko	Conical-shaped bamboo basket used to carry loads on their backs
Ghiu	Clarified butter made from buffalo milk
Goth	A barn where animals and straw are kept
Khola	Small river
Khukuri	Curved knife traditionally carried by Gurkha soldiers
Lipnu	To spread a covering of mud and cow dung over the surface of a house or courtyard
Lungi	Straight length of material sewn into a tube and worn by the women as a skirt
Namaste	The Nepali greeting
Namlo	Tump-line that passes over the forehead for carrying loads
Patuka	Waist band worn usually by women but also by men.
Pradhan Panch	Elected leader of local area council
Puja	Hindu form of worship
Rakshi	Spirit usually distilled from millet
Roti	Flat unleavened bread made from any kind of grain
Serac	Padded cotton bed cover
Syo	A rain-shield made from bamboo and leaves
Tika	A mark put on the forehead, often of red paste
Topi	Small woven hats worn by the men
Tun	A runny sauce usually made from some kind of vegetable